THE PUBLIC EYE

The Public Eye

Ideology and the Police Procedural

ROBERT P. WINSTON
Associate Professor of English
Dickinson College, Carlisle, Pennsylvania

and

NANCY C. MELLERSKI
Associate Professor of French
Dickinson College, Carlisle, Pennsylvania

St. Martin's Press   New York

© Robert P. Winston and Nancy C. Mellerski 1992

All rights reserved. For information, write:
Scholarly and Reference Division,
St. Martin's Press, Inc., 175 Fifth Avenue,
New York, N.Y. 10010

First published in the United States of America in 1992

Printed in Hong Kong

ISBN 0-312-07274-0

Library of Congress Cataloging-in-Publication Data
Winston, Robert Paul.
The public eye : ideology and the police procedural / Robert P. Winston and Nancy C. Mellerski.
  p. cm.
Includes bibliographical references (p.   ) and index.
ISBN 0-312-07274-0
1. Detective and mystery stories—History and criticism. 2. Crime in literature. I. Mellerski, Nancy C. II. Title.
PN3448.D4W55 1992
809.3'872—dc20   91-32751
                                                              CIP

To our mothers
and
To the memory of our fathers

Contents

	Acknowledgments	viii
1	Aspects of the Police Procedural	1
2	Brave New Sweden	16
3	Anatomizing the Other	52
4	The House of Keeping	90
5	A Family Affair	127
6	Imperfect Invigilation	163
	Notes	197
	Select Bibliography	226
	Index	233

Acknowledgments

This book had its origins in a team-taught Freshman Seminar at Dickinson College in the Fall of 1982. "Detective Fiction: Aesthetic, Social, and Cultural Analysis" evolved into "Ghouls, Gumshoes, and Gunslingers," a seminar which took a broader view of formula fiction. Along the way we became increasingly interested in the ways in which contemporary theoretical materials opened up new possibilities for analyzing various forms of popular literature. In this regard, a 1986 summer study group funded by Dickinson College enabled us, along with our colleagues Karyn Hollis, Sharon O'Brien, Terry Poe, and Tom Zoumaras, to read extensively in Marxian cultural analysis. Dickinson College generously provided sabbatical supplement grants for 1986–87, allowing us to do substantial work on the project.

Throughout the writing process, colleagues have been uniformly supportive. In particular, we wish to thank Judy Gill, Wendy Moffatt, Bob Ness and Sharon O'Brien, all of whom read portions of the manuscript and offered their suggestions. In addition, Clarke and Peggy Garrett, Mike Kline, Ashton Nichols, and Tom Reed gave us the benefit of their encouragement and advice throughout. Others have contributed, sometimes quite unknowingly, to the completion of this manuscript: Birgitta Angiolillo, Robin Ashton, Richard Crockatt, Peter Rabinowitz, and scholars of popular culture generally. Dan Buchan, of Dickinson College's Computer Center, deserves special mention; he was always there to take our frantic late-afternoon phone calls and to rush over with his kit to minister to our footnotes. Christine Bonney and Jennifer Haff, our student assistants, proofread the manuscript with meticulous care. Eric Homberger, the general editor of the New Directions in American Studies series at Macmillan (London), has been understanding and helpful throughout our relationship with him.

Finally, we wish to thank our spouses, Debbie Fulham-Winston and John Mellerski, for patience above and beyond the call.

Parts of this study originally appeared in essay form and grateful acknowledgment is made to the following publishers for permission to reprint, in altered form, these materials: in Chapter 2, "Sjöwall and Wahlöö's Brave New Sweden," *Clues: A Journal of Detection*, 7 (1986): 1–17; in Chapter 4, "The Detective in the Intertext: Freeling's Dialogue with Chandler," *Texas Studies in Literature and Language*, 31 (1989): 611–633. *Texas Studies in Literature and Language*, copyright © by University of Texas Press.

ROBERT P. WINSTON
NANCY C. MELLERSKI

1
Aspects of the Police Procedural

The subject of this book is the complex role which crime fiction, particularly the police procedural, plays in mass culture. Superficially, the offer of potential criminality and transgression of the law provides readers with a fantasy freedom of action which is generally unavailable in advanced capitalist societies. Ernest Mandel notes that the fact that crime stories in general maintain their popularity among bourgeois readers is proof of the "partial, contradictory, and self-negating nature of that civilization." Because bourgeois civilization is characterized by various forms of discipline such as the pressure of market forces, the "despotism of the nuclear family, authoritarian schools, and repressive sexual education," it remains civilized through "fear of punishment." At the same time, however, this civilization is marked by violence at its margins: against the Third World, the poor, foreigners, women, workers, and those who generally fail to conform. For these reasons, the crime novel responds to the "sublimation of violent drives [that] take the frustrated form of harking back to vicarious violence" (69). Mandel goes on to claim that such fiction, as a general category, is simply a means of escape "from the monotony of daily life into vicariously enjoyed adventures" which counterbalance the numbing security of daily existence (71).

By concentrating on crime fiction primarily as escapism, Mandel cannot take into account the more complex role which popular forms of culture in general play in post-industrial society. In his essay "Reification and Utopia in Mass Culture," Fredric Jameson argues that mass culture must be understood primarily as a vehicle for "managing" audience desires under contemporary capitalism.[1] A form of mass culture like popular fiction is, for Jameson, a mechanism "which strategically arouses fantasy content within careful symbolic containment structures which defuse it, gratifying intolerable, unrealizable, properly imperishable desires only to the degree to which they can again be laid to rest." Mass culture is not, therefore, "empty distraction or 'mere' false consciousness," as the Frankfurt School, and Mandel, would have us believe, but a method of explicitly presenting a society's "anxieties and fantasies" precisely in order to control them. While modernism offers the reader "compensatory structures" to cope "with the fundamental social anxieties and concerns, hopes and blind spots, ideological antinomies and fantasies of disaster, which are their raw material[,] . . . mass culture represses them by the narrative construction of imaginary resolutions and by the projection of an optical illusion of social harmony" (141).

According to Jameson's analysis of the function of mass culture, one of the most effective "containment structures" ought to be that sub-genre of detective fiction known as the police procedural. It allows its readership to experience vicariously the "pleasures" of criminal "attacks" on a repressive society even as it assures its audience that they are not guilty of criminal behavior themselves. Furthermore, it arouses in readers their fears of the technological elites and state apparatuses which seek to control their behavior while positing a police bureaucracy composed of "ordinary" citizens intent only on ensuring the preservation of "social harmony" from the depradations of society's "outsiders."

The police procedural as a particular sub-genre of crime fiction does not therefore propose merely an escapist structure. Instead, it works upon its audience in a more sophisticated fashion to defuse the potential for violent transgression by foregrounding the police, a dominant Western symbol of social control. By shifting reader identification from the criminal element to the state apparatus which opposes it, the procedural reshapes the potentially destructive impulses of individualism into successful participation in a corporate structure, the police squad. At the same time, however, the series we will examine generally debunk the "optical illusion of social harmony" which should be the primary structure offered to manage the fantasy of individual and social rebellion. They may recreate many of the socially reassuring myths of earlier forms of detective fiction, but they generally end on a note of barely controlled chaos rather than restored and validated order. In order to understand more clearly the "transformational work" of this latest sub-genre of detective fiction, specifically during the last twenty-five years, we must first, albeit briefly, turn to the evolution of the genre.

Detective fiction of the Golden Age is intentionally conservative in its outlook; the formula constrains an author to present a momentary, individualized disruption of an otherwise perfect world. In the late Victorian and Edwardian periods, with their emphasis on the apparent ability of the individual to dominate the socioeconomic spheres of action, the role of the Great Detective essentially reproduces that of the entrepreneurial capitalist. He controls the direction of events by exposing the murderer, who is always portrayed as personally responsible for the evil he has unleashed. By removing this single source of disorder, the detective restores the utopian society which existed prior to the first page of the novel. The fact that the detective often reveals the criminal's identity at a social gathering, like a banquet, re-validates the society which has been disrupted, and the identification of the criminal thus becomes a "ritual celebration of the renewal of the social order and its salvation, not merely from divine wrath, but also from unworthy leadership" (Jameson, "Reification" 142).

As Uri Eisenzweig points out, however, the function of classic detective fiction is to obscure real historical discourse and real historical space (189). That is, Golden Age detective fiction holds the social and economic forces of entrepreneurial capitalism blameless for criminal behavior and insists on an illusory individual culpability: "The illusion is, however, important. It indicates that believing in the existence of authentic detective fiction is equivalent to adhering to an order of things in which identity is natural rather than cultural, absolute rather than historically determined, spiritual rather than material" (189).[2] Clearly, then, Golden Age detective fiction is constituted so as to manage the most troubling anxieties of its readership by proposing the illusion of control through the agency of the Great Detective.[3] Nonetheless, the socioeconomic context cannot be ignored; it makes its presence felt both narratively and ideologically.

As John Cawelti indicates, during the heyday of the classic detective novel, "the middle class encountered two new threats: the political emergence of the lower classes, and a new concern with psychological urges toward aggression and sexuality that were in sharp conflict with the ideal of the family circle. Both socially and psychologically, this new threat manifested itself as a revolt from within" (*Adventure* 102). While earlier in the nineteenth century the middle class had conceived of its identity as a challenge to existing aristocratic structures, by the early twentieth century the middle class found itself in the same position *vis-à-vis* the lower classes which questioned the former's hegemonic rights under entrepreneurial capitalism. The crisis of hegemony provoked by the oppositional stance of the working classes thus called into doubt the confidence which had marked middle-class success. At the same time, the insistence on self-reliance and individual achievement which characterized middle-class child rearing confirmed middle-class guilt by eliminating earlier "objective" standards of success. One indicator of the anxieties centering on the family circle is the high proportion of domestic murders in Golden Age detective novels. Cawelti thus contends that such fiction confirms the existing social order by making crime purely individual, deflects "an increasingly serious moral and social problem into an entertaining pastime," and allows readers to strike out at the repression of the family in a game without sanctions (*Adventure* 102–5).

At the same time, however, these novels insist that they do deal with the "reality" of social life, quite consciously constructing their reality in the form of documents – real cases reported by real people (Watson's reportage of the exploits of Sherlock Holmes, for example). Classic detective fiction stresses its reality when it calls attention to itself as the "true" report of a case: it is "entirely characterized by a series of rhetorical and narrative processes which locate the origin of the story in the very universe of its fiction" (Eisenzweig 154–55). While Eisenzweig's point is that classic detective fiction deflects the anxieties of readers by substituting its own "reality" for that of the world, such a fictional technique does enable one to read the novels as documenting precisely those "real" elements they seek to avoid. That is, the novels become encoded documents which, when carefully examined, reveal the management of the fears of the middle class and the threats to the society's dominant ideology.

By the 1920s and the 1930s conditions in the United States led authors to reject what they perceived as the ahistoricism of earlier English detective fiction since the fears which underlay American self-doubt no longer resembled those of Victorian and Edwardian English middle-class readers. The inability of individuals to overcome market forces which could bring about social disruptions as profound as the Great Depression undercut the myths which had shaped the earlier formula and required new strategies of containment.[4] As a result, hard-boiled detective fiction remains true to the myth of individualism by focusing on a single private investigator, but it simultaneously insists on his powerlessness by generalizing the evil he confronts. No longer is there a single villain in an otherwise perfect world; instead, corruption is seen to be systemic and socioeconomic structures are explicitly indicted.[5] Nonetheless, "the hard-boiled story also affirms the basic success ideology. The private eye's quest seems not so much a criticism of success as a means of resolving the anxieties of the success ethic by imagining a model character whose actions demonstrate that the successful are corrupt, while at the same time he achieves the rewards of success by maintaining his honor and integrity" (Cawelti, *Adventure* 157). In spite of his apparent victory, though, the best the hard-boiled dick can hope to accomplish is to stave off the next, inevitable wave of evil. Although the private investigator finds it impossible to bring order to a corrupt and decaying world, the individual citizen threatened by the overwhelming forces of unchecked capitalism can take comfort in the presence of one honest man who can – and will – ride to the rescue.

Even here, however, at the juncture of two apparently divergent formulas of reassurance, the cultural determinations that arise from literary tradition still prevail. Despite the rise of corporate capitalism, a reorganization so pervasive that it reshapes even the criminal element into its own set of corporate structures, popular fiction still foregrounds the individual protagonist.[6] The hard-boiled novel thus creates its own version of Golden Age ahistoricism as a way to manage the fears of readers manipulated by larger market forces. That is, the "primary text" of the culture, the economic and political structures which determine the rhythms of everyday life, remains bound by residual elements from an earlier era, even at a moment in which ideological struggle reaches a crisis.

By the end of World War II, however, when the shift from a "market to a managed economy" (Wright 174) had become so entrenched that it could no longer be effectively hidden by the ahistorical displacement techniques of the Golden Age novel, the hard-boiled formula was forced to accommodate itself to a new set of strategies that would lead inexorably to another narrative transformation: the development and refinement of a modern police procedural. As Will Wright argues in his study of the structure of the Hollywood Western, a similar evolution can be seen in the change from the "classical" form to the "professional" one. The individual hero who dominated Westerns until the late 1950s was transformed into a group, "an elite body" with "unusual strength, skills, and status" (170). This technological elite was seen as best adapted to achieving practical goals in late capitalism, replacing the individualistic, aggressive businessman who could no longer possess all the skills necessary for success (Wright 178).[7] The transition to the corporate hero, marking the "deep conceptual correlation between . . . narrative structure and the ideological requirements of modern industrial society" (Wright 180), inevitably marks the "third stage" of detective fiction as well. Both Wright and, later, Mandel thus essentially argue the same point about contemporary popular culture: where the professional Western proposes elite groups as models of action, the crime story is likewise transformed into a "modern scientific business enterprise" (Mandel 55).

There can be no doubt that the rise of the police procedural after World War II suggests a response to the technological penetration and increased bureaucratic complexity of post-industrial society which operates by proposing a squad of individualized detectives, each possessing certain crucial skills which enable them to work collectively to investigate the same systemic evil that the hard-boiled detective nostalgically confronted alone. Thus, the formula of the police procedural reacts to the new socioeconomic reality by requiring a corporate detective, a squad sufficiently diverse to cope with the complexities of a world controlled by corporate powers. At the same time, though, the procedural particularizes the detectives, suggesting that the formula is managing widespread distrust of surveillance by a faceless bureaucracy, even in an era in which the public perceives itself to be threatened by increasing criminal activity. It is precisely the individualizing of the members of the corporate squad which mediates the public's fears of an overextended and inhumane police power.

In this sense, the police procedural proposes a different model of the professional elite than that which Wright examines in the Western. In the latter case, the group maintains only a "utilitarian" relationship to the institutions around it; members of the group interact primarily with each other, remaining "independent of the need for other social contracts" (171). Thus, "in technological society, the group of elite, specialized men in the professional Western relate to ordinary society only professionally; their need for a social identity is totally satisfied by membership in the group" (Wright 180). Likewise, viewers derive their own satisfaction by identifying with the elite group of outsiders rather than society as a whole.

The purpose of the procedural is almost exactly the opposite. By emphasizing the human face of state power, the procedural insists explicitly that the police derive their satisfaction from solving their case and thus gaining the approval of society at large; it is this utopian vision of cooperation between the police and society which becomes the source of reader satisfaction.[8] The procedural therefore raises the spectre of absolute state control solely in order, simultaneously, to manage that fear by insisting that such power cannot be seamlessly coercive since only fellow citizens, individual policemen within the squad, can exercise it.

Alan Clarke's work on British television police series between the 1950s and 1970s articulates the "cluster of contradictions" that surrounds this popular form. He notes that "the ideology of 'law and order' is contradictory, its emphasis on freedom under the law resting uneasily with its call for an extension of surveillance necessary to protect this freedom" (37). One cannot, in other words, "read" the increased popularity of police series only as a response to a perceived increase in crime in society since to do so is to reduce the text to a simple outgrowth of crime statistics and to deny that other issues, like the freedom of the individual, for example, are implicated in the transition from unofficial (private) to official (public) responsibility for policing the society.[9]

It is precisely these "other issues" which must be understood in order to propose an adequate reading of the police procedural. In this regard, the whole question of surveillance and social discipline explored by Michel Foucault in *Discipline and Punish* furnishes a useful perspective from which to examine the rise in importance of the police procedural. According to Foucault, the purpose of discipline in a society is to control the populace so completely that the coercive agencies charged with discipline can effectively atrophy and disappear. His model for this "closer penal mapping of the social body" (78) is Jeremy Bentham's Panopticon. Panopticism is the sign of the "disciplinary society," where surveillance is no longer exceptional but generalized throughout the entire social body (209). Thus:

> The ideal point of penality today would be an indefinite discipline: an interrogation without end, an investigation that would be extended without limit to a meticulous and ever more analytical observation, a judgement that would at the same time be the constitution of a file that was never closed, the calculated leniency

of a penalty that would be interlaced with the ruthless curiosity of an examination, a procedure that would be at the same time the permanent measure of a gap in relation to an inaccessible norm and the asymptotic movement that strives to meet in infinity. (227)

The discourse of the police procedural can therefore be construed as one step toward this "ideal" penalty. Its frequent appearance in serial form constitutes the literary equivalent of Foucault's "indefinite discipline": a precise and repeated reproduction of the stages of interrogation, investigation, and judgment which maintain such discipline over time – but in a conciliatory and therefore non-threatening manner.

The aestheticization of crime which began at least as early as De Quincey's "Murder as One of the Fine Arts" (1827) is thus no longer just a displacement of criminality into a game or puzzle, as it was in the Golden Age novels, but it is also a vehicle of control by which the state is able to insist upon its definitions of normality.[10] As Foucault defines the police, they are "an apparatus that must be coextensive with the entire social body and not only by the extreme limits that it embraces, but by the minuteness of the details it is concerned with. Police power must bear 'over everything': it is not however the totality of the state nor of the kingdom as visible and invisible body of the monarch; it is the dust of events, actions, behaviour, opinions – 'everything that happens' . . . " (213).[11] By choosing to write in the mode of the police procedural, then, an author, too, can go beyond the state apparatus itself to survey "everything that happens." The fact that the procedural is generally written in serial form confirms that the ongoing Panopticism envisioned by Foucault is in fact occurring in this category of mass culture.

The need to rehearse the surveillance of deviance in this fashion also indicates, however, the reluctance of individuals to accept this level of state control. Once again, though, this popular form effectively manages audience resistance. A society's boundaries, whether they be specifically related to criminality or more broadly involved with questions of class, race, gender, or family, can be subject to scrutiny in a non-threatening way since the "transgressions" identified by the text's "society" are always deflected away from the reader to the fictional criminals against whom the police are called to act. What is striking about the procedural, however, is that it does not always conclude with a satsifying restoration of order which confirms the value of the society being scrutinized. While the specification of an individual criminal and the absence of recidivism defuse the fear that urban society is inexorably devolving, the constant rehearsal of the process (weekly in the case of a television series, often yearly in the case of novels) indicates that the nexus of social fears raised in procedurals remains troubling and must again be examined in the next broadcast or in the next book in the series.

Previous work on the procedural has generally concentrated on identifying its formulaic characteristics rather than on identifying the mechanisms through which it enters into ideological debate. In *The Police Procedural*, for example, George Dove defines the sub-genre according to two simple criteria: "First, to be called a police procedural, a novel must be a mystery story; and second, it must be one in which the mystery is solved by policemen using normal police routines" (47). In his view, there are five component parts to the formula. The police are portrayed as "ordinary mortals" who are "competent as cops but lacking exceptional ability or reputation" (114). Theirs is a "thankless profession" because the work is less exciting than they had expected and the public fails to appreciate them (119–20). As a result, the police form a "tight enclave," a "community" quick to defend itself against dangers from superiors or uninitiated civilians (121). Unlike the Great Detectives of Golden Age investigations, the police must often depend upon "fickle breaks" or luck (126) and are constrained by "the tyranny of time," the pressure to solve a crime quickly if one is to solve it at all (128).

According to Dove, the formula is constructed in order to embody a series of myths. The first is "the myth of the Moral Absolutes, which represents police work as engagement in the struggle of Good versus Evil, Right versus Wrong," though Dove notes that some authors "dissent" from this myth and see police work as more problematic (134–35). Second, procedurals frequently underscore "the perception of the war that can never be won, the battle that must always be fought over" (135). The last two myths, that police work is dull and boring and that unsolved cases are a major problem, are, however, generally included in procedural novels only to be denied by the narrative at hand (136). That is, all of these myths must ultimately be shaped so as to provide a plausible and convincing "sense of reality . . . in the context of [these] conventions" (143).

Dove's primary aim, therefore, seems to be to demonstrate that police procedurals derive their continuing popularity from a series of formulaic elements which originate in folk wisdom about the police and embody a cluster of myths which are the "means of interpreting the world and organizing our experience of reality" (*Procedural* 132). By establishing an essentially ahistorical and non-contextual definition of reality, however, Dove cannot account for the ways in which police procedurals mediate and manage social fears and anxieties. Nor can he account for the distinctions among procedural writers from different cultures.[12] While his work is certainly useful for its cataloguing of shared generic features, it must be seen primarily as a starting point for a more specifically ideological study of the encoded texts which constitute the heart of the procedural.

Likewise, to analyze the procedural by means of reflection theory, as Mandel does, is to reduce the appearance and popularity of police procedurals written since 1965 to a simplistic and finally distorting mirror of the culture which produced it. A focus on "purely" economic forces, for example, neglects other determinants that, however indirectly, mediate the relationships between cultural and social practice.[13] For this reason, the simple one-to-one connection between text and context obliterates the "specifically cultural mediations through which social and political developments pass in order to connect with and influence the level of cultural practice" ("Popular Culture and Hegemony" 28). Our aim, therefore, is to examine five series of police procedurals in order to establish the ways in which they enter the ideological space of the cultures from which they derive.

Sjöwall and Wahlöö's Martin Beck series intervenes in an ongoing political debate among Swedish leftists during the 1960s and 1970s concerning the nature and evolution of the welfare state. The authors set out to analyze the effects of the institutions created by the Social Democrats to improve Swedish life; in so doing, they focus on the moral ecology of the physical, social, and political environment. The investigations of Martin Beck and his colleagues on the National Homicide Squad enable their creators to indict the conspiracy between a supposedly socialist government and the capitalists in whose interests they govern. As crime spreads throughout Sweden, the police are confronted with an increasingly alienated population that denies the myth of a homogeneous and harmonious society based on "cooperative individualism." Marginal groups within the population – the elderly, the adolescent, the poor – are systematically scrutinized as targets of exploitation by the combined forces of the state and private enterprise.

Sjöwall and Wahlöö's choice of the police procedural as a vehicle to propose counter-hegemonic strategies recognizes its value as a means to enter into an ongoing ideological debate. By using an agency meant to enforce the dominant ideology to embody their analysis, they call into question the code by which deviance is defined; the police themselves deconstruct from within not only the force but the laws they are called upon to serve. Sjöwall and Wahlöö thus transform a conservative form into a revolutionary one in order to liberate its power for a progressive, even radical critique.

In his Kramer and Zondi series, James McClure anatomizes an even more problematic society, South Africa. Although his announced aim is "entertainment," his underlying purpose seems to be to endorse a liberal model of evolutionary change in the apartheid state. By proposing a racially mixed detective team, McClure should be able to examine the full range of South African social pathology. From the first novel in the series, however, it is clear that Kramer and Zondi will largely, and inevitably, be concerned with the defense of white South Africans against threats to their dominance. The crimes are largely white on white, and blacks are valued only as sources of information (by the police) and as cheap labor (by whites generally). Blacks are therefore portrayed as irremediably "Other," inhabitants of an anti-world who are constrained to play out roles assigned them by white mythology. Conflicts between blacks and whites are thus muted if not wholly absent, and to deflect attention away from the threat of racial war within South Africa, McClure foregrounds instead the tensions between Boer and Anglophone South Africans.

The Kramer and Zondi relationship, a theoretical embodiment of possible reconciliation, at first appears to propose a rebellion against the apartheid system. As the series progresses, however, it becomes apparent that Zondi is hopelessly compromised by his role within the white power structure. As a black civil servant, his loyalty to his employer supersedes his identification with his own race, and he comes to represent – and to enforce – black accommodation to white rule. Although McClure attempts to paint the relationship between Kramer and Zondi in positive terms, the net effect of the series is to suggest no solution to the system of separateness upon which the South African state depends. The fact that McClure chooses to focus on a single black and white team reinforces the vision of individual cooperation that lies at the heart of liberalism; the virtual absence of any collective black action defuses the potential for political change growing out of generalized violence throughout the system. McClure's series is thus a portrayal of a non-conformist Boer and a conservative African who, together, are meant to represent a hopeful vison of racial harmony, but in fact they serve only to vacate the political questions which lie at the heart of South Africa's future.

Nicolas Freeling sums up his Van der Valk series as an attempt to transform a tired and inferior genre into a medium that would focus on contemporary social concerns. In order to do so, Freeling consciously interrogates both bourgeois civilization and the three forms of crime fiction it has produced. First, he subverts the Golden Age formula by creating a historical perspective, often embodied in outsiders, exiles, and foreigners, that enables him to transcend a frozen moment in time and elucidate a vision of pan-European history in which Dutch society becomes a microcosm of Europe's cultural crisis under late capitalism. Like Amsterdam's House of Keeping, Freeling's series submits Europe to the judgment of History in order to examine instances of deviance which are themselves manifestations of larger social dysfunctioning.

As he insists upon exhuming the problematic past ignored by his Golden Age predecessors, so, too, Freeling brings another formulaic precursor under scrutiny: the hard-boiled protagonist. Through Van der Valk's vacillations between unofficial and official methods of inquiry, Freeling demonstrates that the individual investigator cannot possibly cope with the complexities of life in the third stage of capitalism; at the same time, he questions whether the creation of the corporate hero of the police procedural is not itself emblematic of social alienation. By intruding the work of Raymond Chandler into his series, and thereby confronting one formula with another, he undertakes an intertextual investigation of the police procedural as an effective response to the suppression of History. The inability of the bureaucratic state apparatuses and their representatives to understand deviance leads him to propose a series of versions of the ideal police squad, ranging from the wholly public to the wholly private. These various attempts to reinsert creativity and imagination into the process of surveillance call into question Freeling's chosen form at the same time that they anatomize anomic European culture, and his Van der Valk series thus becomes a study in generic irresolution.

In his Castang series, Freeling's concerns with formula are less important than his analysis of the myths which govern French society. While he is not participating in an ongoing political debate from within a particular party, as were Sjöwall and Wahlöö, he is nonetheless very much a part of a continuing ideological controversy prompted by a perceived breakdown in authority of the sort Hall *et al.*, following Gramsci, have called "a crisis in the management of the state, a *crisis of hegemony*" (214). In Freeling's view, such a crisis is rooted in simultaneous failures of both the family and the State to maintain the putative consensus which governs all relations among the citizenry. This endemic dysfunctioning is posited so as to offer two options to resolve the crisis: a return to individual moral responsibility rooted in the family or a continuing faith in the coercive power of the state.

In the Castang series both these solutions are shown to be problematic. On the one hand, the authority of the family has been subverted to the service of right-wing political organizations which attempt to substitute their extremist programs for the compensations of traditional family life. On the other hand, the nation itself has come to be seen as a nostalgic fiction; the citzenry has lost faith in the values of the centralized bureaucracy that has regulated every aspect of French life. As a result, in Freeling's France neither the family nor the state apparatus can resolve the crisis of hegemony. The series thus articulates in a sophisticated fashion the extent of the breakdown of authority, but it ends in ideological irresolution because it, too, cannot offer a coherent vision of what policing on either the private or the public level can accomplish.

If Golden Age detective fiction assumes a fundamentally stable society temporarily violated by an aberrant force from within, Janwillem van de Wetering is at pains in the police procedural novels he has published since 1975 to show that a formerly close-knit Dutch society is in fact breaking down. In Dutch cultural mythology, industrious sixteenth- and seventeenth-century burghers staved off primeval nature to create a neat, prosperous, orderly society, with Amsterdam as its crown jewel. In the twentieth century, however, the efforts of the merchants of the Golden Age have been undercut by the confusion at the heart of contemporary reality. Thus, while van de Wetering systematically evokes the mythology of the past, he does so primarily to demonstrate the dislocation central to contemporary Dutch reality.

This dislocation has several sources. One of the most important is the return of the Netherlands' colonial past to haunt the streets of contemporary Amsterdam and call into question established values. Figures from both the Dutch East and West Indies people the novels, often challenging the adequacy of the imperial legacy of the Golden Age. Thus, the "return of the repressed" is explored in two related realms: the ways in which Dutch society continues to manifest the culturally agreed inheritance of the burghers of the Golden Age and the ways those assumptions are challenged by individuals who come to the Netherlands from former overseas colonies. Of course, if the myths of order and prosperity which had governed Dutch society are in fact invalid, then the entire legal structure which supported – indeed, enforced – those myths can also be called into question. Over the course of his series van de Wetering explores the roots of the State's code of laws in a higher system of Law and raises the thorny issue of extralegal police action in a variety of contexts. Ultimately, however, van der Wetering's novels function to deflate the enterprise of policing itself. By self-consciously parodying elements of the police procedural, he demonstrates that when the moral, economic, and political geographies of the nation become too disorderly for the myths (and laws) which had heretofore imposed restraint, then fiction alone is elastic enough to recontain the chaos.

Each of these series arises, then, from a European tradition of ideological and political debate which is itself more sophisticated than its American counterpart. As a result, the post-World War II American progression from the hard-boiled protagonist of Mickey Spillane to the police detectives created by "Dell Shannon" (Elizabeth Linnington) articulates the simple-minded, and often right-wing, responses of American detective fiction to perceived threats against a mythic "America." Shannon, for example, calls her Luis Mendoza series a version of "the morality play of our time," dealing with "truth versus lie, law and order versus anarchy, a moral code versus amorality" ("Lieutenant Luis Mendoza" 148). Even a superior proceduralist like Ed McBain, with his insistence on the physical details of the "bitch city," is more concerned with portraying his squad as a "family" than with exploring the structural weaknesses of American society ("The 87th Precinct" 92).

While one could certainly apply our methodology to the works of Shannon and McBain, their presentation of the role of the police in society is far less self-consciously problematical. Shannon, for example, like the British "moral entrepreneurs of the

New Right," subscribes to a theory of crime fiction as "a vehicle to call for the restoration of standards, the maintaining of discipline, . . . legitimizing the tendency to authoritarian solutions" (Clarke 53–54). Her "morality plays" are necessarily reductive in nature precisely because they never question the moral absolutes which are their starting points. Because she is intent upon reinforcing a conservative ("law and order") view of the police, she can be far less self-conscious about the form in which she writes and need not question the formula she has chosen to embody her views. Americans like Shannon and McBain thus offer no alternative to the hegemonic culture.

By contrast, the authors whom we are studying understand that "post-war popular culture has constituted one of the key sites implicated in the struggle for hegemony" and are concerned with detailing the relationship that exists between economic and political development and "the active practice of culture" ("Popular Culture and Hegemony" 26–28). Their works are therefore sophisticated interventions in the ideological crisis of late capitalism which problematize the police procedural and thus reveal the variety of ways in which literate – and articulate – human beings test the limits of mass culture.

2
Brave New Sweden

> The stern and venerable Goddess of Justice may seem a displaced person in the ideological vacuum of the demo-bureaucratic Welfare State, and displaced she is indeed, after having moved from a temple to a machine, a construct of social engineering. The essential thing, however, is that she still has an altar where she is worshipped, though sometimes as an unknown deity or under strange names.
>
> Stig Stromholm

It is a critical commonplace that Maj Sjöwall and Per Wahlöö's Martin Beck series is a collection of police procedurals with a social conscience.[1] Wahlöö himself, in a l966 essay, stated that they wished to "use the crime novel as a scalpel cutting open the belly of an ideologically pauperized and morally debatable so-called welfare state of the bourgeois type" (Lundin 1553). K. Arne Blom validates this claim when he notes that "In all ten novels, there is a strong Marxist orientation and the tendency found in many fictional works to exaggerate, to reveal some unpleasant truths – in this case, about Sweden" (334). Bo Lundin, on the other hand, argues that Sjöwall and Wahlöö "have been misunderstood by some American critics with muddled politics who claimed that the series sharply criticized the socialist society of Sweden"; he insists instead that "they have succeeded in a serious literary attempt to expand the borders of the detective story and use it to discuss and comment on a much wider and, in many ways, more criminal world" (1554). While Lundin is certainly right to note that Sjöwall and Wahlöö do not limit their focus exclusively to Sweden, his insistence that their critique is of a "wider . . . and more criminal world" seems, essentially, to repeat the usual claims made about hard-boiled detective fiction since Dashiell Hammett. In fact, Sjöwall and Wahlöö's project is even more ambitious. They use their discussion of Sweden as a vehicle to indict contemporary capitalism as a system, and any attempt to defuse such criticism by returning to simplistic questions of human morality in general deflects attention from the historical moment and the social, economic and political forces they analyze. Moreover, Lundin's attempt to elevate Sjöwall and Wahlöö's efforts to those of a "serious literary attempt" paradoxically weakens their trenchant critique of contemporary Sweden by denying the possibility that popular fiction can contest rather than merely reproduce the dominant ideology of the culture which generates it. The arguments of both Blom and Lundin seem, therefore, to undercut Sjöwall and Wahlöö's primary purpose: the former apologizes for an alleged "tendency" to "exaggerate"; the latter defuses their political stance, possibly with the intention of making the series more palatable to conservative American readers.

Even when critics have focused on what they see as the explicit ideological content of the Beck series, they have generally limited themselves to the later novels. James F. Maxfield, for example, says that the first two books "have no apparent political significance: both focus on the investigation of sex murders committed for pathological reasons" (71). Such a claim echoes Lundin's assertion that "The first two or three books would be almost totally apolitical; later ones would put down the mask and speak loud and clear" (1553).[2] In point of fact, the social and ideological critiques of Swedish society begin a good deal earlier than these critics have recognized, and one must evaluate the entire series as a portrait of modern Sweden from a distinctly Marxist perspective in which both the fantasy and the reality of the welfare state are simultaneously confronted and deconstructed.

From the very beginning, the authors knew that "The series would consist of only ten novels. They chose the crime novel as a form because of its strong connection between people and society: it is impossible to be a lawbreaker – or a law enforcer – without a law, laid down and maintained by a society based upon certain political and economic realities and opinions" (Lundin 1553). That is, by choosing to write police procedurals, Sjöwall and Wahlöö inevitably focus their attention on the social contract that permeates Swedish life;[3] detective fiction itself is based on a similar contract between author and reader because an author's announcement that she or he is writing within the confines of a particular formula creates generic expectations on the part of the reader. The fact that

Sjöwall and Wahlöö conceived of a finite series of works, and thus knew in advance what their endpoint would be, suggests that the series should be seen as a single work of epic proportion. Such a view emphasizes the novels' organic relationships to one another and suggests that thematic and structural strands need to be seen as indissoluble; each novel builds on the reader's recollections of both plots and characters of the preceding books and simultaneously extends and expands the ideological targets under scrutiny.[4]

In this sense, Sjöwall and Wahlöö do not attempt to alter the formulaic elements of the police procedural, but they bring to the form a new, overtly ideological purpose. Because readers become increasingly familiar with the individual detectives who comprise the corporate identity of the "hero" and because we recognize the teamwork involved in solving a case, it is evident that Sjöwall and Wahlöö are deepening our reader's awareness of the issues they confront, rather than revising the formula in which they are working. This in turn confirms the organic wholeness of the entire Beck series. From *Roseanna*, the first novel of the series, the basic elements of the authors' "contract" with the reader are clear.

What makes Sjöwall and Wahlöö so interesting is that, as sophisticated readers of the form, they consciously seek to isolate what have heretofore been covert texts and make what is usually hidden overt. Even the titles of their novels suggest this awareness since many of them function ironically, seducing readers with a promise, for example, that they will accompany the police on their hunt for a *"Cop Killer,"* while later we discover that the only cop killers in the novel are a wasp and one of the murder squad's own detectives. Likewise, *The Abominable Man* turns out to be yet another policeman rather than a conventionally "abominable" criminal. With their choice of *The Locked Room* they clearly give away the game by using a formula from an earlier era of detective fiction in order to shatter the preconceptions of readers intent on finding that Hercule Poirot has mysteriously migrated to the land of the midnight sun. In the archetype, the locked room can be seen as an allegorical figure which characterizes the insular society of detective fiction. Another reading, however, suggests that the locked room symbolizes what is "unnarratable, . . . unassimilatable by a story, by History. By explaining how a murderer could pass through a locked door . . . , the detective . . . in fact guarantees the internal cohesion of the nation by reestablishing the continuity of the historical discourse which legitimizes it" (Eisenzweig 234).[5] This is precisely what

Sjöwall and Wahlöö are *not* intent upon doing. The locked room of the title is never penetrated by the killer, only by the police, and their entry into it in turn opens a window on the plight of old-age pensioners in the welfare state. The second locked room the police invade is in fact not even locked, and what results is one of the most comic episodes in the entire series. Together, the two episodes enable Sjöwall and Wahlöö to deconstruct the locked room formula while they simultaneously deconstruct what they see as the locked room of lies embodying the Swedish welfare state.[6]

Their purpose in the series, then, is not to deflect the previously unnameable realities of History but to open the genre to a full-scale exploration of contemporary capitalism, using Sweden as their focus. In order to do so, they recur constantly to a fixed series of themes which function as a kind of shorthand for larger categories of social problems. That they should choose to do so in a series which was inaugurated in 1965 is no accident. The year 1964 marks the moment in Swedish social and political life when debate about the failure of Social Democratic promises crystallized. As Communists, Sjöwall and Wahlöö could hardly avoid participating in the debate within the party concerning its "atrophy" in Swedish political life. As Hancock notes, "Ideological renewal emerged as the dominant theme of the party's twentieth congress in January 1964" (Hancock, *Sweden* 86). In an attempt to distance itself from Moscow, the party turned its attention to "the failure of the Social Democrats to extend democratic principles from the political spheres to economic and social relations" (Hancock, *Sweden* 84–85). The new Left-Party Communists were particularly concerned with "perceived contradictions between democratic-humanistic values and the actual performance of the Swedish system" (Hancock, "Post-Welfare" 235). In particular, the failure of the welfare state was traced to an inability to achieve a truly egalitarian society.[7] As Hancock pointed out in 1972, "the nation's economic growth has not affected all citizens equally. Some strata have benefitted more than others, and structural adjustments within the economy . . . have led to major problems of unemployment, reeducation, and industrial relocation" ("Post-Welfare" 231). The remaining questions of equality involved not only lower-wage groups that are still disadvantaged, but also "Various minorities, such as the aged, the handicapped, and social misfits . . . . Such groups are burdened with lower incomes, poorer service, and reduced standards of living in a society that is primarily created for those who are effective producers" (Gyllensten 286).

Ingemar Wizelius notes that Swedish writers of the 1960s turned toward an examination of their country, "spearheading what might be called an 'agonizing reappraisal' of our basic social values chiefly in the light of demands for paying greater heed to the wishes of different minorities" (244). This new moral engagement forms part of a "radical critique" that is "coupled with rejection of high-brow culture" (Gyllensten 291) and seeks to influence the masses directly in order to "enhance individual moral consciousness and existential freedom" (Hancock, *Sweden* 87). That Sjöwall and Wahlöö should choose to participate in this political debate by writing popular fiction is hardly surprising, given the huge reading public in Sweden; in addition to having the highest per capita newspaper circulation in the world (Hancock, "Post-Welfare" 244), Sweden's general literacy rate is "phenomenonally high" (Childs 6). While dominant groups in Sweden were arguing that the nation had attained a level of social homogeneity and political consensus which precluded ideological conflict,[8] radical dissent focused on "a participatory ... political culture in which individuals would attain more immediate influence on the social, political, and economic terms of their day-to-day existence" (Hancock, *Sweden* 88).

Commentators examined the failures of institutions largely created by the Social Democrats which were meant to protect the individual residents of "the People's Home."[9] In every case they evinced a "common moral concern with the relation of the individual to his social environment" (Hancock, *Sweden* 73). Sjöwall and Wahlöö in particular demythologize a series of welfare state institutions which reveal the consequences of post-industrial modernization. One of the most compelling examples of their method is their manipulation of setting, and their condemnation of the "gross ecological malfeasance" (CK 18) perpetrated in Sweden begins as early as *Roseanna*.

The use of landscape as a medium for social commentary is not original with Sjöwall and Wahlöö; it is a thread that runs through the American hard-boiled detective novel as well. Ross MacDonald, for example, makes "a sustained attack upon the criminal class of polluters, developers, entrepreneurs, politicians and heedless consumers whose selfish ravages have spoiled the Garden" that is California (Babener 84). Sjöwall and Wahlöö have clearly borrowed from this tradition and have systematically connected the use of landscape in the Martin Beck series to their ideological aims in order to create a moral ecology of Sweden.[10]

Dennis Porter points out in *The Pursuit of Crime: Art and Ideology in Detective Fiction* that, "In its broadest sense . . . the landscape which is represented as the backdrop to crime in a detective novel is as ideologically significant as stylistic level and the type of hero" (189).[11] While Porter is not explicitly discussing the police procedural here, his claim clearly applies to Sjöwall and Wahlöö's depiction of the Swedish landscape as it evolves over the course of the Beck series. They consciously manipulate both urban and rural landscapes to indict the Swedish state for what they describe as its consistent disregard for human values in a changing social environment. This is most evident in the use of parks as the loci for crime in the early novels, especially in *The Man on the Balcony*. Here, every important criminal act in both the primary and secondary plots of the novel is set in one of Stockholm's green spaces. An institution meant to provide relief from the burdens of urban life becomes the source of relentlessly increasing terror.

Even though *The Man on the Balcony* begins on June 10, when the summer vacation has already started, the city is still "full of people who . . . would have to make do with the makeshift country life offered by parks and open-air swimming pools" (20). While most Stockholmers are presumably trying to make the best of the recreational opportunities the city offers them, Lennart Kollberg of the National Homicide Squad must confront the reality of what is hidden in Vanadis Park: "It was summer. People were swimming. Tourists were wandering about, map in hand. And in the shrubbery between the rocks and the red paling lay a dead child. It was horrible. And it might get worse" (31). The reader is prepared for this juxtaposition of violence and idyll by the original discovery of the first victim's body. A sunny Saturday morning reveals "two seedy figures" who enter the park in search of a quiet place to drink themselves into oblivion, finding refuge from the harsh reality of their lives in a bottle rather than in Stockholm's version of "country life." Instead of relief they find the violated corpse of Eva Carlsson, "lying with the top part of her body half hidden under a bush. Her legs, wide apart, were stretched out on the damp sand. The face, turned to one side, was bluish and the mouth was open" (22). The police photo used to identify Eva pictures her as she should have been seen in Vanadis Park, "leaning against a tree and laughing up at the sun" (25). The distance between Eva in death and in life embodies the transformation of Stockholm's green spaces from idyllic to demonic.

Sjöwall and Wahlöö repeat this pattern with the discovery of the second murder victim in Tanto Park. Here, the park is even more clearly meant to be an oasis in a squalid desert: it is surrounded by allotment gardens for those too poor to have country homes, scrapyards, "ramshackle wooden huts," the "Högalid Institution for alcoholics," and the "Tanto workingmen's hostel" (49). While Martin Beck's characterization of the situation as "almost hopeless" (49) is intended as a reflection on the difficulty of capturing the murderer in such a neighborhood, the reader necessarily interprets his thought in a wider context: once again the urban refuge has been polluted by violence.

With this second murder, the entire city is transformed into a hunting ground, and the level of violence increases exponentially. Each park becomes a stalking place for groups of vigilantes intent upon preventing crime. Kollberg is blackjacked in Tanto Park by two armed, well-meaning civil engineers; an old-age pensioner is "battered in Haga Park. He was standing having a leak" (126). As Kollberg himself puts it, "everything's going to hell" (126).[12] Of course, these allegedly law-abiding citizens are themselves criminal, and their actions ironically recapitulate those of the mugger whose activities are detailed in the opening chapters of the novel and who is the focus of its secondary plot. A discussion between Beck and Larsson suggests that Vanadis Park has been transformed into a jungle by "a lunatic [who] prowls about the parks bashing people on the head . . . " (6). Larsson's frustration, in particular, centers around his concern that "this man knows his business. He only goes for defenseless old men and women. And always from behind. What was it someone said last week? Oh, yes, 'he leaped out of the bushes like a panther'" (7). Larsson's recollection of an earlier victim's description is especially apt, since Sjöwall and Wahlöö insist throughout the novel that Stockholm's parks epitomize the urban jungle the Swedish capital has become.

Such deterioration cannot be attributed solely to the work of a single mugger, no matter how efficient or ruthless he may be. In fact, both the Swedish police and the mugger use Stockholm's parks as hunting grounds to stalk their respective prey. Chapter 5 opens with a detailed account of the way in which the mugger isolates and targets his victims. Like the panther he supposedly resembles, the mugger is both patient and alert: "He had been in the park or its immediate vicinity for over two hours, observing people closely and calculatingly" (17). The mugger is not, of course, the only individual to use the park for illicit purposes. Although he rejects them as victims, the mugger observes the sexual adventures of two Stockholm teenagers with detached humor. While he is "no Peeping Tom" and has "more important things to do" (18), his close attention to detail ultimately saves him from being wrongly convicted of the sex murders which are the focus of the novel's primary plot.[13] These same powers of observation immediately enable him to identify, overhear and finally evade two policemen in a red Volvo who enter the park just as the teenage couple leaves. Sjöwall and Wahlöö emphasize the inferior skills of the police in this situation by juxtaposing the policemen's apparently aimless walks through the park and their decision to go for a cup of coffee with the mugger's attack on his prey: "He caught sight of her as soon as she entered the park and knew at once which path she would take" (19). The cold-blooded violence of his attack, the victim's defense of her handbag "as if she'd been protecting a baby," and the mugger's characterization of her as a "silly old bitch" (19) set the tone for a description of more horrifying events that have, unbeknownst to the police, taken place at precisely the same time in precisely the same park.

As the two plots converge, it becomes evident that no green space in Stockholm is exempt from violence. The third murder victim's body is discovered in St. Erik's park, "one of the smallest in the city; in fact it is so insignificant that most Stockholmers don't even know of its existence" (161). Nonetheless, this park, tellingly characterized as "forming a kind of unnatural end to the long street of Västmannagatan" (161), is the site of a "macabre corroboration" of the police theory that the "murders would get more and more horrible" (161). While the first victim was discovered by two drunks and the second by two little boys, the third is found by her own mother who "had broken down completely and was already in the hospital" (162). As the pace of the hunt quickens, the police focus more and more of their attention on the parks, flushing more and more criminals into the open. For example, in "the park by Rosendal Manor a young man broke into a run when a policeman asked to see his identity card and in panic he ran right into the arms of two other policemen. He refused to say who he was and why he had run. When they searched him they found a loaded 9-millimeter Parabellum in his coat pocket and he was taken straight to the nearest police station" (168). Kollberg caustically points out: "'In this way we'll soon have pulled in every criminal in Stockholm except the one we want'" (168).

The ineffectiveness of the police as hunters is epitomized by their seizing the wrong man in the parkland of South Djurgården. Here, surrounded by evidence of old wealth and a safer, more secure way of life rooted in class privilege ("manor houses, mansions, dignified villas and small eighteenth-century wooden houses . . . all surrounded by beautiful gardens" [167]), the police grill Wilhelm Fristedt who sums up the transformation of nature in Stockholm by quoting Fröding: *"I am the sick lime-tree that withers while still young./Dry leaves I scattered to the wind when on my crown they hung"* (170).

Such a description could be aptly applied to the real murderer, Ingemund Fransson. Although connected to rural nature by his Småland background, he too has been transformed by the urban environment. Over the course of his life, he has worked for the parks department in Malmö and as a gardening laborer in Stockholm's park system, and this familiarity with Stockholm's green spaces allows Fransson to select the "best" sites for his assaults on young children. Moreover, the connection between urban green spaces and death is reaffirmed by the fact that Fransson has evaded capture for days by sleeping in cemeteries. Ironically, Fransson is caught only by accident, and then by the two least skilled "hunters" on the police force, Kristiansson and Kvant. In an action which recalls the episode of the old-age pensioner beaten by vigilantes, Kvant captures the murderer when he stops to answer the "call of nature" (175). Reducing the solution of the major criminal investigation to a comic accident which deliberately echoes the misplaced attempts of the citizenry to hunt down the murderer stalking their parks suggests that the urban jungle can no longer be effectively patrolled.

In *The Man on the Balcony*, then, Sjöwall and Wahlöö attempt to show that an institution meant to improve the quality of urban life has become a matrix of all types of illegitimate behavior. The robbery, assault, murder, sex, voyeurism, alcoholism, drugs, vagrancy and lynch mobs that characterize daily activities in Stockholm's parks is echoed in later novels, forming a kind of leitmotif that continues throughout the Beck series and leads to the conclusion that all of Sweden's institutions are in danger of falling prey to different forms of pollution.[14] Thus, the third novel of the series begins what Frank Occhiogrosso calls "a record of the altered perception of [Swedish] society" (175). That is, even this early the novels "move in a definite direction: their central vision is pessimistic, and the societal change they chronicle is basically a process of deterioration" (Lesser 19).

Such a view is confirmed in *The Man Who Went Up in Smoke* where Sjöwall and Wahlöö turn to parks to convey the depressing quality of life in modern Stockholm, using images which deliberately echo scenes in *The Man on the Balcony*. For example, immediately after Martin Beck and Lennart Kollberg piece together the identity of the murderer of Alf Matsson, the scene switches from their office to Vasa Park:

> The wind had dropped and in Vasa Park the light rain was falling peacefully down onto the double row of tombola stalls, a carousel and two policemen in black rain capes. The carousel was running and on one of the painted horses sat a lone child: a little girl in a red-plastic coat with a hood. She was riding round and round in the rain with a solemn expression on her face and her eyes focused straight ahead. Her parents were standing under an umbrella a little way away, regarding the amusement park with melancholy eyes. (126–27)

The mournful nature of this scene indicates the morally unsatisfactory outcome of the investigation. Because the victim has in many ways deserved his fate, and because the murder itself was for all intents and purposes an accident, the members of the homicide squad can derive little satisfaction from their work.

The same depression which characterizes the portrait of the little girl allegedly amusing herself in Vasa Park plagues Martin Beck himself the morning after he delivers Gunnarsson to the prosecutor. He gazes from his balcony at "nature" below: "It was called a grove, but hardly lived up to its name. The ground between the evergreens was covered with pine needles and trash, and the little grass that had been there in the early summer had long since been trampled away" (152). While Beck then leaves Stockholm for his delayed vacation in the natural beauty of the Swedish archipelago, he has clearly lost all pleasure and enthusiasm at the prospect (152). Thus, while *The Man on the Balcony* uses parks in an active role to indict Swedish institutions, *The Man Who Went Up in Smoke* employs them in a passive role, as emblems of the state of mind of the Swedish people in general and Martin Beck in particular. Obviously, there is no consolation to be found in urban nature.

Cop Killer, the ninth book of the series, most clearly reprises Sjöwall and Wahlöö's earlier indictment of the perversion of nature in modern Sweden. By bringing murder to the only explicitly rural setting in the entire Martin Beck series, the authors demonstrate that the violence and crime which they had once confined to the "artificial" nature of urban green spaces is in fact endemic to all of Sweden and has corrupted the heretofore idyllic rural world. In so doing they go beyond Dashiell Hammett's "dark myth of the unredeemable city"; rather than "shattering . . . the pastoral dream on the concrete surfaces of the urban wasteland" (Porter 198), they undercut the very assumptions upon which the pastoral idyll has been based.

The body of Sigbrit Mård is discovered by a botanist on a fall outing with a group of hikers. While searching for "a large and beautiful specimen of a parasol mushroom" (149–50), the botanist comes upon a "curious, moss-covered mudhole":

> He saw black mud bubbling up into the holes left by his feet.
>
> And then he noticed something else, rising slowly out of the mire and moss and spruce twigs about a yard from the depression where his left boot had been.
>
> He stood very still and wondered what it might be.
>
> The object took shape before his eyes, and it took a fraction of a second for his brain to register the fact that what he saw was a human hand.
>
> And then he screamed. (150)

Sigbrit's corpse profanes what appears superficially as an isolated and peaceful marshland near a small village that has no history of violent crime. Beck himself has difficulty believing that murder could intrude upon such a setting: "Martin Beck smiled. It was a miserable and tragic situation, but there was something rural and idyllic about it nonetheless. As opposed to the usual grim atmosphere of heavy suspicion and threatening billy clubs" (157). The discovery of the corpse is followed, however, by the usual forensic investigation, made difficult by earlier invasions of nature: heavy forestry machinery has churned up the access road, and the army has staged exercises in the area (154). Where both hikers and reader expect to find only a rural idyll, they find instead "a rather badly decomposed corpse in a mud puddle in the woods" (151). Such a discovery recalls the ways in which a series of innocent individuals had earlier stumbled upon the corpses of young girls in Stockholm's parks in *The Man on the Balcony*.

The reader is prepared to recall such a connection as a result of Sjöwall and Wahlöö's earlier recounting of Lennart Kollberg's accidental killing of a fellow policeman in Stockholm's Långholm Park (CK 11–13). Kollberg's subsequent renunciation of violent methods, embodied in his refusal to carry a gun, contrasts strikingly with the increase in violence which pervades even the Swedish countryside. The authors reinforce this notion of a "spreading stain" (Porter 40) of violence by means of a secondary plot involving Ronnie Casparsson and his partner, who are accused of having killed a policeman in the course of a routine check following a burglary.[15] Sjöwall and Wahlöö note specifically the unlikely setting for such violence: "All of this took place on the morning of November 18, 1973, in the farthest corner of the Malmö Police District. For that matter, in the farthest corner of Sweden. Several hundred yards away long shiny waves surged in against a curving sand beach that seemed to be endless in the fog. The sea" (CK 197). Thus, what began as a relatively unimportant series of botched burglaries in an isolated area of the Swedish countryside becomes the center of intense police activity. Casparsson subsequently becomes a desperado, hiding out with a professional criminal, the Breadman, who has himself accidentally killed a woman in the course of a routine robbery in Uppsala (8). The two transform their woodland hideout – "an ordinary Swedish crofter's cottage" (298) – into an arsenal stocked with "two Army model submachine guns and three automatic pistols of varying make and caliber" as well as "plenty of ammunition, including two whole boxes for the tommy guns" (299). Much as *The Man on the Balcony* fused two plots through the transformation of urban parks, so, too, both primary and secondary plots in *Cop Killer* involve the transformation of a rural setting into a locus of violent crime.

As the penultimate novel in the series, *Cop Killer* not only gathers the plot threads of earlier books[16] but also reprises a crucial theme: Sweden as a whole is being polluted both morally and physically. Thus, just as in the novels of Chandler and Hammett, the land is "no longer a source of regeneration" (Porter 198); instead, the entire environment provides evidence for the degeneration of Swedish society. For example, *Roseanna*, the first novel in the series, opens with an image that will later be echoed in *Cop Killer*. As a dredging machine plows through a clogged channel below the locks at Borenshult, a process which began only after months of bureaucratic haggling, "the dredger's bucket had just gobbled up a new mouthful of Boren's bottom slime and was on its way up out of the water . . . . Filthy gray water streamed out of the bucket as it hung over the hold . . . . A white, naked arm stuck out of the bucket's jaw" (2). The arm, of course, is that of Roseanna McGraw of Lincoln, Nebraska, an unsuspecting tourist lured to her death on a sightseeing boat on Sweden's canals.

Just as the body of an American tourist, a victim of individual violence, pollutes Sweden's waterways, so, too, in *The Fire Engine That Disappeared* Swedish waters are befouled by a double source of pollution, societal and individual. The bay at Malmö contains "filthy water and an empty beer can and a limp contraceptive" (136). It also contains an ancient Ford: "among the tipped-up seats with their rusty springs and blackened frames sat a muddy corpse. One of the most horrible [Månsson] had ever seen. With empty eye-sockets and the lower jaw torn away" (139–40). While nature has ironically contributed to the horror of the scene (scavenging eels have eaten away at the corpse), the principal responsibility for both kinds of pollution lies with society. Indeed, the pollution which Sjöwall and Wahlöö see spreading across Sweden is so great that the results of crimes wash up on the shore of the health resort at Dragør in Denmark. In *Murder at the Savoy* a young boy wandering on the beach finds "the wreck of a green plastic boat . . . , an empty milk carton, a beer can, and a condom" (154). He also finds a crucial piece of evidence that will enable the police to solve the murder of Viktor Palmgren: the gun box, "lined with polystyrene, compressed from the kind of plastic particles that get washed up in countless millions on the Swedish and Danish beaches on the Sound, the Baltic and the North Sea" (155).

In addition to these concrete images of the pollution of nature that crystallize over the course of the Martin Beck series, images which should embody progress are transformed into ones which suggest social corruption and a declining quality of life. Buses become the sites of massacres (*The Laughing Policeman*) when they are not merely the source of lethal carbon monoxide pollution (FE 50); subways are crowded and unfriendly and contain "even more poisonous layers of air" (FE 50) than do the buses, and this poisoned atmosphere is concretized in the booming pornography business that takes place in the central train station (MB 13) as well as in the vandalized cars that litter the Swedish environment. A description in *The Abominable Man* of the alleged improvements in Stockholm epitomizes the sorry state to which urban renewal has ironically reduced the city:

> The center of Stockholm had been subjected to sweeping and violent changes in the course of the last ten years. Entire districts had been leveled and new ones constructed. The structure of the city had been altered: streets had been broadened and freeways built. What was behind all this activity was hardly an ambition to create a humane social environment but rather a desire to achieve the fullest possible exploitation of valuable land. In the heart of the city it had not been enough to tear down ninety percent of the buildings and completely obliterate the original street plan, violence had been visited on the natural topography itself. (36)

The rhetoric of violence that characterizes this description predicts the havoc that occurs at the end of the novel. Once again, Sjöwall and Wahlöö deliberately move from individual violence to large-scale, social mayhem. The chaos of the police action that eventually nets Åke Eriksson amply demonstrates the dangers of an urban bureaucracy gone mad and reminds series readers of the frequent connections between violence against man and violence against the environment.

The sources of the violated environment lie principally in a conspiracy between government and big business. The plot against Sweden's culture and resources is exemplified by redevelopment, and those responsible are either targets for murder (Viktor Palmgren in *Murder at the Savoy*) or precipitators of violence against others by those who are their victims (Eriksson in *The Abominable Man*; Rebecka Lind in *The Terrorists*).[17]

In other words, the centralized effort to improve the quality of life in a supposedly socialist country has clearly had the opposite effect. Along with other "Critics in both the leftist and non-Socialist parties [Sjöwall and Wahlöö assert] that the technocratic power structure constitutes the principal determining factor in urban planning in the larger cities, with citizens exercising virtually no influence in decisions" (Elvander 308). The result of this faceless and apparently inhuman technocratic power, then, is that Stockholm, once a *locus amoenus*, has been reduced to the mechanical: "The buildings tightened along the road and the city rose up beneath its dome of light, huge and cold and desolate, stripped of everything but hard naked surfaces of metal, glass and concrete" (AM 2). As the buildings tighten their grip on the environment, so too the city tightens its grip on Stockholm's "million frightened people" (MB 77). This image of "the anonymity of urban existence" (Lesser 18), already present in the second novel, is developed and elaborated throughout the series.

The theme of urban alienation, then, can be seen as a second major leitmotif unifying the ten novels. In presenting Swedish society as a collection of isolated and frightened individuals, the authors attack the social myth, promulgated especially by the Social Democrats but endorsed by other political power groups as well, that Sweden is a fully homogeneous society where citizens work through mutual support ("cooperative individualism") to achieve a constantly improving quality of life.[18] It is present as early as *Roseanna*, where the subject is ironically introduced under the guise of tourism. In order to reconstruct the events leading to the murder of Roseanna McGraw, the National Homicide Squad must essentially recreate her canal boat tour of Sweden. One of the primary vehicles they use to do so is a collection of photographic souvenirs taken by her fellow passengers. The home movie they view is typical of those taken by tourists in Europe, complete with shots of "the king's guard in Stockholm," "pretty Swedish girls with turned up noses sitting in the sun on the steps of the Concert Hall," and the canal that "curved through a long, soft distance between tree-covered shores" (111–15). Rather than studying the landscape, however, the police must focus on the passengers themselves, seeking the individual who might have wished to take the life of a young American woman. That is, by transforming a home movie into an investigative tool, the police inevitably reify the passengers, turning them into objects of study upon which to practice their surveillance.

In this sense, they are already alienated from the landscape they are viewing by the nature of their task. In turn, readers are similarly distanced from any effect of recognition, and the act of reading itself repeats the alienation which is the central thematic focus. Thus, the authors' use of the Swedish landscape results in an experience that is very different from Porter's notion of "reassurance" projected by "the mythic landscapes that are Doyle's London, Chandler's Southern California, and Simenon's Paris" (217). In these cases, "The gestures made in the direction of mimesis . . . are often cultural references designed to trigger recognition by means of the same metonymic figure used by tourist brochures when they signify London and Paris with the silhouette of the Houses of Parliament and the Eiffel Tower respectively." Porter therefore claims that "Detective novels provide reassurance . . . because they propose a world of fixed cultural quantities. They effectively suppress the historical reality that they seem to represent and draw for solutions to the problems posed on cherished, but frequently anachronistic, cultural values" (217–18). Because the tourist experience in *Roseanna* is vacated by the fact that it becomes an investigative tool in which the reader must participate, the Swedish landscape must be seen as strange and unstable, rather than as a "fixed cultural quantity." That this effect is intentional is clear from the fact that Sjöwall and Wahlöö continue to deconstruct rather than celebrate the tourist's Stockholm; they repeat the structure of the home movie in the narrative, providing the reader with a series of unsettling tours of the city as the police shadow their suspect, Folke Bengtsson.

Like the landscape that is "blotted out" by the more important search for the killer, the streets of Stockholm lose their Baedekeresque quality. As Åke Stenström tails Bengtsson, he charts the suspect's progress by providing Beck with a list of landmarks, but the net result is to efface the city and, more importantly, its citizens: only the hunter and his quarry have life. Although Bengtsson is finally shown to have been motivated by a pathological fear of being "soiled" by women, in fact the sex murder is clearly intended to have larger implications. He kills Roseanna because she invades the protective shell he has built for himself in order to cope with life in contemporary Sweden. Thus, while Bengtsson is clearly an extreme version of the frightened urban dweller, he nonetheless indicates the disturbing nature of life in Stockholm. As Sonja Hansson, the policewoman who finally entraps him, puts it: "'. . . I said that it was no city to be alone in, and he agreed, although he said he rather liked to be alone'" (174). The atomized existence that finally drives Bengtsson to murder an American tourist is underlined not only in the meaninglessly labyrinthine quality of his repeated trips through the city, but also through the character of Detective Lieutenant Elmer B. Kafka, Homicide Squad, Lincoln, Nebraska, U.S.A. It is Kafka, perhaps not ironically, who tells his Swedish colleagues to "'Set a trap'" (162) for Bengtsson. Kafka's presence in the novel unleashes a network of associations which highlight the grim absurdity of both the case and the dystopian society which provoked it.[19] Bengtsson will reappear in *Cop Killer*, now "rehabilitated" after several years in a mental institution, only to become a suspect in yet another murder. Surely Sjöwall and Wahlöö had Joseph K. in mind.

The atomization and alienation that are outlined here are systematically developed in later works. In *Murder at the Savoy*, for example, Gunvald Larsson notes that it is Swedish society itself which is responsible for "what are called unpremeditated crimes":

> Unhappy people, nervous wrecks, were driven into desperate situations against their wills. In almost all the cases, alcohol or drugs were of decisive importance. It may have been partly due to the heat, but more basic was the system itself, the relentless logic of the big city, which wore down the weak-willed and the maladjusted and drove them to senseless actions.
>
> And the lonely. He wondered how many suicides had been committed during the last twenty-four hours and felt almost relieved that it would still be a while before he found out. (121)

The city itself, then, is a "system" which inevitably produces the "nervous wrecks" who are "driven" according to a logic which is beyond their control, and that logic, like the pollution found in *Cop Killer*, is spreading inexorably even to the countryside. It is no wonder that in *Cop Killer* Beck's colleague, Allwright, concludes that, "'Even if conditions are pretty good right here [in rural Anderslöv], still there's something wrong with society as a whole. I wouldn't have wanted to try and raise kids here. The question is whether it can be done at all'" (46). These very general reflections on the dysfunctioning of Swedish society are confirmed by a variety of more specific investigations of particular institutions in the bourgeois welfare state.

One of these targets is paradoxically a source of pride to the Social Democratic architects of the reforms that were carried out in Sweden during the 1950s and 1960s: the care of the aged. While the Swedish government has assumed the responsibiity for maintaining the elderly in old-age homes, these institutions serve to isolate their inmates and reduce them to complete dependence on the state.[20] Sjöwall and Wahlöö return at least twice to the subject, focusing on Martin Beck's mother's deteriorating health, and foregrounding the boredom, gloom and desperation that characterize life in an old folks' home.[21] Though his mother is among the luckier ones,

Beck reflects on the fate that awaits other pensioners who have no personal funds whatsoever:

> To grow old alone and in poverty, unable to look after oneself, meant that after a long and active life one was suddenly stripped of one's dignity and identity – fated to await the end in an institution in the company of other old people, equally outcast and annihilated.
>
> Today they were not even called "institutions," or even "old people's homes." Nowadays they were called "pensioners' homes," or even "pensioners' hotels," to gloss over the fact that in practice most people weren't there voluntarily, but had quite simply been condemned to it by a so-called Welfare State that no longer wished to know about them. It was a cruel sentence, and the crime was being too old. As a worn-out cog in the social machine, one was dumped on the garbage heap. (LR 62)

Ironically, then, the "cradle-to-grave" security system that Sweden began instituting after World II turns out to be nothing more than a "concentration camp" for the nation's "gray Negroes."[22] By imposing the "cruel sentence" of confinement for the "crime [of] being too old," the Swedish bureaucracy can eliminate the "problem" of caring for the indigent old; in this fashion government agencies can effectively avoid true responsibility in "the People's Home" without losing the rhetorical opportunities necessary to continue bureaucratic functioning. Thus, the elderly are relocated in what Foucault calls the "carceral city" precisely because they are no longer seen as "normal," because their old age with its accompanying infirmities automatically marginalizes them and ensures that they become the objects of power rather than its possessors (298–99; 308).

In this sense, the elderly are no better off than the young, who are themselves forced to society's margins when they begin to demonstrate "deviant behavior" that might, in the eyes of the disciplinary state, lead to social disorder. As Bertil Olofsson's mother tells Einar Rönn in *The Fire Engine that Disappeared*,

> "I can tell you one thing . . . . He was actually a very nice boy once. But he got into bad company and was easily led and he opposed me and my husband and his brother, well, practically everyone. Then he went to a reformatory and that didn't make

things any better. There he just learned to hate society even more. He also learned to become a real professional there and how to use drugs." (101)

Once again, as is true for Ronnie Casparsson's fate in *Cop Killer*, an element of the system upon which Sweden particularly prides itself is condemned for subverting the public good. While this particular description of the "kid gone bad" may sound all too familiar to the American ear, it in fact reflects at least two decades of controversy with regard to the treatment of youthful offenders. After several juvenile riots during the early 1950s, Sweden hesitated between incarceration and leniency. The more dangerous offenders were sentenced to reformatories, while the less violent were supervised while at liberty (Fleisher 220–25). These options more or less reflected a continuing split over punishment through the 1960s: there were those who sanctioned the idea of revenge, and others who supported the "curative approach" (Stromholm 107). Currently the National Board of Health and Welfare runs eighteen delinquent centers. Some of the institutions are quite restrictive, while others are quite open. In no case can a youth be incarcerated for more than two months. Specialists on the National Board openly admit that they are unable to rehabilitate the vast majority of young offenders; in fact, "80 percent end up in adult jails – they cannot be kept in delinquent centers after the age of eighteen – in mental hospitals or on the dole for the rest of their lives" (Childs 27–28). The greatest rates of recidivism are for offenders "sentenced to youth prisons and internment – 86 percent and 79 percent respectively" (Childs 28).[23]

The case of Bertil Olofsson is emblematic of the failure of well-intentioned efforts at juvenile reform. Sjöwall and Wahlöö confirm their interest in this theme by stressing more and more frequently over the course of the series that Sweden is losing its young and hence its future. In a general sense, they do so by increasing the frequency of their passing references to young people who are either addicted to or incapacitated by drugs and noting the lengths to which they will go in order to buy them. In contemporary Swedish society, where religious beliefs are declining (Childs 2), the Marxian metaphor of the "opiate of the masses" is no longer figural. As early as *The Man on the Balcony*, for example, Beck is accosted in the train station by "a girl in her early teens": "She was barefoot and dirty and looked the same age as his own daughter." She offers him nude photographs of herself, knowing full well that even if she fails with

Beck, "Before long some idiot was sure to buy her photographs. Then off she would go to Humlegården or Mariatorget and buy purple hearts or marijuana with the money. Or perhaps LSD" (13). This anonymous girl has quite literally reduced herself to an object of exchange, and Beck's reflections on the incident mark the changes in Swedish society since his joining the force twenty-four years earlier: "In those days girls of fourteen and fifteen had not photographed themselves naked in photo machines and tried to sell the pictures to detective superintendents in order to get money for a fix" (14).

Gunvald Larsson is, characteristically, even harsher in his assessment of a young prostitute: "'I think you're rather ugly. You've got flabby breasts and bags under your eyes and you look sick and wretched. In a few years' time you'll be a complete wreck and you'll look so damned awful, no one'll want to touch you with a bargepole'" (FE 75). In a sense, Larsson's "catalog" is another example of the human-made-object, but beneath his exterior gruffness Larsson is just as moved as his colleague: "He felt sticky and unhealthy. His confrontation with that sixteen-year-old girl in her grimy room had given him a feeling of purely physical discomfort. He went straight to the Sture Baths and spent three thought-free hours in the gentlemen's Turkish baths" (FE 75). To have the most action-oriented member of the National Homicide Squad escape the reality of daily life, if only for "three thought-free hours," is surely to mark his own frustration and powerlessness to change the system. With no employment and no place to go, the future of wayward Swedish youth is at best grim, and their plight is little different from that of the mass of Swedish citizens who have fallen through the cracks in the walls of the "People's Home."

Some of these unlucky citizens are the subject of a description late in *The Man on the Balcony*, where a giant manhunt for Ingemund Fransson gives Sjöwall and Wahlöö the opportunity to reflect on the homeless people "who, though fit for work and for the most part capable of holding a down a job, cannot find anywhere to live, since bungled community planning has resulted in an acute housing shortage" (163). As a result, they are to be found in parks, on quaysides, under bridges, in backyards, on construction sites, in train stations and elsewhere, subject to frequent identity checks by the policemen who are seeking a child murderer (163–64). Although the Social Democrats recognized the need for decent housing for the working classes, and planned to build 70,000 new units by

1965 (Fleisher 121), according to Sjöwall and Wahlöö, "the housing shortage had been kept alive artificially for many years, . . . and the rents were close to astronomical" (SAV 83). While a journalist like Fleisher describes the new housing projects as light and airy, emphasizing landscaping, "simplicity of style, and ever-changing originality of design" (121), Sjöwall and Wahlöö point out that many of the projects resemble the one managed by Hampus Broberg in *Murder at the Savoy*: "an isolated group of high-rise apartments, slapped together quickly and carelessly, whose sole purpose was to make as large a profit as possible for the owner while at the same time guaranteeing unpleasantness and discomfort for the unfortunate people who had to live there" (83). Many of Sweden's public housing projects thus serve to reinforce the marginal status of their inhabitants while simultaneously confining them to specific environments which are readily monitored by the state apparatus. The anomic results of such a living situation are exemplified in *The Locked Room*, where the sources of Monita's depression and desperation, as well as the causes of the crimes she commits, are traced to yet another vestige of the carceral network, "a big housing project out in the suburbs where everyone seemed to be erecting barriers around his own privacy" (179). It is only after Monita escapes to Yugoslavia with the money from the bank she has robbed – an evasion of the law and its surveillance that is clearly sanctioned by the authors – that she is able to realize the promises that were broken by Sweden's "Middle Way."

Monita's flight to Yugoslavia is, in itself, an ironic commentary on the economic conditions in her homeland, where "guest" workers from the Mediterranean basin are regularly exploited by both employers and landlords. Once again, Sjöwall and Wahlöö are not analyzing a problem unique to Sweden; the whole question of Southern European and North African workers has been hotly debated throughout the industrialized countries of Northern Europe for the past three decades. By 1968, Sweden had established a Commission on Immigration to discuss the status of immigrant workers. The Commission's work resulted in a law which recognized "the transformation of one of the most homogeneous people to a multi-ethnic nation. The new law set three goals: equality between immigrants and Swedes, cultural freedom of choice for immigrants, and cooperation and solidarity between the native majority and the various ethnic minorities" (Childs 161). While Sweden has made some progress in integrating these new ethnic groups (since 1973, employers have had to provide paid leave for language instruction in Swedish, for example), it is clear that, for Sjöwall and Wahlöö, integration remains an unfulfilled ideal. There is no overt racism under scrutiny here; instead, questions about the conditions faced by immigrants revolve around issues of class. In this respect, guest workers are only one of the most obvious examples of exploitation by privileged classes which should have no place in a supposedly socialist state. Indeed, the fact that immigrants appear relatively infrequently in the novels suggests that Sjöwall and Wahlöö are more concerned with focusing on Sweden's own home-grown exploitation.[24]

Building on the evidence they have assembled that the least powerful segments of society – the elderly, the young and the homeless – are constantly exploited, Sjöwall and Wahlöö make it clear that Swedish society seems to be fast approaching open class warfare.[25] The fourth novel of the series, for example, demonstrates that the murder of nine people on a Stockholm city bus has its roots in the twisted desire of Björn Forsberg to defend "myself and my family and my home and my firm" (LP 218). Forsberg kills in order to cover up his earlier murder of Teresa Camarão, a woman who threatened his marriage into a prosperous business concern. At the end of the novel, Forsberg still does not realize that the murders he has committed are unjustified; he essentially employs a distorted theory of self-defense to excuse himself; his repetitious use of the possessive "my" to refer to his family as well as his firm suggests that people are mere objects of ownership and that by virtue of his socioeconomic position he can claim the right to the lives of his victims. Gunvald Larsson is given the task of evaluating Forsberg, in terms which both reveal his own leftist leanings and convey obliquely the authors' own views:

> "I feel sorry for nearly everyone we meet in this job. They're just a lot of scum who wish they'd never been born. It's not their fault that everything goes to hell and they don't understand why. It's types like this one who wreck their lives. Smug swine who think only of their money and their houses and their families and their so-called status. Who think they can order others about merely because they happen to be better off. There are thousands of such people and most of them are not so stupid that they strangle Portuguese whores. And that's why we never get at them. We only see their victims. This guy's an exception."

"Hm, maybe you're right," Rönn said. (LP 218–19)

The fact that Einar Rönn, perhaps the most apolitical member of the squad, agrees with Larsson underscores the validity of the charges. Here Larsson is articulating the essential critique of Sweden's New Left, that "the bourgeoisie still dominate[s] society and indirectly the political system as well" (Hancock, *Sweden* 84). In other words, "Although the Social Democrats . . . dominate politically in Sweden, a political hegemony is said to exist in the form of capitalistic or bourgeois thoughts, values, and behavior patterns." The supposed socialists are thus tools of private enterprise (Gyllensten 288), and true class equality in Sweden is merely a convenient myth.

In *Murder at the Savoy*, it is the murderer himself, Bertil Svensson, who is "anxious" for the police to understand why he impulsively killed Viktor Palmgren: Palmgren had had him evicted, forced him to move, laid him off from his job, and ultimately cost him his marriage. For these reasons, "It became clearer and clearer to him who was the cause of all his troubles: Viktor Palmgren, the bloodsucker, who lined his purse at the expense of other human beings, the big shot, who didn't give a damn about the welfare of his employees or tenants" (197–98). Once again, it is the police who are left to evaluate the alleged criminality of the accused, and this time it is Martin Beck who says, "Hope he gets a light sentence" (198). All of Palmgren's associates, his accomplices in perfectly legal and perfectly horrible robbery, will flourish. Beck knows that it is only "a shipyard janitor, who in the course of time would be tried for second-degree, maybe first-degree, murder, and then have to rot away the best years of his life in a prison cell. Chief Inspector Martin Beck didn't feel good at all" (204).

Perhaps the clearest denunciation of criminal capitalism can be seen in *The Terrorists*, where Crasher Braxen, Rebecka Lind's defense attorney, systematically exposes the exploitation of the powerless by a hegemonic coalition of the state and private enterprise:

> "The fact is, Rebecka Lind has on repeated occasions during her short life been confronted with a system whose arbitrariness we all have to submit to. On not one single occasion has society, or the philosophy that created it, given her any help or offered her its understanding. . . . In fact, Rebecka's action had political foundations, although she herself does not belong to any political

group and certainly lives in happy ignorance of the political system that dictates practically everything that happens to us in this country. Let us not forget that the preposterous doctrine that war is the logical conclusion of politics is still valid today, and that this maxim has been created by well-paid theorists in the service of this capitalist society. What this young woman did yesterday was a political act, even if unconscious. I maintain that Rebecka Lind sees the corrupt rottenness of society more clearly than thousands of other young people. As she lacks political contacts and has little idea of what is involved in a mixed-economy government, her clarity of vision is even greater." (285)

The crime with which Rebecka Lind is charged is the assassination of the Swedish Prime Minister, although to call a thoroughly apolitical killing an assassination is, perhaps, to overstate the case. Nonetheless, it is evident that, however unconscious her motives may be, Rebecka Lind is one of those who has been victimized by the powerful elites of Sweden.[26] What is crucial here is that the "malaise" which Sjöwall and Wahlöö see taking over Sweden has clearly extended itself to those beyond the overt political debate, thus creating a sense of despair that is exemplified in the method by which Rebecka chooses to escape her sentence: she kills herself in a mental hospital "by throwing herself against a wall with such force that her skull was shattered. Her death was listed as accidental" (287).[27]

Rebecka Lind's suicide is no doubt the logical conclusion of a series that includes numerous examples of crimes against their fellow Swedes by the nation's captains of industry.[28] Sjöwall and Wahlöö's perspective is obvious. The police of contemporary Sweden are forced to defend a "society, which boasted of a prosperity actually reserved for a small privileged minority while the great majority's only privilege was to keep moving on the treadmill that turned the machinery" (LR 180). In so doing, the police of the Martin Beck series are forced simultaneously to question not only the particular function they fulfill in maintaining public order, but also the role of the entire criminal justice system.

By including fundamental questions about the law itself, Sjöwall and Wahlöö's novels clearly diverge from earlier detective fiction and police procedurals. Porter, for example, argues that "What is particularly notable about detective stories . . . is that they only exceptionally raise questions concerning the code; the law itself is accepted as a given. . . . The dimension that is missing from formulaic works in the detective genre is, in fact, any recognition that the law itself, with its definitions of crimes and its agencies of law enforcement and punishment, is problematic" (121). The Beck series is one of those exceptions to Porter's rule in that it openly recognizes the procedural as a "site for ideological struggle and the negotiation of hegemony" (Clarke 37).[29] By transforming a state apparatus into a vehicle for analysis, they foreground the very code that defines deviant behavior. When the damage being done to Swedish culture by the legal apparatus is articulated from within, the attack on the code is necessarily more trenchant. While it would be easy for self-described Marxists to make the police a monolithic, fascist organization, Sjöwall and Wahlöö are unwilling to do so. Their point, rather, is that the police represented by Beck and his colleagues are finally in much the same position as the rest of Swedish society, susceptible, for example, to a version of the same marginalization which affects other less privileged groups. In fact, their position may well be worse since the "Great General Public" expects them to be soldiers in the war against crime while, simultaneously, insisting on their right – or perhaps privilege – to be left alone by yet another state agency interfering in their lives.[30] The notion of the police as "good soldiers" is present as early as *The Man on the Balcony* which ends with the suggestion that, though the battle against Ingemund Fransson has been won, the war will inevitably go on: "'Good God, Lennart,' [Beck] said, 'it's over.' 'Yes,' Kollberg replied. 'For this time'" (179). The ambivalence of the public, then, is mirrored by the ambivalence of the police themselves as they come to learn more and more about the "police action" in which they find themselves engaged.

The notion of a local war fought in Stockholm is represented emblematically in the leitmotif of another, more public war that runs throughout the series: America's involvement in Vietnam. Through Gunvald Larsson, the authors explicitly link the two "police actions": "Why don't they blow up the whole of Stockholm to bits in one go instead of doing it piecemeal? They ought to do what Ronald Reagan or whatever-his-name-is said about Vietnam: Asphalt it and paint on yellow stripes and make parking lots of the goddam thing. It could hardly be worse than when the town planners get their way" (LP 70). Larsson's reference to Vietnam is apt; whether the cause is indiscriminate urban renewal or unchecked urban crime, modern Stockholm has become a war zone – the jungles of southeast

Asia and the "jungle" of contemporary Sweden have become one.[31] The connection has already been implicitly made, since *The Laughing Policeman* opens with an account of a demonstration outside the American Embassy in Stockholm where

> 412 policemen were struggling with about twice as many demonstrators. The police were equipped with tear gas bombs, pistols, whips, batons, cars, motorcycles, shortwave radios, battery megaphones, riot dogs and hysterical horses. The demonstrators were armed with a letter and cardboard signs, which grew more and more sodden in the pelting rain. (1)

The demonstration ends in chaos and is ironically juxtaposed with the commission of a real crime, that of the massacre on the bus in another part of Stockholm. The misdirected efforts of the police are thus emblematic of a larger ideological misdirection at the heart of contemporary Swedish politics; the real threat against the citizenry of Stockholm comes not from the expression of free speech, but from entrenched bourgeois businessmen like Björn Forsberg who are willing to slaughter in order to protect their financial interests and social status.

It is no secret that Swedish opposition to America's involvement in Vietnam was widespread by the mid-1960s, although the government clearly lagged behind the populace as a whole. Nonetheless, by 1968 even members of the government had begun to voice their disapproval. On February 21, 1968, for example, Olof Palme, then education minister, participated in an anti-war demonstration along with the North Vietnamese ambassador to Moscow. In 1972, when he was Prime Minister, Palme compared the Christmas bombing of Cambodia to Nazi genocide (Childs 139–43). It is small wonder that the United States recalled its ambassador and began to pressure the Palme government to tone down its opposition, threatening economic reprisals against Sweden (Hancock, *Sweden* 254). Nonetheless, Sjöwall and Wahlöö argue that much of their government's opposition to the war was hypocritical in that an official stance against American oppression in Vietnam was counteracted by repressive measures against Swedes who took to the streets to voice their own objections.

Thus, it is particularly telling that Sjöwall and Wahlöö's description of the police who are detailed to "protect the American ambassador against letters and other things from people who disliked

Lyndon Johnson and the war in Vietnam" (LP 3) sounds suspiciously like that of the American soldiers who were sent to fight a war they didn't understand:

> They had been mustered from every available precinct in town, but every policeman who knew a doctor or was good at dodging had managed to escape this unpleasant assignment. There remained those who knew what they were doing and liked it, and those who were considered cocky and who were far too young and inexperienced to try and get out of it; besides, they hadn't a clue as to what they were doing or why they were doing it. (LP 1–2)

A later demonstration, in *The Locked Room*, involves an even more bureaucratized reaction to those who might "throw an egg at the United States ambassador, or perhaps a tomato at the embassy, or set fire to the Star-Spangled Banner" (205). When the National Police Commissioner tries to lead the demonstration to a "safer spot" away from the Embassy, the demonstrators meet up with a "crowd of soccer fans" and, once again, total chaos ensues. Significantly, "Gunvald Larsson suddenly [finds] himself sitting in a helicopter, staring down at the long line of people with banners and Viet Cong flags" (206), helpless to intervene as his nominal superior transforms peaceful protest into injurious riot from which he must be evacuated, saying "'None of this must be allowed to come out'" (207).

The connection between American brutality in Vietnam and police brutality by some elements of the Swedish police is explicit in *The Abominable Man*. There, readers discover that Åke Eriksson, a former policeman dismissed from his duties after leaving his post during an anti-war demonstration, has murdered Stig Nyman, the reactionary lieutenant who allowed Eriksson's wife to die while she was mistakenly held in police custody. Nyman himself was Kollberg's sergeant for paratroop training in which Kollberg learned the finer points of killing quietly by experimenting on live animals (58–59). While Kollberg's reaction is to shy away from unnecessary violence after the war, Nyman is presented as a policeman who takes the metaphor "war on crime" quite literally and pursues it with the same sadism he demonstrated during World War II. The spiralling violence of contemporary Sweden is dramatized by Eriksson's final stand on the roof of an apartment building. As the Police Commissioner insists again and again on the efficacy of a high-tech "solution" to capturing Eriksson, sending in helicopters, specially-trained police commandos, and "stormtroopers" (165), Eriksson employs his own police training to shoot them from the sky. The scene is one of horrific comedy: the level of violence precipitated by the police is truly frightening, while their reliance on what seem to be high-tech toys for maladjusted adults renders their entire enterprise absurd.

With this sort of police activity dominating the public scene, it is no wonder that Beck and his squad are frequently treated as if they were an occupying army.[32] Like the "unpopular war" fought in southeast Asia, the local Swedish war is being fought not only to maintain order but to protect business interests. For example, the aptly-named district attorney, Bulldozer Olsson, believes that "To violate society's banks [is] to commit an outrage against its very foundations" (LR 49). In short, the state is committed to a view of crime which celebrates private property at the expense of human beings. Supposedly socialist Sweden is thus no different from its more overtly capitalist neighbors. As Foucault has noted, "the shift from a criminality of blood to a criminality of fraud" brings about "a higher juridical and moral value placed on property relations, stricter methods of surveillance, a tighter partitioning of the population, more efficient techniques of locating and obtaining information" (77).

To defend society's "foundations" requires a strong police force, and so a good deal of police attention is devoted to bolstering its numbers. As Sjöwall and Wahlöö put it, the method is simple. By manipulating statistics and by including incidents provoked by the police during anti-war demonstrations, the Commissioner can argue that attacks on the police, and thus the public order, are mounting astronomically and need to be met with even greater force: "It had all started with demands for a more militant and homogeneous police force, for greater technical resources in general, and for more firearms in particular" (LR 49–50). Once the police are more "militant" themselves, of course, they are met by a more militant citizenry, and the consequent escalation of violence, insecurity and fear is amply documented by Sjöwall and Wahlöö (LR 50–52, for example). For policemen like Martin Beck and Lennart Kollberg, however, such methods are repulsive; after all, Beck himself had originally joined the police force to avoid joining the Army during World War II (FE 5). As a result, their presence in a national, paramilitary police force is an anomaly which can only lead to disenchantment and, in the case of Kollberg, eventual resignation from the force (CK 294ff.).

The notion of the police as an occupying army has its roots in Sjöwall and Wahlöö's distrust of the nationalization of local police forces in 1965: "the entire force now came under a single hat, and from the outset it had been obvious that this hat was sitting on the wrong head" (LR 49). As we noted earlier, the national police force manipulated statistics in order to justify both its existence and its continued growth, not unlike the U.S. military's use of inflated body counts to justify sending more troops. The local, Swedish results are quite the opposite of those intended, however. Just as the presence of more and more American troops in Vietnam failed to produce a victory, so, too, more and more policemen in the streets of Sweden cannot halt crime. In fact, the continuously inflated statistics undercut the effectiveness of more police because "Violence breeds not only antipathy and hatred, but also insecurity and fear. In the end things had come to such a pass that people were going about being scared of each other and Stockholm had become a city containing tens of thousands of terrified individuals. And frightened people are dangerous people" (LR 50–51).

The nationalization of the Swedish police effects an extension of what Foucault calls a "society of the disciplinary type" (215). In this regard, the police represent a state apparatus "whose major, if not exclusive, function is to assure that discipline reigns over society as a whole . . ." (216). A burgeoning government bureaucracy that reactively seeks to control all aspects of social interaction authorizes the kind of discipline that Foucault sees as "comprising a whole set of instruments, techniques, procedures, levels of application, targets; it is a 'physics' or an 'anatomy' of power, a technology" (215) embodied in the augmented man- and firepower that the authors present as defining the new concept of the police.

The nationalized police force is therefore symptomatic of the increased surveillance that certain Swedish officials of the 1960s and 1970s had come to see as necessary to the smooth functioning of society. As Martin Beck notes, the previous decade "had been an auspicious period in the history of the Stockholm police" because "Military thinking ceased to be so popular, and reactionary ideas were no longer necessarily an asset." The movement away from "the Prussian spit-and-polish of the regular police" came to an abrupt end, however: "nationalization in 1965 had broken the positive trend. Since then, all the good prospects had been betrayed and all the good intentions laid to rest" (AM 45–46). Indeed, as Kollberg later reflects in *The Locked Room*, "The regime had backfired. As for its deepest motives, they remained shrouded in darkness – a darkness, however, in which some people detected a tint of Nazi brown" (51).

The ultimate symbol of the nightmare of bureaucratic attempts to create a brave new Sweden is the unfinished national police headquarters, begun early in *The Man Who Went Up in Smoke* and still unfinished at the conclusion of *The Terrorists*. This headquarters will be peopled, according to Lennart Kollberg, with the "rats of fascism" (LR 52) and is designed to extend the tentacles of the police "in every direction and hold the dispirited citizens of Sweden in an iron grip. At least some of them. After all, they couldn't all emigrate or commit suicide" (LR 130):

> What the police, or to be more precise, some persons within its ranks, actually wanted, was power. This was the secret ingredient that in recent years had been guiding the department's philosophy . . . .
>
> The new building was to be an important symbol of this new power. It was to facilitate a planned central directorate of a totalitarian type, and it was also to be a fortress against the prying eyes and ears of persons having no business there – which meant, in this case, the entire Swedish nation. In this context one line of thought was important: Swedes had gotten into the habit of laughing at the police. Soon no one would laugh any more. Or so it was hoped.
>
> All this, however, was so far no more than a pious aspiration, screened from all except a few; something which, with a little luck and if the right political breezes blew, could ripen into a Ministry of Terror. (LR 130–31)

The new National Police Headquarters is, then, emblematic of a new locus of power. No longer will "the prying eyes and ears" surveying Sweden be those of the citizenry; instead, they will belong only to the police whose object of attention will be the faceless, undifferentiated "nation."

Not surprisingly, therefore, the description of the National Police Headquarters is strikingly similar to that of the Panopticon analyzed by Foucault: "The Panopticon . . . must be understood as a generalizable model of functioning; a way of defining power relations in terms of the everyday life of men. . . . it is in fact a figure of political technology that may and must be detached from any specific use" (205). In other words, the headquarters becomes a nonspecific threat to the entire populace of Sweden, representing in its very secrecy a new relation of power between the rulers, here the police, and the ruled. It does so, "Because, without any physical instrument other than architecture and geometry, it acts directly on individuals; it gives 'power of mind over mind'" (Foucault 206). While Foucault argues, following Bentham, that "There is no risk . . . that the increase of power created by the panoptic machine may degenerate into tyranny [since] the disciplinary mechanism will be . . . constantly accessible 'to the great tribunal committee of the world'" (207), it is obvious that Sjöwall and Wahlöö do not share this benign opinion of the possible consequences of panoptic power. Instead, they believe that, even in the sort of disciplinary society anticipated by the architects of the Swedish Panopticon, "all varieties of crimes flourished better than ever in the fertile topsoil provided by the welfare state" (SAV 82). While Sjöwall and Wahlöö exempt the National Homicide Squad from their general condemnation of the repressive state apparatus, they nonetheless equate the treatment of the Swedish people by police bureaucrats like Stig Nyman and Stig Malm with the exploitation they have earlier shown through figures like Björn Forsberg and Viktor Palmgren, and they anticipate that public reaction against the "state within the state" (CK 125) will affect the Homicide Squad as well.

The consequence of the historical and proposed changes in the structure of the Swedish police is the production of civil servants who are themselves, in many cases, as alienated from the state as those they are intended to protect – and control. Police officers themselves, for example, are susceptible to investigation by SEPO, the security police in charge of rooting out "deviant" thought. Thus, just as they predict the increase in power among the "rats of fascism" from the very beginning of the series, Sjöwall and Wahlöö adumbrate police alienation as well. Even though the complaints about nationalization increase dramatically in number as the series progresses, discontent with the conditions under which the squad must work – and the methods they find themselves using – begins in *Roseanna*. The novel ends on a note of personal despair for Martin Beck, who reflects that "They had all sat in their offices in Motala and Stockholm and Lincoln, Nebraska, and solved this case by means that could never be made public. They would always remember it, but hardly with pride" (201). This same sense of failure in the midst of technical success dominates the endings of virtually every novel in the series, suggesting that the members of the Homicide Squad are working despite, rather than because of, the institutions which surround them.

A constant theme running throughout the series, therefore, is a commentary by the policemen themselves on the effects of the loss of individual and local control brought about by the nationalization of the Swedish police. As Dove points out, a crucial element in all procedurals is the "paramilitary nature" of any police system: "The police force . . . is a small army; criminals are the enemy, orders are to be obeyed no matter how ridiculous, and the team always comes first" (*Procedural* 68). This paramilitary system necessarily fosters the creation of a "Tight Enclave, a conception of the police community whose members cover for each other's derelictions and infractions, who take a superior, exclusive attitude toward the non-police community, and who are ready to avenge at all costs any threat of violence to their fellow officers" (Dove, *Procedural* 121). The existence of this separate community in turn produces tension because of the policeman's position within the larger society:

> As a member of the community the policeman is not only responsible for the preservation of the order and security of society, but he is in turn affected by the common condition, because he and his family share the fruits of security or suffer the dangers of disruption felt by the rest of the community. He is, moreover, by the nature of social organization, the servant of the community that pays him, judges him, and ultimately controls his success or failure as a law officer. (Dove, *Procedural* 68)

That is, the typical police detective is pulled in two very different directions, the first involving his loyalty to his colleagues, and the second arising from his citizenship in a broader community. The ultimate question Sjöwall and Wahlöö ask, of course, is whether the "broader community," as it is constituted in contemporary Sweden, is worth saving at all.[33]

The National Homicide Squad is, as a group, deeply aware of what Sjöwall and Wahlöö describe as their untenable position. In *The Man on the Balcony*, Lennart Kollberg, "Like most of those who were to deal with this case[,] . . . was jaded before the investigation started" (29). Although repulsed by the viciousness of the sex murder of young Eva Carlsson, Kollberg is initially struck not so much by the pathological nature of the act itself, but by "the swift gangsterization of this society, which in the last resort must be a product of himself and of the other people who lived in it and had a share in its creation" (29). Kollberg realizes, then, that he is ultimately at least as much to blame for society's ills as those he apprehends. His efforts, even when they are successful, can only temporarily improve the quality of life. Even the recent technological advances in police work so loved by the National Police Commissioner are finally no comfort because they can offer nothing that might alleviate the pain that victims and their relatives experience. That technology is designed to operate on objects of power rather than on recognizably human beings; Beck and his squad, however, are constantly portrayed as confronting vividly human victims. Thus, it is no wonder that Beck and Kollberg reflect later on "their powerlessness and . . . their ambivalent attitude to the society they were there to protect" (MB 61). If in the first novel of the series Beck and his colleagues are already sickened by the methods they must employ to capture a murderer, by the second novel they are suspicious of the entire enterprise in which they are involved.

In order to question the legal apparatus from within, Sjöwall and Wahlöö create a dialogue within Beck's National Homicide Squad. By portraying Beck as troubled but ultimately loyal to his profession, they open a space for another figure to serve as a sounding board. In this respect the formula is made polyphonic; decentering the hero makes it possible for other voices to articulate the increasing disenchantment of policemen with their roles. It is through Lennart Kollberg in particular that Sjöwall and Wahlöö explore the ambivalence that characterizes the attitude of the police toward their work. In order to strengthen his function, he is made "capable of penetrating and analyzing his own situation clearly" (SAV 103), and he is increasingly aware that he is a victim of "the policeman's occupational disease":

> Twenty-three years of daily contact with police officers had made him incapable of maintaining sensible relations with the rest of the world. In fact, he never felt truly free, not even with his own family. There was always something gnawing at his mind. He'd waited a long time to build this family because

police work wasn't a normal job, but something you committed yourself to. And it was obvious you could never get away from it. A profession involving daily confrontations with people in abnormal situations could only lead in the end to becoming abnormal yourself. (SAV 102–3)[34]

Kollberg's reflection here that the private sphere is inevitably contaminated by the "fear, distrust [and] open contempt" (SAV 103) of everyday police work crystallizes the conflict that defines his profession. It is particularly affecting that the consequences of disenchantment be exemplified in Kollberg, since by comparison to Beck, his family life is normal and happy.

It is small wonder, then, that Kollberg eventually must resign from the force in order, quite literally, to save himself. Throughout the series, he has steadily distanced himself from the typical cop sought by the System. He refuses, for example, to carry a weapon because, as we have seen, prior to the beginning of the series he accidentally shot and killed a colleague. He is, typically, the member of the squad sent on missions that require the most sensitivity in dealing with witnesses and suspects. He is also the most profoundly affected by the display of overkill that frequently characterizes police operations in the later novels, and by the consequent orders of his superiors to cover up their failures. In his resignation letter, while denying that his decision to leave is a "political" one, Kollberg makes it clear that he "cannot feel any sense of solidarity with the kind of organization the police department has become" (CK 294–95). Imputing the rise in violent crime to the fact that policemen are armed, and noting that weaponry can lead "to even poorer contact with persons outside the police force," he concludes by saying that "After twenty-seven years of service, I find that I am so ashamed of my profession that my conscience will no longer permit me to practice it" (CK 296). The loss which Kollberg's resignation from the force entails is ironically made clear in the final novel of the series, *The Terrorists*. There he has taken a job cataloguing both antique weapons and handguns turned in by their owners following a new parliamentary statute (182). When Martin Beck seeks out his friend for advice on how to prevent a planned terrorist attack on a visiting U.S. Senator (closely resembling Barry Goldwater), a target which deliberately recapitulates earlier commentaries on the U.S. war in Vietnam, Kollberg in fact gives him the solution to his problem, the likely site of the attempt. He also inadvertently predicts the outcome of the novel's second plot when he describes to Beck the sort of weapon Rebecka Lind will use to assassinate the Prime Minister (186-87; 285).

Lind's actions return the novel, and finally the series as a whole, to the "question of conscience" raised by Kollberg in his resignation letter. If we recall here Wahlöö's notion that the authors intended "to use the crime novel as a scalpel cutting open the belly of an ideologically pauperized and morally debatable so-called welfare state of the bourgeois type" (Lundin 1553), it is clear that the growing frustration of Lennart Kollberg and "ordinary citizens" like Lind is symptomatic of Sweden's malaise. While it would surely be too simple to argue that Sjöwall and Wahlöö are merely attempting to divide Sweden into categories which they label "good guys" and "bad guys," there is a sense in which they are attempting to identify the varieties of infections which afflict the body politic. The medical analogy used by Wahlöö is especially suggestive if we see the authors as social physicians anatomizing the society, revealing, for example, the persistence of class and "the disparity between public squalor and private affluence" (Back 55) which in fact accounts for much of the nation's allegedly "criminal" behavior.

In so doing, they have cast themselves in the role of another venerable figure of Swedish origin, the ombudsman, whose "task is to redress wrongs committed by the authorities against citizens and [who is] vested with far-reaching powers to inspect all public authorities, including courts and municipal institutions" (Stromholm 104). The three ombudsmen who currently operate in Sweden, while considered to be the public's protectors, act "more on a general, abstract level than on an individual, concrete level." For this reason, the ombudsmen, rather than helping particular complainants, support instead more general improvements (Hancock, *Sweden* 238). As a result of the "proliferation of government agencies and statutory and administrative regulations" in Sweden in the late 1960s, the number of cases coming to the ombudsmen skyrocketed: "As an instrument of social change, law has therefore contributed to the intensified activity of Sweden's ombudsmen by extending the domain of their responsibilities. At the same time the dissemination of new forms of critical consciousness associated with the rise of radical liberalism and the New Left has added additional demands on their services" (Hancock, *Sweden* 239). In effect, then, Sjöwall and Wahlöö have helped to expand not only the jurisdiction of the ombudsmen, but have generalized and extended the forum in which complaints can be heard and aired. Like their official counterparts, Sjöwall and Wahlöö necessarily address themselves to abuses of state power.

By choosing, paradoxically, to write within a formula which focuses on the coercive power of the state apparatus – the police – Sjöwall and Wahlöö have succeeded in liberating the power of the Panopticon which Foucault sees first expressing itself in the "plague-stricken town, traversed throughout with hierarchy, surveillance, observation, writing; . . . immobilized by the functioning of an extensive power that bears in a distinct way over all individual bodies" (198). Stockholm and its environs constitute, in their eyes, the "carceral city." Their aim is not further "surveillance" and "discipline"; instead, they propose a new "countersystem," which would be characterized by "continual change as individuals and groups engage in a ceaseless dialogue to reformulate the goals of public policy in response to new and unforeseen consequences of postindustrial modernization" (Hancock, *Sweden* 277). As an element in this countersystem, the unfinished National Police Headquarters can now be seen in a new light. If the radical critique in which Sjöwall and Wahlöö are participating can succeed in wresting power from the "rats of fascism," the possibility of a utopian future remains. Sjöwall and Wahlöö's role, then, is quite literally revolutionary: by subverting a popular formula to their overtly ideological aims, they have created "a situation in which the hitherto prevailing set of relations between rulers and ruled through which the former had been able to represent itself as embodying the claims of society as a whole has been *put into crisis* by the development of alternative, counter-hegemonic strategies on the part of opposing social classes or their representatives" ("Popular Culture and Hegemony" 17). They contribute to the "crisis of hegemony" by questioning the aims of the social engineering that has made a mockery of the utopian promise of "the People's Home."

3
Anatomizing the Other

> ...if the symbol of the administration of justice in South Africa is a two-edged sword, the edge that menaces the black population has become increasingly sharp, while the edge that restrains white officials and police grows increasingly blunt.
>
> Albie Sachs

> *Quis custodiet ipsos custodes?*
>
> Juvenal

Per Wahlöö's notion that the crime novel can be used "as a scalpel cutting open the belly of an ideologically pauperized and morally debatable" society (Lundin 1553) should be peculiarly appropriate to James McClure's police procedurals, set in South Africa, which undertake to anatomize the ailing body politic of his homeland.[1] As Nadine Gordimer notes, quoting Gramsci as her epigraph to *July's People*, "The old is dying, and the new cannot be born; in this interregnum there arises a great diversity of morbid symptoms." Indeed, it is hard to imagine fiction about South Africa which does not at some level confront these signs of mortal illness, yet when such a confrontation is formulated by European or American authors, many white South Africans resent it: "'What angers me,' one man said, 'is that you see in me your own underbelly'" (Crapanzano 47).[2] Such an argument implies, of course, that those non-South African writers are simultaneously displaying their ignorance and displacing their own racial fears, and perhaps racism, in their fascination with South Africa. As a result of this displacement, South Africa has become "a symbolic element in the discourse of the West..." (Crapanzano 308). Thus, on the one hand, the abstract notion of an apartheid state has been the consistent – if distant – object of protest for at least the last forty years; on the other hand, the reality of life in the Republic remains Other: the daily existence of both blacks and whites under the system of apartheid remains, by and large, mysterious to those who have never experienced it.[3]

As a former resident of South Africa, now living in Great Britain, McClure ought to be able to provide a dual perspective: he is both insider and outsider, theoretically both an informed witness and a knowledgeable judge. Because he is no longer living under the system of apartheid, his works ought to transcend the literature many white South Africans have produced to describe themselves, a literature which "is repetitive, mythic, closed in on itself – a series of variations on a single theme or a small group of related themes. It is morally and politically charged. It gives a frozen and ultimately unrealistic picture of social reality that requires confirmation and reconfirmation through endless repetition" (Crapanzano 27). However, McClure's angle of vision has several limitations as well. While he can ostensibly write freely and objectively about a country in which he no longer lives, his very distance (since 1965) has ironically frozen his portrait in time.[4] Like Ed McBain, whose 87th Precinct novels are based on the New York City police department's regulations and procedures of a fixed point in time,[5] McClure's series, "repetitive" by nature, "mythic" and "closed in on itself," does not keep up with the changing society in which it is set. For this reason, the Kramer and Zondi series paradoxically communicates a sense of stability that has been absent in South Africa for the past twenty years. Readers of the series will find only an oblique reference to the riots in Soweto in 1976, and no mention at all of Nelson Mandela and the African National Congress, Gatsha Buthelezi and Inkatha, Eugene Terreblanche and the Afrikaner Resistance Movement, parliamentary "reforms," or indeed any of the current figures in the political struggle and recent events in the upheaval affecting South Africa over the past two decades.

It is therefore problematic that reviewers of the series have nonetheless consistently characterized McClure's work as "a grotesquely vivid picture of life under apartheid" (Bailey 89) and a "picture of apartheid that will teach American readers a good deal about how South Africans think and operate" (Callendar, 1974, 14).[6] While Sjöwall and Wahlöö were, by virtue of their involvement in a radical critique of Sweden, simultaneously insiders and outsiders to its political system and therefore able to trace what they saw as the constant devolution of the welfare state, McClure's "portrait" is necessarily static. If Sjöwall and Wahlöö could produce in their series a cinematographic treatment of "the People's Home," McClure can provide only a still picture taken with a telephoto lens. It is apparently accurate in its quotidian detail, but it clearly deflects the reader's attention from the changing rhythms of South African life.[7]

Because McClure does not appear to have an explicitly revolutionary agenda, he can "safely" write police procedurals which foreground the repressive state apparatus.[8] In so doing, he reproduces the fixed ideology upon which the political and social "survival" of the ruling white minority depends. For this reason, McClure cannot be seen as an "impartial observer" (Callendar, 1981, 31). At the same time, however, McClure should not be seen merely as a spokesman for the ideology of the system of apartheid; rather, the Kramer and Zondi series, with its white and black detective team, also articulates the liberal hope for slow and evolutionary change which contends with other, more progressive strategies in the ideological arena of South Africa. His aim, then, is to anatomize the surface of apartheid while simultaneously embedding one scenario for change. In this respect, the autopsy is a particularly apt metaphor.

Given McClure's distance from the scene and his fixed position as observer, the finely-detailed autopsies which mark each of his Kramer and Zondi novels suggest a mode of reading these procedurals at the same time that they recall the "morbidity" Gordimer isolates as characteristic of South African life. The inert figure on the mortuary table is emblematic of the unchanging body politic of McClure's South Africa; although history indicates that the state is clearly dying, McClure can only begin to speculate on the new nation which "cannot be born." Thus, the organic dynamism of Sjöwall and Wahlöö's Beck series gives way in McClure to the dissection and probing of a static system: his privileged voice lays bare a divided community but cannot speak for the black majority in a repressive system whose existence depends upon their very silence. McClure's novels thus reproduce the forensic investigations of a medical examiner like Dr. Strydom, which in their turn reproduce the bodily surveillance upon which the South African regime depends.[9]

According to Foucault, punitive methods have evolved since the eighteenth century into a "political technology of the body" (24) in which ritual public torture has been replaced by, first, hidden penal repression and, more recently, a system of discipline and surveillance which has been generalized throughout social institutions (293–306). Although South Africa generally eschews public execution and its accompanying carnivalesque celebration of power, precisely because such a celebration of sovereign power also contains the possibility of popular revolt against that power (Foucault 59–65), it has not dared merely to internalize discipline. Its infamous prisons are the sites of daily beatings and torture, and its system of surveillance, superficially as omniscient as the panoptic model of Bentham, must supplement the power it exercises over the mind by acting directly on the body through concealed but widely recognized and acknowledged physical abuse.[10] In South Africa, where the state regularly practices corporal punishments like flogging, the body of the condemned is still the place "where the vengeance of the sovereign [is] applied, the anchoring point for a manifestation of power, an opportunity of affirming the dissymmetry of forces" (55). The persistence of this pre-nineteenth-century mode of discipline, along with more "modern" techniques of ideological manipulation, thus mark the stasis which prevents the evolutionary change that McClure endorses in his Republic.

McClure's dissection of a moment in South African history in turn reproduces the work of his policemen; they are themselves intent upon recreating an event, and their investigations enable McClure to anatomize South African society. The investigation of a murder, for example, is an attempt at reconstruction which parallels Dr. Strydom's attempt to isolate a cause of death through an autopsy:

> The Last Great Journey into the Unknown had properly begun now for Edward 'Bonzo' Hookham. He lay unzipped from pubic arch to jaw bone, and looked as though he was passing through Customs. Zealous rummaging had left his colourful contents in gay disorder; his heart, lungs, liver and gullet had been seized and sliced open on the sink's draining board, his kidneys rested in a kidney bowl on the third table along, and his intestines awaited further inspection in an enamel bucket. (BE 46)

The reification explicit in Hookham's final metamorphosis, into a suspicious-looking suitcase, points to the technology of surveillance practiced by the state apparatus – the police, here synecdochically represented by "Customs." As a result of the autopsy performed upon it, Hookham's body becomes a source of knowledge which is integral to the ongoing investigation of his death, and his corpse thus has an inherently political function: "This political investment of the body is bound up, in accordance with complex reciprocal relations, with its economic use; it is largely as a force of production that the body is invested with relations of power and domination" (Foucault 25–26). Hookham's body becomes a force of productive knowledge at the moment it is "caught up in a system of subjection" (Foucault 26). In short, the technology of the autopsy enables the police to master the body's forces, to externalize its internal relations and turn them to their own investigative, and hence ideological, uses.

In other words, while Foucault addresses himself to the productive powers of the living body, the police procedural, by its nature, fetishizes the dead body by endowing the corpse with economic value precisely because of its usefulness to the state apparatus which is the focus of the formula. In McClure's work in particular, the repeated emphasis on the autopsy scene encodes the hierarchy of power central to the ideology of South Africa. For this reason, the corpse of any white victim has far greater real and symbolic value than that of any non-white.[11] Hookham's autopsy, for example, is juxtaposed to the removal of a body by a black family "in a long electric appliance carton that they'd salvaged from somewhere" (48). Here, because the black cadaver is not a valued object of forensic inquiry, the body is simply vacated. Indeed, it is only when the more prized appliance has been safely installed that the shipping carton can serve as a temporary coffin for the deceased black. Similarly, in *Caterpillar Cop*, Strydom's conclusion that a malnourished rural Bantu has died of "'natural causes'" (49) is followed by the victim's removal to a "splintery coffin, made by a timber firm that also churned out fruit trays for farmers" (50). This very routine corpse, which has itself recently nourished the fresh-water crabs in the irrigation ditch in which it has been lying (49), is thus quickly dispensed with, so that Strydom can pass on to Boetie Swanepoel's more interesting white cadaver.

In most cases, then, the black corpse is valueless, to be discarded; when black cadavers are valued at all, it is only as objects of experimentation which will help the police solve a crime involving a white.[12] It comes as no surprise, then, when Nxumalo, a black constable assigned to the mortuary, recounts that Van Rensburg, his immediate superior, has ordered him to "chuck out" the head of a black victim who has died in Peacevale Township because "it's just some idle kaffir's head," a piece of "junk" that is "cluttering up the place" (BE 37). Because both power and knowledge are reserved to the white ruling class, even black detectives are prevented from viewing white corpses; in *Blood of an Englishman*, for example, Zondi is chastised by Prinsloo for sneaking a peek at Hookham's body as it lies in the trunk of a car (38).[13] The so-called "sacred" quality of the white corpse is such that black eyes are not fit to contemplate it. Clearly, white citizens who have died violently symbolize a temporary breakdown in discipline which the state must remedy. As Zondi thinks in *The Sunday Hangman*, contemplating the curiosity of black children who have found the hanged body of Tollie Erasmus, "If I were a child . . . then I would have been greatly excited by what I saw today. It was a dead white man, and now I know that a white man can die, the same as my father. I have seen this frighten other white men, and I want to see why the police come here to do so much writing . . . . What strange things are happening . . . " (24).

It is therefore McClure's white victims who embody the particular social pathologies brought about by South Africa's repressive system. Over the course of the series, these pathologies evolve from apparently apolitical, often sexually motivated crimes to those which are more explicitly political in nature. Boetie Swanepoel, the puritanical Afrikaner boy who has joined a Detective Club in order to seek out and identify liberals and communists, is murdered by a displaced English captain willing to kill in order to protect the Jarvis family name from sexual scandal (*The Caterpillar Cop*). Hugo Swart, hired by the Bureau of State Security to spy on the congregation of a liberal church, is knifed by one of the parishioners whose personal rather than political confessions have made him Swart's blackmail victim (*The Gooseberry Fool*).[14] Sonja Bergstroom, the snake dancer, is strangled by Peter Shirley, a psychopath whose Oedipal problems transform a sexual encounter into a murder (*Snake*). The victims of "the Sunday hangman" are the objects of experimentation by Gysbert Swanepoel, whose own illegitimate son was hanged by the state (*The Sunday Hangman*). Edward Hookham is killed by Archibald Bradshaw, who does not want his cowardice during World War II revealed (*The Blood of an Englishman*). Naomi Stride dies at the hands of Bruce Newbury and Vicki Stilgoe, as part of a complicated plot to regain the wealth and status they lost when Rhodesia became Zimbabwe (*The Artful Egg*). This movement away from a primary focus on repressed sexuality to a more overtly political motive for murder has, however, already been foreshadowed in the first novel of the Kramer and Zondi series, *The Steam Pig*.

The four white city councillors who recreate their separate childhood gang experiences by coming together in a new, adolescent "gang" at the Albert Club attempt to escape the rigid sexual repression of their middle-class lives in South Africa. While their initial pursuits involve nothing more than passing around banned magazines like *Playboy*, they eventually tire of vicarious eroticism and move on to "clean dirty fun" (SP 215) with Theresa le Roux, a prostitute they nickname the Steam Pig. In so doing, they fall victim to a blackmail plot organized by Jackson who, intent on winning lucrative construction contracts, knows that Theresa le Roux is only passing for white and that the gang of four has thus inadvertently transgressed the Immorality Act by engaging in sex with a colored prostitute.[15] Le Roux is killed by her brother Lenny, her pimp and an employee of Jackson, because he resents the fact that "'She was a bitch, a whoring filthy bitch who thought she had a right to get out of this sodding country and leave us . . . [since] she'd be okay anywhere . . . '" (SP 240). As Don Wall points out, "it is apartheid that causes the murders and other suffering which take place" ("Apartheid" 348). For Wall, the real focus of the story is the tragedy of Theresa le Roux who, because her father was suddenly reclassified as colored, cannot continue a promising musical career ("Apartheid" 348–49). There is no doubt that McClure is intent upon exposing the personal dislocations brought about by apartheid, but *The Steam Pig* goes beyond the private to the structural.

The political is adumbrated in the personal throughout the novel, but one of the clearest examples of such layering can be found in the descriptions of the Albert Club. The four councillors led by Trenshaw themselves constitute an *arriviste* class within the club itself: "The new secretary, an upstart who had never seen action, was allowing the tone to go to pieces in a damnable fashion. Once the black ball had dealt summarily with counter-jumpers Jews, and Nationalist party wallahs – now, alas, there were increasingly few men of honor left to do their duty at membership meetings. The whole world was going to hell . . . " (SP 213). McClure interpolates here the point of view of older, largely Anglophone club members who are forced to recognize that the official establishment of apartheid in 1948 has inexorably changed the white world as surely as it has affected the non-white. The new "intruders" know only the world of apartheid, and for them the Albert Club is merely a mark of class and wealth rather than a bastion of shared fellowship and culture. They are drawn to the myth of club life, but within it they must establish their own sub-culture to derive even the vaguest satisfaction: "In short, the adult world proved a grievous disappointment and their regression to covert childhood was natural enough" (SP 213). Nonetheless, they have "even learned a compassion for the fierce old bachelors who had lived in an officers' mess all their lives and wished to die in one; there was an almost irresistible attraction in such firm concepts of good, in articulate English spoken slowly round a sip of Cape brandy, in killers who had the innocence of children" (SP 213).

For Trenshaw and his cohorts, violence is separated from any "firm concept of good" and becomes merely an expression of self-interest. These are the men, we recall, who were identified by the fact that "Nothing they did, even with claymores that bizarre night in the billiard room, could be regarded by adults as anything but childish" (SP 213). It is no wonder, then, that they can accept Jackson's argument that "after all, gentlemen, she was only a colored. It was not quite the same thing as killing a white. Look how she deceived you, shamed you, humiliated you in the name of eroticism yet really because she hated you for something you could not help – being white" (SP 217). The larger implications of their actions are, therefore, necessarily political. The Empire of an older generation of "fierce old bachelors" has been transformed into the petty and sordid empire of misguided late adolescents willing to sink to the level of blackmailers, pimps, and murderers in order to defend their respectability, their status, and their new-found wealth. The fact that their amoral behavior is prompted by their fear of apartheid's Immorality Act is itself an indictment of that system.

The ease with which these whites can accept the murder of Theresa le Roux points to analogous "caste" distinctions within the white community itself. Because non-whites are so absolutely different, they cannot "enter in any meaningful way into the formation of white identity" (Crapanzano 39). Thus, "The two prominent white groups are caught in an asymmetrical play of identity. Through the rejection of the other, through opposition to the other, they affirm the significance of the other" (Crapanzano 37). This process whereby rejection ironically confers meaning can most clearly be seen in *The Caterpillar Cop*, where the English Captain Jarvis is willing to murder the Afrikaner boy Boetie Swanepoel with no more compunction than Trenshaw and his cohorts exhibit when they acquiesce in the murder of Theresa le Roux. Jarvis is a survivor of the "disappearing Empire" (CC 184) who has been a "manager on a rubber plantation in Malaya," a district commissioner in Kenya, and "a police chief somewhere else" (CC 183-84). Nonetheless, he remains an "outsider" to Africa. Kramer is struck, for example, by the fact that the hall in Jarvis' house is decorated with the remnants of battle – "old pistols, swords, a crossbow, a daisy of daggers, and a battleax" (CC 129). However, while Jarvis has "paintings of horsemen in red blazers jumping over farm fences," Kramer looks in vain for "anything from Africa" (CC 129). Thus, Jarvis is the sort of Englishman who complains that "the wogs weren't grateful and they forgot to put ice in his drinks" (CC 184). Not surprisingly, then, Jarvis greets Kramer with ill humor, noting that he does not speak Cape Dutch (CC 130) and quoting Winston Churchill's ironic compliment to the Boers, "the finest mounted warriors since the Huns" (CC 131).[16]

Jarvis' victim, Boetie, is from a lower-middle class home, but he is, even at his age, clearly aware of the various white social strata within South African society. He knows, for example, that he must learn to speak English "because all the big business in this country" is run by English-speakers (CC 89). Boetie's involvement with English South Africans does not revolve entirely around social climbing, however. He is a member of a Detective Club, sponsored by an Afrikaner magazine run by a prominent member of the government and "open to all Afrikaner boys aged between twelve and sixteen who had never committed a criminal offense . . . . If they were accepted, then they would be sent a card, initialed by the head of the South African Police, that gave them the right to 'cooperate' with local representatives of the force" (CC 73). This Detective Club, which McClure says really exists in South Africa (Wall, "Interview" 11), reinforces the notion that Afrikaners are the bulwark of the society, those who must protect the state from the depredations of blacks, liberals, English traitors, and communists. Boetie has been a most active member, checking servants' passbooks and bike licenses and arresting "Bantu youths for loitering" (CC 72). As a result, he is universally despised by the servants of the area (CC 65-66), but he is safe from any harm by virtue of his race. It is only when he extends his "investigations" to include the Jarvis family, members of the white elite itself, that he is killed.

In working out the murder of Boetie Swanepoel, McClure articulates one of the most deeply rooted conflicts within white South African society. According to Crapanzano, all hostility between

Afrikaners and the English is inevitably traced to the second Anglo-Boer War (1899–1902):

> It describes the bitterness, the frustration, the sense of having been wronged, the defeat of the Afrikaner. It describes the outrage of the Afrikaners at having been made into lower-caste citizens and having their cultural heritage, their language, ignored, denied, or eliminated. It also describes the arrogant shame of the British, their sense of being enmeshed in a conflict that sullies them, their imperial aspiration and its demise, a threatened sense of superiority, and their victory in a war in which it makes little sense to talk about victory. (50–51)

The broadly drawn portraits of both Boetie and Jarvis must therefore be seen as stereotypical reproductions of a conflict which threatens white hegemony in the region, and the fact that Boetie's death is originally thought to be a perverse sex murder marks the depth of that conflict: the upstanding Boer is victimized by the decadent English. That both characters are utterly unsympathetic confirms that McClure fears the uncontrolled destruction which the conflict could produce and situates him firmly in the ideologically liberal camp.

The antipathy that characterizes Anglo-Boer relations is reinforced throughout the series, in an almost choral fashion. In this respect, Tromp Kramer, an Afrikaner like virtually all his colleagues in the South African police, never misses an opportunity to treat the English as objects of scorn. In *The Blood of an Englishman*, for example, he reflects that "Names like Digby-Smith had always irritated [him]. They smacked of English-speaking snobs with horse-dung under their fingernails and – after drug-crazed alcoholic clap-struck half-castes – there was no breed of human he distrusted more profoundly" (30). *The Artful Egg* contains a panoply of stereotyped characters like "'Major Hamish MacTaggart, Cameron Highlanders Retired,'" one of those "old lunatics, who should have been dead and buried long ago, but persisted in staining their corners of the globe Empire Red with shakier and shakier pourings of the port-bottle" (22). While Kramer rather likes the MacTaggart sort, an amiable counterpart to the far more vicious Jarvis, he is less sanguine about being required to mediate a domestic dispute in the English suburb of Morningside, where "the violence would be all verbal, and they'd be saying intellectual things about each other in English that the average constable had a hard time understanding" (21). Kramer also reserves harsh criticism for arty English liberal types like the Carswells, who argue pompously that "'Every nation, as someone once said, must look to its artists to act as the watchdogs of its soul and its future!'" (70). Kramer's only comment on Carswell's abstract paintings is, "'I'm sorry, but I don't think you stand a hope of getting it banned'" (70–71). In this regard, Kramer echoes a typically Afrikaner perspective on the English dissident, who will criticize apartheid and call for reform, but at the first sign of disorder or chaos will immediately emigrate to another Commonwealth nation.[17]

Kramer's awareness of the conflict that separates Afrikaner and Englishman is usually expressed in terms of his distaste for a particular person rather than in larger, explicitly historical terms. Nonetheless, McClure emphasizes Kramer's deep-rooted distrust of the "other" whites when he attributes to him several long, metaphorical descriptions of the premier English city in South Africa, a city that is ostensibly colonial and genteel, conservative and racist, emblematic of the hypocrisy that Afrikaners see in English critics of apartheid (Crapanzano 84–85). For Afrikaners like Kramer, however, Durban is

> not his kind of city. He liked his women to be big and strong and primitive, yes; but also dignified and clean. Durban was a whore.
>
> A cheap whore who sprawled lush, legs agape at the harbor mouth, beside the warm Indian Ocean, which was not a sea but a favor that she sold. And they came in their thousands, these people who craved to pleasure their bodies, hurtling down the roads from the prim, dry veld of the interior. Some died in their eager haste – shredded by shattered windshields and buried beneath cairns of transistor radios, beach balls, teddy bears, peppermint packets, and hand luggage. But most arrived safely to wander nearly naked in the palm-lined streets and be tempted by garish signs which stood out like face paint against dirty-skinned buildings.
>
> Of course she had lice; half a million humble parasites who knew nothing wrong in dwelling with her and sharing the take. (SP 169)

The comparison of Durban to a cheap, painted whore reflects, of course, the vestiges of Kramer's own puritanical Boer mentality, but it also reveals the repressed sexuality of South African society ("the prim dry veld of the interior") in which upstanding Afrikaners are seduced by the English pimps of Durban; those not killed in the journey will be infected with the "lice" of liberalism and immorality.

A second description of Durban, later in the series, goes further to suggest that Durban is the soft underbelly of South Africa itself, the vulnerable gap in the South African *laager* which can allow it to be conquered by seaborne, foreign forces following hard on the heels of the infiltration of "radical" ideas and lifestyles:

> Any one of the waves, for example, could have creamed from the bows of a Chink battle cruiser to come all the way across to splash over a man's kids. Just like the waves that had thrown up other people's rubbish along the shoreline, all those Miami apartment blocks and English beach hotels and Spanish ranch houses. If you flew high enough . . . then Durban looked like a high-water mark, with all sorts of tiny, nasty things crawling about among the pastel shells and the glitter. (SH 88)

Kramer's reflections center here quite literally on Boer fears of foreign forces and ideologies ("Chink battle cruiser") which threaten hearth and home ("a man's kids"). It is thus the English city that endangers the Afrikaner vision of a stable, secure, orderly South Africa: Afrikaners "will resist the temptations of the Old and New Worlds. They will fight incursions from the East, the Soviet Union and China, and from the *natuurvolk* of Black Africa who in their innocence have succumbed to the communist devil. Their identity seems at times to be constituted by their defense against outside influence of whatever sort" (Crapanzano 183–84). For Kramer, the English city therefore embodies the threat of softness opening up the country to destruction from outsiders. Its liberal attitudes towards blacks particularly threaten white, especially Afrikaner, hegemony.[18]

Such attitudes can lead to the empowering of the heretofore dispossessed, and there are numerous indications of this "threat" throughout the series. They are frequently unobtrusive, simply part of the background which McClure's narrative "assumes." For example, as Kramer and Zondi drive from Trekkersburg in search of an informant, McClure notes that the fast section of the highway lasts the length of Peacehaven, a black quarter: "It took the vulnerable white motorist through as quickly as possible, reducing the shacks and shanties to a colorful blur, and provided an excellent surface for the deployment of military vehicles in the event of a civil disturbance" (SP 77). While the speed of the automobile obliterates the black area, "blurring" its outlines and obscuring its identity, white fears of the disorder and chaos that might arise within its confines are nevertheless real.[19] In this respect, South Africans exhibit a curious kind of paranoia: on the one hand, the black is so totally different that his existence appears to have no significance; on the other hand, the threat of pollution, loss of purity, and finally assault and violence by non-whites is articulated in every aspect of South African life, revealing itself in even the smallest gestures of revulsion. Housewives shopping in Trekkersburg in the morning are described as darting "from car to store like tropical fish," even flicking "away from the gray-skinned beggar crabbing his legless way down the gray paving stones" (SH 53–54). Here, though the color gray seems to render the beggar a part of the sidewalk, and therefore invisible, the threat of mere contact is underscored.

Through white eyes, then, blacks are in a curious position: they are both seen and unseen, absent and present. As Nadine Gordimer describes it, "The weird ordering of the collective life, in South Africa, has slipped its special contact lens into the eyes of whites; we actually *see* blacks differently, which includes *not seeing*, not noticing their unnatural absence, since there are so many perfectly ordinary venues of daily life . . . where blacks have never been allowed in, and so one has forgotten that they could be, might be, encountered there" ("Living in the Interregnum" 21). Such a view dominates even police thinking. In *Snake*, for example, Kramer is struck by the blindness of both the press and his colleagues to the dangers of minimizing a series of murders of black shopkeepers by a gang of black assailants. While the newspapers are unwilling to report stories of "Another coon killed in Peacevale," they "crucify" white shoplifters. Although they report "wog death sentences," Kramer insists that the press's reproduction of apartheid barriers in their rigid separation of unimportant (i.e., black) and important (i.e., white) crime is finally dangerous because it means that the media are blind "In thinking it's two worlds apart. That what happens in one doesn't mean anything in the other" (24–25). Kramer is ultimately proven right, of course, when he discovers that the "black on black" murders were in fact organized by a Portuguese immigrant, Da Gama, in preparation for the murder of his uncle whose chain of shops he plans to seize.

When blacks do intrude themselves into white vision, they are immediately displaced. Occasionally their situation becomes a matter of public record, as in the case of a group of epileptics,

> Five women and two men, old to middle-aged, all black, who had been discharged from hospitals and left to fend for themselves. They had somehow grouped together on the [vacant] lot five months ago, and had dwelt there quietly ever since, rain or shine, with the crippled woman tending the fire while the others scavenged in garbage bins for food. They would almost certainly keep a sharp eye on anyone who came near them, fearing eviction or something worse. (BE 110–11)

While Meerkat Marais, a petty criminal in Trekkersburg, would like nothing better than to kick information out of them, he refrains because "he did have a horror of unwanted publicity and, for the last three days or so, these horrible objects had been very much in the news. Some Christian kind of black or other had discovered them, told his minister about their way of life, and since then the *Gazette* had been digging up all sorts of excuses to drag the thing out" (BE 111). Because these people are physically impaired and thus inherently less powerful, they are "safe" objects of sympathy. Thus, the group of epileptics is luckier, in one sense, than other blacks whose displacement is carried out far from public view and as part of a deliberate government policy.

While the epileptics may finally receive charity from "a smart [white] lady from Morninghill way" (BE 111), the blacks at Robert's Halt in *The Gooseberry Fool* fare much worse. Victims of a Black Spot eviction, they are ordered into silence while the police load their furniture, strip their roofing, and finally bulldoze their vacated homes.[20] When they are "resettled" at Jabula, they are almost literally invisible, even to a black detective like Zondi:

> He had not spotted the inhabitants before because they were seated in the shade of their homes, silent, motionless in different attitudes. His immediate reaction was instinctive: a prickling along the spine, a tightening of sinew that halted him in his tracks. Then he realized there was nothing ominous in this, for not a head turned to inspect him. These were people lost

in themselves and totally listless. He had once seen something
of the kind after a whirlwind flattened a township near Kokstad
– but that had nothing to do with anything. (GF 66)

Although these "voluntary emigrants" (GF 68) are to receive rations, they – and the reader – know they will not receive enough, and because the land is hard and infertile, as well as devoid of water, the government has taken the trouble to blast graves into the surrounding rock for those who will surely die (GF 68).

McClure is careful not to intrude a great deal of explicit authorial commentary on the Black Spot policy, but he makes his position clear through metaphor. When Zondi muses on the initial eviction from Robert's Halt, his observation of the process of removal is itself displaced to other activity in his immediate surroundings: "He watched a dung beetle carve a perfect sphere from a pile of droppings near his feet" (GF 42). If comparing the South African government to a dung beetle and reducing blacks to "a pile of droppings" is not enough to make McClure's position clear, he goes on to present a conversation between Brother Kerrigan and the officer in charge of the eviction squad. Here, though, McClure backs away from more forceful criticism. While Kerrigan attacks the resettlement policy and the policeman defends it, the argument is finally suspended with the comment, "'Ach, don't let's argue politics . . . . We aren't politicians, are we, hey? Just two blokes that have got to see laws are kept. You've got your Ten Commandments – and I've got my orders from above, hey? Ha ha. There was no trouble'" (GF 45). Thus, although McClure clearly deplores this Black Spot eviction, the fact that such an event occurs only once in the series connects him to those "liberal and religious opponents of removals" who "tend to react to each one as if it were an isolated outrage, a throwback, an aberration that can be stopped or delayed if the outcry is loud enough" (Lelyveld 149).

The incorporation of specific incidents of black displacement and their consequences, both literal and figural, is, however, less important than the process of reification that often governs the depiction of non-whites in the Kramer and Zondi series, and which is occasionally underlined by the rhetorical figure of the zeugma. In a description of the Swanepoels' lower-middle class home in *The Caterpillar Cop*, for example, McClure notes that the plot of land contains "A separate structure, also in yellow brick, [which] served to accommodate a car, a servant, and gardening equipment"

(60–61). Later in the same novel, in the courtyard of the ironically named Colonial Hotel, Kramer snaps his fingers to "activate" the Indian waiter "who stood, motionless between orders, like some kind of robot conserving its batteries, against a far pillar." Kramer's order is simple: "'Brandy and telephone directory, Sammy.' The waiter's name was not Sammy, but his race had been divided by the whites into Sammy units and Mary units to facilitate friendly relationships" (99).

In a society that lives by classification and categorization (Crapanzano 20), such reification inevitably extends itself even to the classifiers and categorizers themselves: "Peacevale petered out in a straggle of lopsided homes and black pedestrians trudging across the shoulder. The high security fences guarding the gray railway yards gradually gave way to the whitewash and white folk of the old part of Trekkersburg, wire gates and palm trees; then slowly the concrete of the tall administration buildings took over, as sharp as paper cutouts against the flat blue sky" (S 26). Indeed, it is the forces of discipline and surveillance embodied in the "tall administration buildings" who "take over" and control the careful segmentation of society, distinguishing precisely among the shades of color (black-gray-white) that comprise their area of domination. The reproduction of the racial categories of black, colored and white in the landscape itself confirms how deeply the policy of apartheid is, here quite literally, rooted in the soil of South Africa.

The figure of the black servant is perhaps the most obvious example of the effects of absolute segmentation on identity. On the one hand, servants are the invisible and passive presence readying the world for the emergence of their white masters. Philip Sven Nielsen, for example, would never "think of stirring until [his] veranda shone like a tart's toenail and the tea was brought in" (CC 38). On the other hand, the same servants frequently take any opportunity to subvert the system that denies them privilege. In *The Steam Pig*, McClure generalizes this process by describing "One of those edge-to-edge mornings that make milkmen feel superior as they skim off its cream while the white boss sleeps" (111). This metaphoric "theft" of the best part of the day becomes literal as well, since "There was not a servant's room in the land that could not reveal some sign of petty pilfering" (CC 126). The smallest gestures, like Zondi's slopping coffee into the saucer of a particularly obnoxious white cop (SP 155), betray resistance to the system. Paradoxically, perhaps the greatest power that black servants can exercise is one of surveillance. One of Zondi's primary functions as a detective, after all, is to interview servants because, as Kramer notes, "'Servants can tell you more about a family than their own doctor, lawyer, and abortionist rolled into one'" (S 157). Interestingly, though, not all servants are willing to "betray" the family secrets; indeed, there are many whose identity has become so closely tied to that of their masters that their own personalities are subsumed.

Dorothy Jele, the kidnapper of Mama Buza's baby in *The Sunday Hangman*, has worked for the Jackson family for thirty years. She has been rewarded with a room that resembles a small palace, but has not dared to ask if the furniture is hers to keep. As Zondi notes, her life is a "deposit" (184); she has forfeited her identity and has even come to adopt "the hipless walk of a white woman" (182). Another, less tangible reward comes in the form of power amidst the powerless, revealed when she stares at Zondi "with the fixity of a slow mind imitating authority" and when "The other servants smiled up at her as if this would make their day easier" (182). It is no wonder that Zondi detects a "contradictory feel" when he enters her room, "contradictory in the sense it didn't have the sharp, acid smell of whites" that ought to accompany the "shoplike unreality" of her pseudo-white decor (183).[21] In an even more striking example of transfer of identity, Naomi Stride's servant, Betty Duboza, has adopted a completely English style of speech and manners (AE 156). Though she betrays her African heritage to Zondi by fearing to return to the scene of the crime, where "the spirits are bad" (AE 156), in her own house she is transformed into a reproduction of her murdered English mistress, "grave and gracious" in her service of the tea, and critical of the manners of Naomi Stride's white guests. Zondi notices that her smallest gestures are those of someone else; indeed, she is so accurate in her reminiscences that by the end of the conversation, both her husband, Ben, and the black detective realize that they have been speaking with her dead mistress (AE 191).[22]

While the blacks, especially the black servants, who inhabit McClure's South Africa are often deprived by their circumstances of any opportunity to establish a personal identity, white South Africans easily and quickly impose identities, however stereotypical, upon them when they see them at all. Blacks are clearly "other," so different as to be barely recognizable as human. Even a charitable figure like the Widow Fourie, Kramer's lover, a woman who can give away household furnishings to help Zondi and his family (S 56–58), nonetheless believes that "kaffirs" quite literally have a different mentality (SP 117). If someone so remarkable for her kindness, a woman who knows Zondi relatively well, can still define another race by mental difference, then it is small wonder that white South Africans see "The world of the Coloured, of drinking, fighting, and promiscuity as white South Africans depict it, [as] a sort of anti-world, contrasting with their own idealized one of gentility, respectability, and, as they say, Victorian morality" (Crapanzano 261).[23]

McClure faithfully recreates this "anti-world" throughout his series, largely by juxtaposing black eroticism with the repressed sexuality of whites. In *The Sunday Hangman*, for example, Constable Willie Boshoff's musings on his jumping onto his horse and galloping off "at the slightest excuse, even if it was only a Bantu female reporting attempted rape at a beer party" (133) slide imperceptibly into fantasies about the adolescent, off-limits body of Gysbert Swanepoel's daughter Suzanne, "shameless and inquisitive and eager": "To think that she'd still be in bed, for it was not even eight yet, and that, in a perfect world, he could be in bed with her, coaxing a new awareness" (135). While Willie must content himself with surreptitious glances at *Lilliput*, an old pornographic magazine, Zondi can employ his more "natural" sexuality to "seduce" a group of black women washing clothing on the bank of a river: " . . . the banter began, with the womenfolk speculating loudly and pessimistically on his worth as a lover, and, in return, being treated to the best repartee he could offer" (139). Zondi wins their confidence by flattering the group leader, and, "pleased with the progress he was making," moves on to the real object of his quest: the identification of a photo of a "white tramp" (140). The point here is that the alleged "anti-world" is ultimately the healthier of the two, even when it is transformed into a vehicle for police investigation. By contrast, Willie Boshoff's attempt to bed the fifteen-year-old Suzanne nearly leads to his being hanged by her obsessed and puritanical father.

A similar juxtaposition of white and black physicality occurs in *The Blood of an Englishman*, where the denizens of the Aquarius Health and Fitness Centre strive mightily, if vainly, to beautify their bodies. Kramer is amused by their exertions: "It was certainly an educative and engaging sight to see so many of Trekkersburg's leading citizens stripped down and running over. What Kramer enjoyed most was the Supreme Court's most pompous and self-righteous judge, so paunchy he looked pregnant, using a vibrating-belt machine with every indication that he hoped, with so much bouncing about, to procure an illegal abortion" (82). The displaced sexual energy of these whites and their "heightened sense of physical well-being" make them an easier target for the black beggar who knowingly "lay sprawled at the entrance to the lane leading to the . . . Fitness Centre" (79).

While Kramer's visit to the health club fails to produce any useful information for his investigation of the primary (white) crime, immediately afterwards Zondi is much more successful in his efforts involving the secondary (black) crime when he visits Mama Benghu's whorehouse. Her "half a dozen drunken customers," the anti-types of the fat, jiggling Supreme Court justice amusing himself with a vibrator at the Aquarius club, await their turn seated on "condensed-milk crates, exchanging lewd predictions." The brothel, "one of the best . . . in the township," is a "large, lean-to shed with walls and a roof made of corrugated iron, and a floor made of crumbly concrete" in which a goat has free run of the premises and serves, quite literally, as Mama Benghu's bouncer (84). The fact that the goat is traditionally associated with lechery and here replaces the expected human bouncer confirms the stereotypical link between black sexuality and animality.[24] Zondi locates an aluminum prepuce-cover in one of the cubicles, the only clue he needs to convict Banjo Nyembezi of murder:

> Once such an object was all that a Zulu needed to wear to consider himself fully dressed, and although modern society demanded rather more of him, the traditions of encasing one's foreskin in this fashion persisted beneath even some quite sophisticated trousers. Not that anyone bothered to have it woven out of palm leaves any longer, when various sizes were available cheap and ready-made at most trading stores. (98)

The prepuce-cover, reminding readers of mythical black sexuality, is also a totemic object, emblematic both of tribal ritual and the loss of that tradition in contemporary South African life. While, for Hellmann, the importance of such totemic objects, magic, and witch doctors among urban blacks "is related to the insecurity of urban existence and the many unpredictable hazards it presents"

(172–73), McClure stresses that the devaluation of such totems and rituals increases black alienation in the urban world.

This same loss of tradition and the commodification of ritual objects by the marketplace permeate other facets of black life as well. In *The Sunday Hangman*, for example, Zondi's search for a baby-snatcher takes him to "the street of the witch doctors in the lower part of town": "Several of them there had wholesale departments, stocked with everything from bulk packets of aphrodisiacs to entire desiccated baboons, and also supplied the fur trappings a black man was no longer permitted to hunt for himself. He went from store to store, from fancy glass counter to self-service emporium, from holes in the wall to sinister back rooms, and from one end of the street to the other" (103). The reduction of myth to profit by the marketplace can be even more destructive. Chainpuller Mabatso, for example, claims to be a powerful witch doctor and is thought of by the black community as a "wizard" (S 74). In fact, the police see him as nothing more than an extortionist and murderer intent on exploiting the primitive fears of the citizens of Peacevale: "Once, another black sergeant had tried to prove that the gifts of cash left near [Chainpuller's] hut were not given in charity but as blood money – payments made to have the donor relieved of a burdensome wife or mother-in-law. This sergeant had died in his sleep before bringing any charges" (S 75). In transforming primitive magic into a vehicle of exploitation, Mabatso demonstrates that, under the pressures of apartheid, indigenous culture can be twisted into a vehicle of "self-destructive violence" (Lelyveld 208) that paradoxically protects whites from black frustration.

Ironically, when Kramer and Zondi abduct Chainpuller in order to interrogate him, they reproduce his own methods and use the same primitive beliefs of neighbors to cover their identity. They disguise themselves with "a sleeve of cheesecloth" and thereby resemble "two demons without faces" (S 87). Because Mabatso's mistress is convinced that he has been kidnapped by unearthly forces, Kramer and Zondi will not be accused of their illegal actions: "the story she'd tell would be half the battle won already" (S 87). In order to soften up Chainpuller, the two detectives imprison him in an empty flat in a high-rise apartment building, completely disorienting him since he has never been that far above the ground. Chainpuller's reaction marks the distance between his world and that of whites; like the snake of the title who, when frightened, "makes himself into an almost perfect ball with his head tucked away on the inside" (S 100), Chainpuller "sobbed and drew himself into a tight ball, rolling over and hiding his face in his hand, keeping his sobs silent" (S 93). By the time Chainpuller realizes that he has not been spirited away by evil spirits, he has also come to realize that he has been seized by something just as dangerous – white man's justice. In reality, Chainpuller has not literally committed the evil acts which enable him to extort money from his fellows; instead, as Zondi explains, "'It was the people's own fears of darkness that made him so great – darkness only in their own minds'" (S 98). McClure thus articulates for his largely white readers a version of their fascination with the "demonic" nature of the non-white world.[25] Because he demonstrates the fraud which Chainpuller perpetrates, one could argue that McClure is challenging racial preconceptions of the demonic. Unfortunately, by insisting on making his example as thoroughly evil as Mabatso, he finally does little to change the larger categories of racial prejudice which underlie the myth of the "demonic" other. More importantly, by apparently approving of the essentially criminal activity of Kramer and Zondi, McClure's text inevitably endorses the notion that any means can be employed against black suspects in order to solve the murder of a white, thus reproducing and, finally, condoning such state-sponsored lawlessness.

McClure's refusal to challenge completely such stereotypical beliefs is even clearer in an episode in *The Caterpillar Cop*. Here another witch doctor is refused by a prostitute because he is obviously infected with a venereal disease. When he brutally beats her and she calls for the aid of a constable, Argyle Mslope responds, only to be attacked himself. Zondi enters the scene to assist his colleague, and he, too, becomes entangled in the violence; leaping on the witch doctor from behind, he is like "a cheetah on the back of a maddened buffalo" (116). The witch doctor is eventually killed with Mslope's spear, and "the beast's massive body lay on its side in a heap, heaving in spasm" (117). Although this episode takes place in Kwela Village, Zondi's home area, a place where Miriam tries to make their two-room house as "civilized" as possible, McClure's language suggests little more than a return to the naked violence of the jungle. Once again, then, the demonic governs the black landscape. By juxtaposing this episode to Kramer and Lisbet Louw's mutual dreaming about a sexual encounter, however, McClure confirms that an equally "primitive" desire lies just beneath the repressed exterior of white South African culture and that the smug distinction between "us" and "them" is ultimately non-existent. The demonizing of blacks, and especially of their sexuality, is therefore nothing more than another aspect of stereotyping: "These bits of knowledge and the resultant images of the other create and preserve a distance between self and other that is at the root of those attitudes from which apartheid, legalized or not, arises" (Crapanzano 272). While the non-South African reader might well see McClure challenging the stereotypes of apartheid here, there is little textual evidence to suggest that an "insider" to the culture, shaped by those very beliefs, might have the necessary distance to recognize anything problematical in the portrayal of these myths or would realize that transforming Zondi into a "beast" like the witch doctor is ideologically problematic insofar as the status of the police is concerned.

The movement from displacement to metaphor and reification to reductive myth in the treatment of non-whites and non-white culture thus reproduces the marginalization of this segment of South Africa's population under apartheid. Although the history of South Africa is the story of ever-increasing numbers of non-white victims of generalized and government-inspired violence, McClure's novels deflect the reader's attention from this reality to the "problem" of white victimization while largely absolving the police, at least as they are embodied in Kramer and Zondi, from any moral culpability for their technically criminal behavior. The primary investigations conducted by Kramer and Zondi always center on murdered whites – or at least those believed to be white. The fact that the autopsies that McClure employs to further his police investigations, to metaphorize the dissection of South African society, and to figure the reading process are never those of non-whites confirms the notion that their presence is nothing more than a shadow which falls across the South African landscape. Like Kramer and Zondi as they hunt Chainpuller Mabatso, they are ghostly figures removed from official participation in the system that acts upon every aspect of their lives. Dead "kaffirs" are of no intrinsic interest to the state; it is only their living counterparts (witnesses and informants) who become the objects of the technology of power embodied in the state, just as they become the objects of white myth-making.

Like other police detectives, Kramer and Zondi necessarily rely on informants. It is a mark of the strength of apartheid that in every case these informants are non-white. In one sense, they are the team's counterparts to the servants of white households in that their marginalized position makes them especially effective observers. Their situation is even more tenuous, however, because typically they are law-breakers themselves. The full and unimpeded power of the state's disciplinary apparatus can therefore be brought to bear upon them. Gershwin Mkize, a suspect in the death of Shoe Shoe, one of Kramer and Zondi's informants, runs "the beggar circus in Trekkersburg, often traveling far into the bush for his exhibits positioned strategically about the town, and he was always on the lookout for new attractions" (SP 43–44). Mkize is the worst sort of entrepreneur, an exploiter of those even more disenfranchised than he, a collector of non-white "exhibits" and "attractions" in the service of money. Although Kramer and Zondi apparently collect enough evidence to convict Mkize of Shoe Shoe's death, his prosecution is never detailed in *The Steam Pig*.[26] Instead, the detectives' sole interest in Mkize is to exploit his knowledge of the death of Theresa le Roux, and they are willing to go to almost any length in order to extract it:

> Gershwin was mouthing frantically as Zondi took up his position behind him.
> They concentrated on the soft parts of the body, the areas where there was no backing of bone to fracture or aggravate capillary damage through excessive resilience. One soft part was particularly favored for its extreme sensitivity and relative isolation from vital organs.
> They did it all with the fingers, never with the fist. (SP 124)

Kramer and Zondi's willingness to resort to the extended torture of a black suspect in order to solve the murder of a (supposedly) white woman appears to be common practice and further implicates them in the criminality which they are nominally to control. Indeed, Mkize is twice the victim of beatings at the hands of the team, and at the end of the first session Kramer notes that the evidence of torture will be quietly cleaned up by a "fatigue party . . . brought up from the cells . . . . By nine the room – with its four cream walls, brown woodwork, two chairs and a desk – would be unremarkable as ever" (SP 112). These scenes of torture have a two-fold purpose. First, they confirm that blacks like Gershwin Mkize are objects of power but never the reason that power is activated. Second, they problematize the roles of Kramer and Zondi, especially the latter, as protagonists in the series.[27]

The treatment received by Yankee Boy Msomi in *Snake* is especially important in confirming Zondi's troubling role. Once again, a black informant is important to the solution of a murder, and once again Zondi is willing to resort to extra-legal violence in order to elicit information (S 36). While initially the case seems to revolve around the deaths of a string of black shopkeepers, in fact it turns out that these murders/robberies have been no more than practice runs and decoys for the murder of a Portuguese storeowner. Thus, even though it appears that Kramer and Zondi are working to solve crimes against blacks, the "ultimate" crime has once again been perpetrated against the white bourgeoisie, and Kramer's interest in the series of murders is largely due to his intuition that there must be some connection between the killings of blacks and future harm to whites. The disparity between the efforts to solve crimes against blacks and those against whites is itself, of course, a criticism of South African society in general, but it raises particularly troubling questions about the "heroes" of McClure's series.

Critics who have written about the Kramer and Zondi series have inevitably focused on the relationship between the Afrikaner detective and his Bantu assistant. Fred Isaac, for example, points to moments of shared laughter between the two detectives and claims that they signify "the sharing of a special point of view and their bond against the world that threatens them. It is an open act of unrecognized friendship, the most lasting sign of their closeness in opposition to both law and custom" ("Black and White" 14).[28] Though Isaac notes Kramer and Zondi's "mutual dependence," he makes the point that "Kramer's solicitude for Zondi only goes so far" because Kramer must protect "his security and his position in society" ("Black and White" 15–16; 13). Building on these personal connections, made clear in the surreptitious rebellions against official racism, it might be tempting to see the teaming of Kramer and Zondi as McClure's effort to show that the artificial divisions created by apartheid are finally unnecessary on the basis of some appealing notion of universal humanity. In fact, such teams are required by the system itself.[29] Black detectives are not allowed to interrogate white suspects, for example, and white detectives, even when they speak the language of black suspects, are objects of such mistrust – and fear – that they are usually ineffective. As Don Wall points out, "It might be supposed that in a country where the police have such enormous powers to detain, threaten, and interrogate, they would have an easy time of it. Ironically, however, the system can be a severe handicap." That is, McClure attempts to use apartheid in order "to complicate the process of detection"; Wall thus argues that at least one of McClure's accomplishments is to demonstrate the "'brokenness'" and "'separateness'" of South African life ("Apartheid" 349; 351). Other critics have gone far beyond such a view, indeed far beyond McClure's texts, to claim that the "deep respect and friendship" which grows between Kramer and Zondi in spite of official strictures means that "the significance of laws can be lessened and the laws themselves can crumble away" (Schleh 106). Such an optimistic view of the Kramer-Zondi relationship ignores the very real questions that their teaming implies.

Zondi's position in South African society is a relatively privileged one; he has at his disposal the powers of the disciplinary state apparatus, though these are themselves circumscribed by the larger social aims which limit the role Zondi can play. He can never, for example, arrest a white. Indeed, Colonel Muller, in a moment of frustration at the lack of progress in solving the murder of Sonja Bergstroom, says, "'You know what I think is going to happen next, Kramer? We're going to have our little black friend Zondi arresting white suspects. It is coming to that'" (S 163). Much to Muller's relief, of course, no such eventuality occurs. Despite such limitations, though, it is clear that Zondi has "made it" within the system, and his reflections on Argyle Mslope, a municipal policeman at Kwela village, articulate the distance between Zondi and a less privileged representative of state authority:

> One of the old school and no mistake about it; mission-educated, a stretcher-bearer with the white soldiers in the deserts of North Africa, a perfect Zulu gentleman and – at times – a fearless fighter. It was a great pity, though, that Argyle had not progressed very far at the mission or he might have been an asset to the South African Police itself. However, he seemed happy enough in the municipal force, guarding beer halls, hospitals, clinics, hostels, and townships. He played the bass drum in its band and put a shine on his brass buttons that contrasted as strongly with the tatty-quality uniform as fresh blood on a stray's fur. (CC 92)

Zondi's patronizing treatment of a fellow black officer marks how far he has traveled within the structures of apartheid and suggests how far he is willing to go to protect his status. Even though Zondi has risen higher within the South African system than Mslope, they both function as "NEW MEN" who are, in white eyes, "the key to stability" (Lelyveld 65). They are particularly useful for the "technical skills" they have acquired as a result of their police training, and because they clearly have no revolutionary agenda, they not only pose no threat to the white power structure (Lelyveld 67) but in fact serve as its bulwark.[30] In other words, because blacks in the civil service are especially vulnerable to attacks from other blacks, they necessarily remain loyal to their employer: "The harassment of Black state employees by the revolutionary forces may in fact drive the threatened dependents closer to their masters than to their opponents. After all, they have more to fear after a Black takeover" (Adam and Moodley 144).

A dialogue between Zondi and his wife, Miriam, in *The Sunday Hangman* reveals that Zondi's fidelity to the state extends even to the upbringing of his children. When Miriam says, "'You are always cross with the children . . . . You don't listen to why they think their education is not so good,'" Zondi replies, "'You have heard what happened in Soweto? I am the one who knows how to work with authority! With children it is always the same; they are too impatient. And they must tell me if they hear of agitators, because those men are very foolish'" (SH 57). Whereas the Soweto riots inaugurated a resurgence of black consciousness and caused the deaths of hundreds of people, for Zondi they are merely the work of "foolish" agitators who must be stopped. Zondi's dismissal of the riots by Soweto students in 1976 has its roots in his own mission school education "in a remote valley of Zululand":

> There the best dreams of his life had been dreamed; all you had to do, the white nuns had said, was learn your lessons well and then, when you grew up, you could be anything you wanted to be. They had been wrong, those stupid, kind women, who believed all men were brothers, totally wrong, but Zondi still could not feel bitter. Unlike his classmate Matthew Mslope, who had gone back with a mob to burn, pillage, and rape. But Matthew had been wrong, too, and Zondi had arrested him, had him hanged. Which was how he met the lieutenant. And how two wrongs could make a right, whatever Sister Therese had said. (GF 43)

Despite the fact, then, that Zondi has been misled by the "stupid, kind women" of the mission school, he nonetheless rejects any notion of open rebellion against the state and its system of apartheid. Instead, the primary goal of his life is accommodation, and it is only logical, then, that he work as an agent of the very system which confines him. He is, in short, a perfect example of the cooperative and faithful black whom a liberal like McClure sees as part of the *laager* against chaos. Zondi's embrace of apartheid is thus one answer to the question which Lelyveld sees as central in the lives of non-revolutionary blacks:

> How then can a black who aspires to normal autonomy for himself and his family, who is drawn to neither the discipline of revolutionary politics nor the indiscipline of the nightly shebeen crawl, put some distance between himself and the grinding conflict that insists, in so many ways, on defining his existence? What exit is there from the tent of white paternalism and control? The system offers him a little respite in the form of a deal: It will leave him alone if he accepts its basic premise, confines himself to the black world, and tries to make a living off blacks. (270)

Clearly, Zondi embodies those blacks who go "along with the status quo," rather than resist, in order to maintain jobs in the civil service (Adam and Moodley 55). Long-term advancement of Zondi's race has therefore been sacrificed to short-term improvement for his family. That is, Zondi has developed a "consciousness of class differences" which is stronger than his resentment at racial discrimination.[31]

Zondi's conditioning, which responds to the hope of the South African state that crisis can be avoided if "collective goals" are replaced with "individual hopes for advancement through education or material rewards" (Adam and Moodley 168), is particularly evident in his attitudes toward his own living conditions. After the family's move to Hamilton in *The Artful Egg*, Zondi reflects on the "amenities" that the government has accorded him:

> Admittedly, the place had only three rooms in place of two, a cement floor, and there was still no bathroom or separate kitchen, but at least the outside lavatory had a proper door on it, instead of the wooden flaps provided at Kwela Village, and everything looked new, having recently been slotted together. Who knows? In a few years, they might even have electricity, and then some of the Widow Fourie's other presents – the secondhand steam iron,

for example – could come into use, too. He began to daydream. To imagine things that he might buy in the meantime. A small black-and-white television set, perhaps, like the people next door already owned, running it off a twelve-volt car battery. No, a paraffin refrigerator would please Miriam more. (238)

Zondi has, in short, responded to the meretricious promises given by the South African regime in order to deflect black attention from their subject condition. To put it another way, "At the core of the cultural diet on which Blacks are fed lies the message that happy Blacks are those who confine themselves to consumerism, who stay aloof from trouble-making politics, and who strive hard to live in harmony with their circumstances" (Adam and Moodley 158). In all fairness to Zondi, though, it is important to realize that he and his family must, after all, eat. Thus, it might be argued that Zondi is a realist or pragmatist, rather than a collaborator with a repressive regime. In this sense, he is extracting benefits, working within the system in order to achieve "maximum advantage in the absence of feasible alternatives" (Adam and Moodley 81–82). The ambivalence of his position is thus emblematic of the complex ideological matrix with which McClure attempts to come to grips. Perhaps the clearest conclusion which can be drawn is that Zondi's acquiescence is an example of the ways in which South Africa achieves "stability" through manipulation as well as coercion.

As a result of his insertion into a white power structure, then, Zondi is both insider and outsider to his own race, much as McClure occupies his own ambivalent position with regard to "his" South Africa. When Zondi questions a Jabula woman about how she has spent her day, she responds, "'I did nothing. What is there to do in this place? Should I clean the dirt from the dirt?'" As a policeman exempt from the sort of Black Spot eviction which has disrupted the life of the Jabula woman, Zondi cannot understand her apathy, and this in turn makes him an object of her hatred: "Perhaps schooling would have been quite the wrong thing for her and the world had been spared much trouble. Zondi despised those of his people who could not stay proud . . . . She spat, so she despised him too" (GF 76–77). In the same scene Zondi miscalculates dreadfully. When he displays his gun to convince a crowd to help him, the community turns and advances on him chanting "'*Bulala! Bulala!*' The three most dreaded syllables in the ears of any lone policeman – the Zulu chant for 'Kill!' Once uttered, the word was an incantation that totally banished fear and replaced it with a wild blood lust only bullets could halt – if you had enough of them. Zondi had four" (GF 83). McClure's depiction of the reaction of Jabula's residents accurately represents the white vision of "what the homelands were all about, . . . that, properly channeled, black anger could be turned against black anger" (Lelyveld 184). It is especially important to note that the hostility of the Zulus is directed against one of their own who has been co-opted into the system which victimizes them, and their rage is thus deflected from more appropriate targets. Zondi's position is made even more problematic by the fact that he has been sent to Jabula on a wild goose chase organized by BOSS in order to protect the identity of their white informer, Hugo Swart. Attacked by his fellow Zulus and schemed against by his white superiors, Zondi is literally suspended between two worlds with no effective allies in either.

Zondi's anomalous position is evident from the first novel in the series. McClure introduces Zondi in terms which adumbrate his cultural dislocation and recall the adaptation to white norms which characterizes servants like Dorothy Jele. He is

> a coon version of Frank Sinatra making with the jaunty walk. The snap-brim hat, padded shoulders, and zoot suit larded with glinting thread were all secondhand ideas from a secondhand shop. The walk was pure Chicago, yet no black was permitted to see a gangster film. No, here was an original, even if someone, somewhere else, had thought of it all before. Zondi walked that way because he thought that way. (SP 36)[32]

In other words, Zondi is himself a "secondhand" individual in cast-off (white?) clothes, creating a fictional pose in order to establish a sense of identity in a world where his Zulu heritage is "inappropriate" except insofar as it is useful to white authority and true integration into the white world is utterly impossible.[33] In fact, it is the very deprivations which Zondi suffered before he joined the police force which have made him especially useful. As a child in the mission school, he "had adapted to making do without his own textbooks. He read fast, read once, and remembered" (SP 36). Later, as a houseboy, he gained "an eye for the details of a white man's abode which was as fresh and perceptive as that of an anthropologist making much of what the natives themselves never noticed. Kramer had found it invaluable more than once" (SP 38). Zondi is thus a useful tool to his employers: "Telling Zondi something was, in effect, as good as feeding it into a small brown computer; it freed one's mind to deal with the broader issues, while every snippet was reliably retained, ready to pop up at the appropriate moment – or, and this no computer could do, at an imaginatively inappropriate moment, which was often just as effective in solving a crime" (BE 106). Kramer's reification of Zondi here is emblematic of the dialectic of exploitation and admiration that characterizes the team.

Of course, Kramer's praise of Zondi's imagination suggests that there is more to their relationship than master and servant. These are, after all, men who have shot and killed thirty men between them, protecting one another in the field (AE 223–24). The smallest gestures reinforce the relationship of mutual respect that McClure is anxious to establish. For example, when Kramer drops his assistant at his home in Kwela Village he waits with his headlights on so that Zondi can get his key in the door (SP 56). Perhaps the clearest evidence of their concern for one another comes in *The Gooseberry Fool* when Kramer is led to believe that Zondi is dying as a result of injuries sustained in a rigged traffic accident. The Lieutenant goes to great lengths to discover Zondi's true condition (he is in fact only slightly injured) and to ensure that he receives the best possible treatment (115–16; 135–36). Although Kramer covers his concern by claiming that "'this boy might have had some information I wanted – he was on an important case'" (116), the sight of Zondi who "looked unnaturally small under the sheet . . . was all he could take" (119). An incident in *The Sunday Hangman* goes even further in demonstrating the distance between the private trust and respect shared by Zondi and Kramer and the necessity of preserving a very different public image. When Zondi returns to the police station in the rain, barely able to drag himself along on his wounded leg, Kramer rushes outside to help him in. Zondi fears not only the exposure of his physical weakness, but also the transgression of protocol ("'No, boss; men would see'" [157]). Kramer picks Zondi up in his arms and carries him to the verandah, taking care to avoid being seen by black colleagues inside. He then explains Zondi's collapse by suggesting he is drunk (158).

Not surprisingly Zondi views Kramer's insubordinate acts, his difficulties with superiors, and his threats to resign, with trepidation: "If the Lieutenant left the force, life would be – . . . " (BE 153). At the same time, though, he understands that much of Kramer's abrasive relationship with his superiors springs from the latter's desire to protect Zondi as an individual and their team from the depredations of a rigid hierarchy inherently suspicious of interracial success. Thus, Kramer often articulates the racial slurs expected of him by colleagues in order to guarantee at least some freedom of action. In *The Sunday Hangman*, when Strydom tells Kramer that he may have no choice but to declare Zondi medically unfit for service as a result of a bullet wound he received, the Lieutenant replies, "'I've had that boy for how many years now? Do you know how many hours I've spent training him? You should know what slow learners some of them are, man, even if you've never had to work with them. But I tell you, and others would say exactly the same, that when you get a good boy, then you want to hold on to him'" (40). For his part, Zondi rarely misses a chance to use that same stereotype to protect the team from "outsiders." He continually calls Kramer "Master" and "Boss"; he "slouche[s] up" (CC 56) when in the presence of Afrikaner colleagues; and he dutifully walks "his usual pace behind in public" (BE 69). For Isaac, these subterfuges are examples of "the mixture of their obedience to the letter of the rules and their personal evasion of their spirit" in Kramer and Zondi's "professional relations with other police" ("Black and White" 15).

Despite Kramer's solicitude and genuine concern for Zondi, however, there is no doubt, as Isaac puts it, that it "only goes so far" ("Black and White" 16). That is, Kramer in no sense views blacks in general as equals or, even, capable of achieving equality. On numerous occasions throughout the novels, Kramer resorts to derogatory terms like "kaffir" and "black bugger" to describe Zondi when he is in a situation which does not in fact call for a "cover-up" of their "friendship."[34] Similarly, his easy use of "Sammy units" and "Mary units" as well as other racial epithets like "wog" (GF 17) suggests that he has thoroughly internalized Afrikaner racism.[35] Likewise, he is singularly unsympathetic to someone like Naomi Stride whose liberal politics and racial attitudes have apparently led to her death. This in turn suggests that Kramer's condemnation of Bruce Newbury and the Selous Scouts as "a homicidal bunch of psychos" (AE 261) implies no independent sympathies for blacks struggling for liberation. Moreover, despite his uneasy relations with his superiors in the South African police, he never questions the validity of the code he is employed to enforce. As a result, it is difficult to conclude that McClure's series is in fact "hopeful" about the future of South Africa as a whole. Even the "best" Afrikaners in government service reproduce versions of the racism evident in other white-black teams in the force.

In *The Artful Egg* McClure creates a distorted mirror image of the Kramer-Zondi team, Lieutenant Jacob Jones and Constable Gagonk Mbopa. The fact that this duo appears only in the most recent novel of the series suggests that McClure feels the need to buttress the value of the Kramer-Zondi relationship by portraying an analogous situation which is far more destructive to the myth of racial progress which the original team has borne. Rather than mutual respect, Jones and Mbopa embody mutual exploitation. Mbopa lets Jones drive, for example, although he is clearly superior behind the wheel, because his partner then becomes his "little pink chauffeur" (82). When they trade ideas on a case, Jones insists on asking the questions so that Mbopa will give him his best leads in the investigation, although even they are not very good (185–86). While Mbopa daydreams about vicious tricks to play on his partner, suggesting that he is playing a role and knows his boss is an idiot (95–96), he nevertheless recognizes that his own career depends upon the vigorous prosecution – and persecution – of his own race and their sympathizers. Thus, Mbopa is the sort of policeman who becomes "heartily sick of questioning domestic servants" because "his idea of an interrogation was something a good deal more lively, less inhibited, and best carried out after dark, well away from squeamish people with sensitive hearing" (AE 81).[36]

Mbopa is, in short, just as paranoid about black aspirations as his white partner. When they visit the ironically named Cold Comfort Farm, where the black workers are "confident-looking, well-fed, and decently clothed," it is Mbopa who wonders whether the Security Branch should be tipped off to this "bloody weird set-up" (90–91). Mbopa's dependence on white patronage causes him to fear and distrust other black colleagues like Zondi, and as a result he attempts on several occasions to subvert Zondi's progress and thus beat him to a promotion. Mbopa's narrow acceptance of the rules and goals of apartheid is perhaps best summed up in his reaction to Naomi Stride's *The Last Magnolia*. Whereas Zondi had earlier read the book and found it true to his experiences (68), Mbopa is stunned by the "ludicrous ambition" of a "half-witted Zulu" who wishes to become a Member of Parliament (159). Both Zondi and Mbopa, then, are cogs in the government machinery, and McClure's attempt to distinguish between them, largely on the grounds of a quality as amorphous as "aesthetic sensitivity," suggests that he is evading rather than facing the problematic role of the black policeman: "Black policemen are considered far more ruthless than Whites, because of the constant hidden suspicion of disloyalty to their White masters" (Adam and Moodley 228). Similarly, his distorted re-creation of Kramer in the figure of Jones merely deflects attention from Kramer's own racism by presenting a thoroughgoing villain whose viciousness is only undercut by the absurdity of his behavior.[37]

A more authentic version of the "uncomfortable" position of the black policeman is seen only occasionally in the series, and only rarely are the scenes developed. When Zondi interviews the headman Absalom Mkuzi in *The Sunday Hangman*, he knows that only a "civility" based on "rigamarole" and "deceit" will overcome the headman's unwillingness to cooperate with policemen, white or black (148–49). In *Snake*, Zondi realizes that, as far as young black children are concerned, "For some years yet he'd just be a bogeyman . . . " (147); they flee before him in Peacevale. The clearest example of the anomalous position of the black cop also appears in *Snake*. When Zondi tries to interrogate Gosh Twala at the brickyard where he works, he is first put off by the white foreman who insists on "completing his scrutiny of Zondi's identity card" before he will talk with him at all: "This delay was beginning to seriously worry Zondi. He had already felt long, sullen glares being made in his direction from the ragged men hand-pushing trucks of brick from the kilns. Many of them knew him, and soon the alert would have reached the farthest corner of the works" (130). As Zondi is led by the *keshla* to the firing house where Twala works, he feels the men's "undisguised loathing for him," and they do all they can to hide Twala from him (131). Although Zondi remarks that the brickyard is "close to a hell itself" (131), he nevertheless captures Twala by drawing his pistol and ordering the men to finish bricking up the furnace in which the suspect is hiding. While at least some of the hostility to Zondi is attributable simply to the fact that he is a policeman and many of the workers at the brickyard have criminal records, the exposition of the scene makes it clear that, insofar as the workers are concerned, Zondi is a candidate for necklacing precisely because he serves the system which has condemned them to work in the "fires of hell."[38]

What the roles played by Zondi and his black colleagues confirm, then, is that the state apparatus designed to implement and enforce the system of apartheid re-creates and reaffirms that system. While it is true that Tromp Kramer's relationship with Mickey Zondi suggests that adherence to the dictates of apartheid is not absolute, an idea itself confirmed occasionally in other contexts,[39] McClure's liberal position finally offers no solution to the structural problem of apartheid. Indeed, a careful reading of his novels suggests the limits of such a position: McClure can demonstrate the injustices of and the suffering under apartheid, but he can propose no solution to the "separateness" upon which the system is built. In fact, McClure himself reinforces the gap between these two social components through his use of multiple plots.[40] While many police procedurals contain concurrent investigations, no doubt for the sake of "realism,"[41] McClure exploits this convention by juxtaposing a "major" crime involving a white victim with one or more "minor" crimes against non-whites. In none of the novels is there a case of black on white crime (though the police may automatically assume this must be the case);[42] rather, McClure structures his novels in such a way as to reflect real social divisions under apartheid. As Lelyveld notes, "Apartheid ensures that the victims of most black violence are black and the victims of most white violence white. That is one of its virtues, its supporters would contend" (207). In this sense, the popularity of McClure's novels in South Africa is easy to understand.

In a different way, however, McClure's decision to write about South Africa by using the sub-genre of the police procedural demonstrates the tenuousness of the Afrikaner hold on the nation. The historical vulnerability of South Africa is demonstrated by the vulnerability to death of its white inhabitants, and the police procedural can thus become an especially appropriate vehicle to explore the body politic of the state and its future. However, while the "real" South Africa is on the verge of disorder, McClure never deals directly with that threat. Instead, his works serve to deflect attention from the real problem – the roles, present and future, of non-whites in South Africa – to an ideologically safer concern with the fate of white "victims" of a non-racially motivated turbulence. Indeed, blacks in the series appear largely as passive victims of state repression; the reality of their resistance is vacated in favor of a reproduction of their "usual" roles as servants, waiters, displaced persons, and petty criminals who obliquely endorse the system by victimizing their fellows.

The "hope" of McClure's liberal ideology is thus no real hope at all but instead, at least as it is expressed in the Kramer and Zondi series, supports a mythical status quo in which apartheid functions smoothly and the various segments of the society are content with their defined social – or extra-social – roles. In this respect, the Kramer and Zondi series functions as "a transformational work on social and political anxieties and fantasies" which appear in the "mass cultural text in order subsequently to be 'managed' or repressed." The relationship of Kramer and Zondi, for example, must thus be read as a "compensatory structure" which represses the "raw material" of "ideological antinomies and fantasies of disaster . . . by the narrative construction of imaginary resolutions and by the projection of an optical illusion of social harmony" (Jameson, "Reification and Utopia" 141). McClure's insistence on the "entertainment" value of his novels and the fact that reviewers "seem to thoroughly enjoy them" (Wall, "Interview" 19–20) bears out Jameson's theory of mass culture: the series reassures rather than forces readers to confront the troubling prospects for South Africa's future.[43]

That McClure's works need to be seen as "optical illusions" is demonstrable from the inclusion of a series of Oedipal plots which become increasingly important as the series progresses. Kramer himself twice relates the story of his birth: his father was a small farmer, a conservative and deeply religious elder in the Dutch Reformed Church. This archetypal Afrikaner is horrified by the possibility that his son might be born on Christmas Day, and thus rival Christ, and to avert the crisis he forces his wife to walk up and down, insists that she ride in a donkey cart, and finally – ironically – calls in a black witch doctor to give her a strong purge to induce labor. Kramer is born on December 24, but his mother dies in childbirth (GF 102; AE 149). The net effect of this trauma on Kramer is his inability to establish a family, though the Widow Fourie and her children serve as a carefully distanced substitute.[44] Another version of this Oedipal conflict is worked out in *Snake* where Piet Fourie's problems with Kramer as a "substitute" father and as his mother's lover are solved by the end of the book, but Peter Shirley's Oedipal crisis, motivated by his father's continual absence from the family on business, distorts his sexuality and leads him to murder Sonja Bergstroom. The fact that Shirley confesses his crime when confronted by the black husband of the nanny who has raised him necessarily suggests a political dimension to the psychological context and at least adumbrates a new hierarchy of power in South Africa's future (162; 171–74; 179).[45]

In *The Artful Egg* the Oedipal conflict between Jannie Zuidmeyer and his father, obviously a political allegory, is introduced by a retelling of Kramer's own story and is linked to the main plot of the novel by clues found in *Hamlet*. Major Willem Martinus Zuidmeyer, a retired member of the Security Branch of the South African police nicknamed "Many a Slip" for the numerous black suspects who died by "jumping" out the window of the tenth floor of Security Branch Headquarters, "falling" down stairs, or "slipping" on soap, finds his wife dead in the shower of their home. While the official line of inquiry is cautious, largely an attempt to avoid implicating the elder Zuidmeyer in his wife's peculiarly appropriate death, Kramer, in his eagerness to convict the elder retired officer, has "already made up his mind to save everything until after the arrest, when it'd be too late for anyone to interfere with him" (215). In fact, Mrs. Zuidmeyer has died accidentally; her son had tried to kill his father, confessing that "'he hates his father, how terribly his mother had suffered each time he had one of his "mishaps" then took it out on her, because he didn't like the reprimands he got from his seniors'" (236). Jannie strikes a final blow at his father by luring him to a lawyer's office on the pretext of settling Mrs. Zuidmeyer's estate; he then leaps from the window of a tenth-floor office, committing suicide directly across the street from the offices of the *Trekkersburg Gazette* and thus ensuring that his death will make news. The ending of the novel suggests that, while Jannie does in fact commit suicide, Kramer will frame the father for his son's death ("'It's a pity you were alone in the room with him, and we have only your word for all this'" [283]). Kramer's unwillingness to exonerate the elder Zuidmeyer of either death suggests two possible interpretations. On the one hand, Kramer may be working out his hatred of his own father's complicity in his mother's death; on the other, Kramer's dislike of his colleagues in the security police, whose interference has often affected his investigations, may also explain why he is eager to punish Zuidmeyer. In neither case, though, can his actions be construed as a coherent frontal attack on the system.

These Oedipal strands combine to suggest that the younger generation of white South Africans has ineluctably inherited not only the system of apartheid but the "baggage" which it brings. Their lives are structured by a system imposed upon them by the patriarchs of the Afrikaner "tribe," and they fear both the inheritance itself and the power of the fathers who have forced it upon them.[46] Jannie Zuidmeyer's attempt to kill his father suggests the possibility that the overthrow of the system may have roots in the white, Afrikaner society as well as in the non-white areas, and his attempt to punish his father can thus be read as constituting McClure's recognition that all is not well even among the most staunchly "loyal" inhabitants of his mythical, ahistorical South Africa. Even here, however, McClure draws back. The rebellion of the sons against the sins of their fathers is finally ineffective. Kramer may have a nightmare in which he cries out, "'It was the father, the father, not the son!'" (AE 239), and Jannie Zuidmeyer may succeed in having his father "pay" for the mistreatment of his wife, but these individual fears – and individual retributions – still fail to address the structural bases of apartheid and the ideology which controls it.[47]

As Leatt *et al.* put it, "The real bone of contention is liberalism's insistence that the individual is the basic unit of social analysis; its refusal to give proper weight to the interests and aspirations of groups in a multiracial, pluralistic society" (63). Such a vision is necessarily based "on an unreconstructed atomistic model of society" (Leatt *et al.* 64). McClure's choice of a police procedural focusing on a single white and black team ignores "the traditionalist and patriarchal family pattern among the Boers" and their "spirit of solidarity – a kind of embattled warriors' *esprit de corps*" (Andreski 33) and substitutes a non-corporate – and non-threatening – minimal unit. At the same time, it marginalizes collective black action against the system and replaces it with a purely personal, "hopeful" vision of individual cooperation. It is not surprising, therefore, that McClure's novels minimize the representation of blacks in their collectivity by deflecting police work to individual (and white) victims of white violence. Nowhere in the series do we find examples of the other, and very real, task of the South African police: riot control. Nowhere does McClure address either the celebratory nature of black crowds (at soccer games or funerals, for example), or the anomie in the townships that reveals itself in unorganized terror.[48] The virtual invisibility of black collectivity, both in the individual figure of Zondi and in the absence of black murder victims, suggests that McClure avoids touching what Adam and Moodley call the "raw nerve" of apartheid – the fact that "law enforcement generally operates in a direct, brutal, and traditional master-servant relationship" (104–5).

Anatomizing the Other

The real potential for generalized black violence, which constitutes a fact of life in present-day South Africa and a possibility for its future, is thus defused in the odd couple of Kramer and Zondi: the eccentric Boer, with his unlikely, non-conformist attitudes, is seconded by a conservative African, himself co-opted into the collaborating elite. The popularity of McClure's series with South African readers is therefore understandable: his agenda offers a reassuring and apparently hopeful vision of accommodation, rather than one of meaningful, though disturbing, collective action.

4
The House of Keeping

> The combination of the *fait divers* and the detective novel has produced for the last hundred years or more an enormous mass of "crime stories" in which delinquency appears both as very close and quite alien, a perpetual threat to everyday life, but extremely distant in its origin and motives, both everyday and exotic in the milieu in which it takes place. Through the importance attributed to it and the surfeit of discourse surrounding it, a line is traced round it which, while exalting it, sets it apart. In such a formidable delinquency, coming from so alien a clime, what illegality could recognize itself?.
>
> Michel Foucault

Sjöwall and Wahlöö's Martin Beck series and McClure's Kramer and Zondi procedurals attempt, with varying degrees of success, to confront the social structures within which their detectives must work. Nicolas Freeling's Van der Valk series, too, deals consciously with its own Dutch environment, anatomizing facets of Holland's social system in the context of a wider European community,[1] but it has another, formal mission to accomplish. Earlier sub-genres of detective fiction seem inadequate vehicles to foreground the sorts of questions Freeling wishes to ask about contemporary society. He recognizes that Golden Age and hard-boiled detective fiction practiced their own "strategies of containment," and that such texts were "staged . . . as an *interference* between levels" which prevented the reader from seeing the underlying contradictions in socioeconomic reality (Jameson, *The Political Unconscious* 53–56). On the one hand, Golden Age novels suppressed historical continuity; on the other hand, hard-boiled fiction allowed the return of history but romanticized a single investigator who was finally incapable of coping with his complex world. The police procedural, as Freeling envisions it, will insist upon those very contradictions, focusing specifically on the period of transition inaugurated by World War II.

While Freeling's reasons for embarking on the Van der Valk series appear to be primarily formal, they also reveal a dissatisfaction with the ability of earlier crime fiction to confront social, and hence ideological, issues. As he puts it in his "biography" of Inspector Piet Van der Valk,

> His beginning . . . sprang from my boredom with existing crime writers' platitudes. I could not see any point or interest in a character (be it the English amateur, mannerisms-and-manservants, or the beat-up Cal-Flor eye; the species never flourished in Salt Lake City) who was no more than tired mechanical catalyzer of a denouement that stayed obvious no matter how many surprise twists it could be given. The whole business of crime writing rested upon a false premise: that it was a somehow inferior genre, not to be taken seriously. Was not the answer to present a crime tale that introduced people one could care about, with problems that were ours? In my youthful enthusiasm I overlooked the difficulties of overcoming nineteenth-century prejudice in this as in other moral questions deeply rooted. ("Inspector Van der Valk" 252-53)

Such an account of his series' inception suggests a dual prospect: Freeling believes that a popular form like detective fiction, evolving from nineteenth-century conventions, can be transformed into a vehicle that can mediate contemporary social concerns; at the same time, he recognizes that he will necessarily confront an audience which may well be opposed to any changes in the literary world they have claimed as their own. In this sense, Freeling is even more ambitious in his undertaking than Sjöwall and Wahlöö and McClure; while he, too, understands that a popular form like the police procedural can be used to examine a society, he is also overtly aware of the precise formal links between genre and ideology. For this reason, Freeling consciously sets out to "test" the limits of a non-canonical literary form by interrogating two popular sub-genres; he can thus assess the adequacy of that form to mediate society's concerns.

Indeed, Carol Shloss, in her discussion of the series as a whole, notes that "we can understand these books to be records of cultural crisis. Freeling's fiction represents a world whose antinomies or dissonances are incapable of full resolution. As such, his books serve as a critique of industrial Europe's social constructs rather than a legitimisation of them" (170).[2] Freeling is particularly attuned to Europe's "cultural crisis"; just as he is an "outsider" to the police procedural by virtue of his interrogation of its conventions, so, too, he is an outsider to Amsterdam and Holland. As an Englishman resident in the Netherlands for most of the time he was writing the Van der Valk series, he brings to bear a broader European perspective on post-war social and cultural development. That is, he is both insider and outsider, but his vision is not obscured by the same problem of distance that characterizes McClure's "exile" from South Africa. His position is thus much closer to that of Sjöwall and Wahlöö whose perspective arises from an "internal distance" afforded by their antagonistic political stance.

Freeling is conscious of the potential problem that confronts authors who no longer have "the everyday contact with the tissue of existence" in the countries about which they write. This was, in fact, one of the reasons he abandoned the Van der Valk series after the tenth book: "The background would have ceased being exact, slipping into the nonsense chambers of commerce print for handouts. As well as degenerating increasingly toward cardboard, Van der Valk, in the pattern of streets and houses that was his, would have slipped out of focus. The sort of thing that happened, in fact, to Maigret, whose Third Republic anachronisms in modern Paris became embarrassing" ("Inspector Van der Valk" 255–56). Freeling here specifically rejects an appeal to the "reader as tourist" that Porter sees permeating the Van der Valk series (73). Instead, he insists upon an exactitude of physical detail which mirrors precision in his creation of character and his presentation of Dutch society as a microcosm of Europe in transition.[3]

Whereas Golden Age detective fiction illuminated a version of society to demonstrate what was fundamentally "right" with it, Freeling creates "his" Holland in order to deconstruct it through the actions of either victims or criminals who are at odds with the expectations of a society which insists on conformity to its order.[4] Freeling's extensive familiarity with the formulas of detective fiction suggests that he is deliberately playing upon a convention that Eisenzweig sees as central to the plots of early spy fiction and classic detective novels, in which criminal guilt is incessantly associated with national or racial otherness. In this version of the formula, where paranoid fantasies about the dangers posed by the

Other invariably link innocence with the Same (215–16), a mythic version of the historical national identity is reaffirmed with every denouement (228). Freeling's novels appear to incorporate a vestige of Golden Age detective fiction: here, too, the detective and the criminal are frequently outsiders, reproducing what Eisenzweig terms the "ex-centric" character of both law-enforcers and law-breakers (125).[5] However, Holland is in no way an ahistorical stage upon which to test the viability of a conservative social and political environment. Instead, Freeling inverts the Golden Age formula in a significant way: the outsiders, foreigners and exiles who play all the roles in Freeling's fiction provide a pan-European lens through which the post-war history of that continent is explored.

Indeed, rather than effacing historical space and discourse, as Golden Age detective fiction was obliged to do in order to propose an illusory timeless framework (Eisenzweig 189), Freeling's fiction seems obsessed with the return of History in its most troubling forms. For this reason, the shadow of the recent past is re-established in virtually every novel in the Van der Valk series. Hence, as we will see, the links to Empire in *The King of the Rainy Country*, as well as the figure of Besançon/Müller in *Double Barrel* and that of Esther Marx in *Tsing-Boom!*, suggest that the face of contemporary Europe is only comprehensible through the memory of the War – and the ensuing colonial wars that prolonged Europe's agony after 1945. The Van der Valk series therefore attempts to establish a historical continuity that is banished from other sub-genres in detective fiction.

In this respect, Freeling's Europe may be seen as an all-encompassing House of Keeping, in which the suspects – the citizens of post-war Europe – await judgment by History itself, meditating upon real or imagined sins, like Martin in *Death in Amsterdam*. The function of the House of Keeping is explained by "Mr. J. F. R. Slotemaker de Bruin. Officer van Justitie" (DA 134). When Martin asks if he can be released because there is "'no presumption of my guilt,'" de Bruin replies,

> "There is, unfortunately, no presumption of your innocence . . . . There is doubt and an open mind. You recall my saying that our individual views must be submitted to the decision of the state. The state provides that a person coming under imputation of a hand in violent death must be held at the state's disposal until obscurities can be examined. The charge that brings you to my office is a formal document setting out the state's intention and

the reasons supporting this. A subpoena, scarcely more. It means neither that you are guilty nor that I think you so. Simply that I am not satisfied, that I do not understand your role in the affair. I hope you find me lucid." (139)

The House of Keeping is, therefore, a primary institution by means of which the state can "examine" anything which it finds "obscure" or unexplained. It embodies the state's unquenchable thirst for surveillance and discipline at the same time that it purports to protect the interests of the accused (138).

The nature of the House of Keeping makes explicit its relationship to the other institutions of surveillance that prevail in contemporary Western society. Martin likens it, for example, to a convent (142) and to "a hostel for the unemployed poor" (144); its routines resemble those of the army (144). In short, it reproduces the discipline of space that Foucault locates in monasteries, military barracks, factories, schools, hospitals, and poorhouses (141–49), and which "allows both the characterization of the individual as individual and the ordering of a given multiplicity," an allegedly deviant sector of the general populace (149). The reproduction of bureaucratic surveillance through the metaphor of the House of Keeping and Van der Valk as protagonist is itself recreated by Freeling's texts. They serve to isolate the citizenry of Europe under the gaze of the author and the reader; in replicating this function of enclosure, Freeling can, without presuming either the guilt or the innocence of his subjects, proceed to bring them under the scrutiny of History.

The seemingly unrelated natures of the two "exorcisms" that Van der Valk undertakes in *Double Barrel* epitomize the dilemma in which all of Europe finds itself. On the one hand, the inquiry involving Miss Burger requires Van der Valk to penetrate a public mask that conceals private repressions: "The crime – what a word – belonged to the town where it had happened. An inevitable, inextricable consequence of a way of life. What were the problems here that had accompanied the laying of a thin veneer of glitter, a coating of wealthy materialism, on the old Calvinist roots of a stick-in-the-mud country market town?" (105). Throughout the novel Freeling's constant references to the witchcraft trials at Salem suggest the hysteria which characterizes a fearful reaction to change. The anonymous letters thus become, at a personal level, a vehicle to deny the value of the evolution imposed upon Zwinderen by the central planners, while they avoid a confrontation at the public level which is in fact the real source of the "problem." Miss Burger's actions thus constitute a denial of the forces of history by the individual while, on the other hand, Van der Valk's relationship with Besançon/Müller introduces a much larger denial of the legacy of History.

Besançon's private mask conceals yet another public functionary, another bureaucrat with far greater responsibilities than those of Miss Burger. The latter's rebellion is a private attack which intersects with her public functions when she uses her position to gather information. Ironically, it is Besançon who is able to provide the key to understanding her actions, through a definition of functionaries who exceed their authority. She resembles Heydrich and Göring, servants of the state "'who behaved with a savagery, a vengefulness, pointing to very personal reasons for behaving as they did'":

> "A bureaucrat is nothing; he serves. Enclosed in a deadening mold of formality. Unless . . . one of them is sufficiently gifted to break out – and receives unusual opportunities of exercising great power . . . . For the civil servant, it is dangerous to do anything but serve. Nothing is so dangerous as the bureaucrat in revolt." (168)

The lethal results of Miss Burger's private vendetta pale by comparison to Müller's crimes, but both are the consequence of power misused in the service of an ideal opposed to change. The lesson is not lost on Van der Valk, who recognizes his own propensities for "revolt" and is morally immobilized by the prospect of bringing Müller under the scrutiny of justice.

The crucial difference, however, between Van der Valk and his distorted mirror images in Zwinderen is that he recognizes the inevitability of change, whether it be for good or ill. That is, he can sneer at Bloemendaal's embrace of *arriviste* values in *Because of the Cats* or satirize the *nouveaux riches* of Lisse in *Strike Out Where Not Applicable*, but he cannot deny his own role in history by opting out of his investigations despite his own hesitation over Müller. Like Freeling himself, who is perfectly willing to scorn the pretensions of the Dutch bourgeoisie, Van der Valk accords his "victims" the human dignity which transcends their petty failings. Thus it is especially appropriate that Van der Valk's legacy in *Auprès de ma Blonde* is also that of a writer: his series of scribbled notebooks, like the series itself, calls for the return of sensitivity in the police bureaucracy and, by extension, in a European culture struggling to come to grips with the changes in society which Golden Age fiction vacates from its texts.

The juxtaposition of a micro-plot involving a specific crime within Holland and a macro-plot concerning the legacy of Nazi crimes confirms Freeling's desire to establish connections between individual maladjustment and larger social disruption. If World War II is the starting point for the broader questions Freeling poses early in the series, by the later novels he is more clearly interested in the legacies of the colonial wars, especially French involvement in Algeria and Indochina.[6] The lesson of Algeria surfaces only occasionally in the earliest novels of the Van der Valk series, as in *Because of the Cats*, where it is used primarily to illustrate the dangers of idealism turned to destructiveness (73–74). The more important interrogation of Indochina appears in *Tsing-Boom!* which foregrounds both the disparate groups of World War II veterans that fought in the French Legion and the denial of history that characterizes French "memory" of the recent past. By re-opening the wounds of Dienbienphu Freeling can concentrate on a specific instance of guilt which is different from the greater, though more diffuse, guilt that characterizes European responses to the Holocaust. The French people as a whole bear the scars of their national misadventure in Indochina, and the depth of their involvement has produced a corresponding repression of responsibility.

Esther Marx's background, while initially dismissed as "dull" by Van der Valk (35), soon becomes "A job for the archaeologists," which means that "we go digging in the past" (41), a process that soon leads Van der Valk into "a wasps' nest" of politics (59). Once again, Freeling insists upon multiplying "plots" in order to stress the relationships between private pasts and the public Past. Early in the investigation, Van der Valk discovers that

> Esther Marx had served in Indochina and had been mixed up with French soldiery. She had been assassinated with a submachine gun, and there was something in her past that was known to the French administration. It was easy enough to believe that this was something to do with the Secret Army, but how in heaven's name did Esther, peaceably married for ten years to a Dutch career soldier, come to have importance to the Secret Army? (58)

Esther's marriage to Sergeant Zomerlust was disapproved of by his superior officers; he was subsequently "punished" for it by being denied rapid promotion and by notations throughout his file that he was somehow, vaguely, "politically unreliable" (26). Inevitably, this thumbnail sketch of Esther Marx and Zomerlust reminds Van der Valk of his own situation as a Dutch career policeman married to a foreigner: "Arlette was a handicap to him . . . . Just as a diplomat who marries a Russian wife runs a considerable risk of being sent to the Bahama Islands and left there, a policeman who makes an unconventional marriage stands an excellent chance of having thirty years in which to look at the four walls of the Bureau of Records" (55–56).

The parallels between the two couples go even further than mere foreignness: "Arlette had been suspected of OAS sympathies, and the sad thing about this was that she did have OAS sympathies. She came from Southern France, from the Department of the Var, had a brother in Algiers, and had, very naturally, been as vociferous as most about 'Algérie française'" (56). Nevertheless, when Arlette finally was forced to acknowledge both the violence of the OAS and that "Algeria belonged to the Arabs after all, she fought a battle between her emotions and her conscience, and her conscience won" (56). Although Arlette came to renounce her romantic attachment to the cause of the OAS, she nonetheless remains suspect because of her earlier ideals. In the same way, Esther Marx remains tied to her past commitments. Thus, Arlette's link with Algeria furnishes a bridge of insight to the origins of Esther Marx's death, which has its roots at Dienbienphu. Van der Valk's "archaeological dig" thus must penetrate layer after layer of the repressed colonial legacy that continues to haunt the present: "So Esther was mixed up with this legend, this traumatic disaster that had bewitched the course of events in Algeria as well as in Vietnam, whose echoes had not ceased rumbling around the world . . . . Like all great catastrophes, this one was encrusted with myth, which nobody could now disentangle" (62). Van der Valk, loyal both to Arlette and to Esther's memory ("'This woman – now that I can no longer protect her, it is my duty to defend her'" [117]), must, like Freeling, "stand and fight" (63) against "the strategies of containment," the myths that refuse History in the name of reconciliation.[7]

Shloss identifies *Tsing-Boom!* as the novel in which the Van der Valk series veers toward the feminization of the investigation, and therefore toward the privatization of the detective's role (167–68).

She bases her conclusion on the adoption of Esther's daughter Ruth by Arlette and Piet, symbolizing "the private union of the investigator and victim" and constituting a "new symbolic family" (167). Yet it might also be argued that Ruth's adoption is equally emblematic of the persistence of History as a determining factor in both the private and the public spheres. Through Arlette, Van der Valk comes to see his own responsibility for the legacy of Indochina. He must both "defend" Esther herself and the offspring of Esther's ideals. Whereas he had earlier tried to sidestep his place in History by refusing responsibility for the arrest of Besançon/Müller in *Double Barrel*, Van der Valk here realizes that if he is to preserve his own integrity in a world which devalues the past, he must embrace the suppressed legacy which Ruth embodies.

Freeling thus clearly distinguishes himself from predecessors who do away with historical discourse in order to assert the mastery of a different, fictional truth (Eisenzweig 200); rather than displace the colonial experience or replace the soldier's sword with the writer's pen (Eisenzweig 198), Freeling's detective seeks to exhume the past in its problematic forms. Freeling thus inverts what Eisenzweig sees as a primary characteristic of Golden Age detective fiction: as the soldier guarded the colonial empire, so the detective guarded the homefront, "guaranteeing the homogeneity of that space, that is, preventing the appearance of ruptures, enclaves, secessions" and ensuring its "narrative continuity" (234). Rather than preserve the Same, Freeling's novels show that the Same becomes the Other; that is, the nation becomes strange, not because of the presence of immigrants, foreigners or aliens, but because of the inevitable return of History.

As we have seen, Freeling is emphatically not reproducing Golden Age conventions uncritically. While earlier detective fiction assumed that the social and cultural conditions which surrounded the fictional world were sound and could be "redeemed" from a momentary disruption by the elimination of a single aberrant element, the murderer, Freeling once again takes into account the increasingly complex world of contemporary Europe in order to underscore the disruption and dislocation beneath superficial stability. Freeling therefore throws into relief the nature of conformist Holland; he suggests that it is the "internal exiles," those who, like Van der Valk himself, live outside the "small-minded and insular" (GB 14) confines of accepted convention, who seem all too often to be criminals or victims. Ironically, Dutch suspicion "Of foreigners as a whole inside Holland . . . and the automatic distrust of anything imaginative, unusual, unconventional" (GB 17) turns out to be well-founded precisely because it forces them to examine their community values.

The emphasis on conformism which runs throughout the Van der Valk series suggests society's desire to see itself as a coherent and harmonious whole. In order to do so, it must marginalize those who, however unconsciously, call into question facets of the fiction which a society has created for itself. In Freeling's work, then, it is these marginal characters who mark the areas in the social fiction which are most troubling and about which society is most anxious. One way to understand Freeling's use of these characters is to turn to a theory of deviance proposed by Kai T. Erikson. According to Erikson, "the term 'deviance' refers to conduct which the people of a group consider so dangerous or embarrassing or irritating that they bring special sanctions to bear against the persons who exhibit it. Deviance is not a property *inherent* in any particular kind of behavior; it is a property *conferred upon* that behavior by the people who come into direct or indirect contact with it" (6). Since all communities are "boundary maintaining," they insist that their members live within a certain "cultural space" in order to preserve a "cultural integrity" (9–10). Because the only way to mark a community's boundaries is by examining the behavior of its members, it is necessary to study the interactions "between deviant persons on the one side and official agents of the community on the other. The deviant is a person whose activities have moved outside the margins of the group, and when the community calls him to account for that vagrancy it is making a statement about the nature and placement of its boundaries" (11). In some sense, every sub-genre of detective fiction has something to say about social deviance and boundary maintenance, but Freeling focuses specifically on this question in a number of his Van der Valk novels, recalling the second function of the House of Keeping. The police procedural is a particularly apt vehicle for analyzing the surveillance integral to defining deviance since it posits a protagonist who is the representative of official order engaged in the surveillance of those very boundaries.[8]

Once again, the subtext in *Double Barrel* provides perhaps the most elaborate example of a community engaged in the process of defining its boundaries against deviance. Here, Freeling uses the case of Zwinderen as it attempts to cope with the transition from "a tiny market town in Drente into an industrial town with model garden suburbs, a place of beauty and joy to live in" (220). The extent of the community's dislocation is made obvious by Van der Valk's insistent comparison of Zwinderen to Salem at the time of the witchcraft trials: "Like Salem, the whole place sounded hysterical, neurotic" (23).[9] The anxiety which pervades village life has its roots in the conflict between an older, stern Calvinism and the perceived amorality of the new order. As Van der Valk puts it, "There was a lot of immorality – a bit too much. He had the file on the past year's police-court cases heard behind locked doors. Incest, mm – never quite unknown in these ingrown intermarried districts. But rather too much rape, indecent exposure, dissemination of pornography, obscene dancing in cafes, underhand prostitution; beneath all the drumbeating and bell ringing on Sundays there was a sort of sexy itch" (23). In the course of investigating the anonymous letters Van der Valk notes that their salient qualities include sexiness, religion, conformism, and a distrust "of anything that came from outside" (110). The source of the letters, Miss Burger, is herself the secretary to the burgomaster, and thus is instrumental in furthering the modernization program in Zwinderen. At the same time, her conservatism, rooted in her loyalty to church and respectability, makes her a primary force for stasis. The conflict between these two different impulses drives her to neurosis and blackmail, and her divided self mirrors not only Zwinderen's own schizophrenia, but Holland and Europe's difficulty in coming to terms with post-war redevelopment.

If such a reading seems to place too much weight on a single psychological crisis, Freeling's sub-plot involving Besançon/Müller expands the framework of the analysis to include a broader European neurosis. The fact that Müller, an ex-Nazi, has been living in a former lunatic asylum in Zwinderen as Besançon, the displaced Jew, suggests that the "plague" of the 1940s has not yet been fully eradicated. Yet even here, the larger community boundaries that define genocide as the most heinous of crimes can somehow remain blurred. Van der Valk procrastinates in bringing Müller to justice because he has come to respect him as a literate and philosophizing "victim," but also because the bureaucratic definition of justice does not cover the crimes of which Müller is guilty (238). Van der Valk's methods are adequate to cope with the crimes instigated by Miss Burger's neurotic conscience, but are wholly insufficient to deal with the guilt created by the inaction of an entire continent.

The crucial problem, then, is not to identify Freeling's exploration of the inability to understand "unofficial" or private life as an end in itself, as Shloss suggests (171–72), since if that were the case Van der Valk's own investigations would be much more successful. The key is the failure of a people – and its institutions – to recognize the force of History in both "unofficial" and "official" realms. A single investigator, however vehemently he may reject the narrow confines of his institutional base, cannot possibly compensate for the universal denial of the forces which shape the changing face of culture.

By choosing to write police procedurals, with their emphasis on the corporate world of contemporary capitalism, Freeling is able to respond more accurately to the repression of history and subsequent dislocations which permeate advanced capitalist society than his Golden Age predecessors could do. A simplistic reliance on the procedural formula poses, however, its own problems. If he cannot simply re-use, or even extend, the Golden Age formula because it assumes an ahistorical framework, Freeling seems equally unwilling to reproduce Ed McBain's archetypal procedural formula in a European context. Although the police procedural enables Freeling to focus on the social and political structures through which History manifests itself in contemporary society, its own insistence on a corporate hero may itself reaffirm the alienation of individuals and insist that they are merely cogs in the machinery of contemporary capitalism. Before he is content to devote himself wholly to the police procedural, then, as he does in the later Castang series, he must bring yet another literary predecessor, the hard-boiled detective novel, within his own aesthetic House of Keeping for scrutiny and interrogation.

Freeling is therefore drawn in conflicting directions even as he writes within the general framework of the police procedural. While he carefully places Van der Valk within the Dutch police bureaucracy, he also isolates him from his colleagues by suppressing the idea of a squad and endowing him with the usual eccentricities associated with the Great Detective (Eisenzweig 274).[10] In addition, Van der Valk's investigations are frequently marked by the same sort of social criticism and unsatisfactory solutions which characterize the hard-boiled detective novel.[11] Such disparate elements undermine the formula governing the police procedurals he is writing. Since, as John Cawelti has pointed out, "literary formulas assist in the process of assimilating changes in values to traditional imaginative constructs" (*Adventure* 36), we should not expect Freeling to challenge his "chosen" formula; we have already seen, for example, that he can attack the ahistoricism of the Golden Age story without re-formulating the archetype of the procedural. That he does so means that his experiments necessarily call attention to themselves as attempts to interrogate the form.

Freeling's Van der Valk novels, especially *The King of the Rainy Country* and *Auprès de ma Blonde* which call into question the formulaic conventions of the police procedural, must therefore be read not so much as confused reworkings – or even laudable extensions – of the latter, but as conscious efforts to establish a dialogue between the single investigative hero of the hard-boiled genre and the collective protagonists of the police procedural through which to explore the problematic of the mystery story since World War II. The ending of *The King of the Rainy Country* furnishes no clear choice between the two formulas available to Freeling; indeed, the unanswered questions are so troubling to him that he returns to them in the final Van der Valk novel, *Auprès de ma Blonde*, but even here the problem Freeling sets for himself results in generic irresolution.

In *The King of the Rainy Country* Freeling consciously and deliberately intrudes an intertext which will serve as an archetype of the hard-boiled formula, Raymond Chandler's *The Big Sleep* (TBS 1939). Laurent Jenny's essay, "The Strategy of Form," underscores the fact that all intertextual references have as a goal the establishment of a "relation to . . . archetypal models [that] is always one of realization, transformation, or transgression" (34). When intertextuality is executed in an exploratory manner for the purpose of rewriting critically or amplifying the original (Jenny 56), such a use creates "a common relational network" (Jenny 51), an ongoing dialogue in which "the borrowed text at once denotes and refuses to denote, is transitive and intransitive, has full value as a signified and full value as a signifier" (Jenny 45). This dialogue confers new meanings on the original text as the reader rethinks it through the focal text and enriches the latter by opening new contexts and modes of understanding. The goal of this use of intertextuality is therefore to perturb,

> to prevent meaning from becoming lethargic – to avert the triumph of the cliché by a process of transformation. Cultural persistence [especially in formulaic texts like detective fiction, for example] indeed provides nourishment for all texts, but it

also poses a constant threat of stagnation, if the text yields to automatism of association, does not resist the paralysing pressure of increasingly cumbersome stereotypes. (Jenny 59)

Freeling's use of Chandler is in fact a case of perturbation, an attempt to question the police procedural's generic archetype, the *architext* (Jenny 42), because it no longer provides a feasible solution to the problematics of the genre.[12] His experiment, however, goes beyond attention to mere formal elements because every work of detective fiction is, as we have shown, necessarily embedded in a social and political context. While the hard-boiled novel constructs its narrative to deflect guilt towards the social order as a whole and thus often makes a single solution to an investigation impossible, the typical police procedural deploys its narrative elements in order to insist on naming specific individuals and holding them responsible for specific crimes. It thereby defuses an attack on the social structures which have prompted criminal activities. Freeling's dialogue between the hard-boiled and police procedural sub-genres therefore indicts not only the excesses of contemporary capitalism, but also a specific popular formula which suppresses rather than reveals the systemic sources of criminal behavior. That is, he rejects the myths perpetuated by other proceduralists like James McClure who attempt to manage the social and political fears currently associated with maintaining law and order – or to recontain these anxieties by simultaneously reenacting and defusing them. Instead, he asks *his* readers to confront the "reality" of contemporary life by asking whether the new "corporate hero" of the police procedural provides an adequate ideological solution to the problems created by the dysfunctioning of contemporary capitalism.

The King of the Rainy Country actually weaves together two parallel networks of intertextuality: the first, drawn from "high art," is explicit; the second, drawn from *The Big Sleep*, is more discreetly embedded in the text. The title itself, of course, is a quotation from the first line of one of Baudelaire's "Spleen" poems; midway through the novel, Freeling even provides a prose translation of the complete sonnet. This first intertext functions, however, less as a literary reference than as a historical one,[13] raising political issues that are explored obliquely as Van der Valk pursues Jean-Claude Marschal at the behest of the Sopexique conglomerate which seeks to dominate him as it dominates the third-world countries exploited for the raw materials of its European empire.

Important as this initial network seems to be, however, the central intertextual reference of *The King of the Rainy Country* is unmistakably Raymond Chandler's *The Big Sleep*. Freeling embeds Chandler in the center of his own text, just after Van der Valk uncovers the murder scene. On the level of plot, then, Van der Valk pursues the reasons for Marschal's death through clues provided by the text of Baudelaire; on the level of narrative, however, Freeling asks his readers to begin their own investigation, to rethink the entire sub-genre of the police procedural as he alternates the Baudelaire poem with quotations extracted directly from Chandler's most famous novel and uses both texts to comment directly on the central death scene itself. Freeling never indicates that he is borrowing whole passages from *The Big Sleep* as he does when he quotes Baudelaire; apparently he has enough confidence in his readers' familiarity with detective fiction to make this unmarked intertext a structuring principle of a novel in which he conducts an inquiry into the problematics of the genre.

The King of the Rainy Country distinguishes itself from other novels in the Van der Valk series by its singular format. It is structured as a flashback from the detective's point of view, so that in a sense it reconstructs its own absent text to the second degree. The novel is therefore genre-referential in a peculiar way: while all detective fiction reconstructs an absence (the initial crime), here the text begins with the aftermath of the investigation rather than the crime which launches it.[14] Freeling begins the novel with Van der Valk recovering from his wounds and recounting his pursuit of the Marschals across Europe. As a result, the expected linearity of the text is perturbed by the frame story of Van der Valk's convalescence. The investigation itself undertakes a dual reconstruction – that of the flight and death of Jean-Claude Marschal, and that of the pursuit and suicide of Anne-Marie Marschal, his wife.

The parallelism that characterizes *The King of the Rainy Country* on the level of plot is reproduced elliptically in the political and historical framework furnished by the title reference to Baudelaire. The sonnet reminds us of a young prince in a decaying royal house when France is at the first stage of market capitalism, opening up her empires in the New World. Jean-Claude Marschal is himself a representative of the latest stage of capitalism, that of the multinational corporate network embodied in his family's firm. The Sopexique is described by Monsieur Canisius, one of its senior employees, as "a trade company with considerable interests in South and North America, and fewer, I am happy to say, in the Africa where it had its beginnings . . . . The Sopex is largely an investment trust, and where trade is still carried on it is principally in raw materials . . . . Everybody has heard of us and nobody knows quite what it is we do, which is just the state of affairs we like." (KRC 12–13)

In fact, the firm is so important that Van der Valk soon reflects that "the Sopexique had just as much drag or more as a firm that was a household word over the entire world. If whatever was good for General Motors was good for the nation it was also a logical conclusion that whatever was bad for the Sopex was bad, very, for several nations" (KRC 18).

That Freeling intends the reader to link past and present empires is underscored by the fact that the text moves immediately to a description of the superb seventeenth-century homes of Amsterdam's "vulgar bankers and burgomasters," homes which now display "degraded and squalid" facades and whose "insides have been devoured like cheese by the cheesemites of a dingier and pettier commerce" (KRC 19) that characterizes contemporary capitalism.[15] Through the frequent references to Napoleon's marshals that dot *The King of the Rainy Country*, reminding the reader of France's nineteenth-century attempts to extend her domination throughout the Western world, Freeling is careful to reinforce the connection between the first and third stages of capitalism as empire. Like the Emperor of France who stationed his marshals to ensure the maintenance of French military and economic power, so Jean-Claude Marschal and his father, "'at times of political unrest'" (KRC 13), have deployed their money throughout the continent in a variety of bank accounts listed under the names of those same Napoleonic soldiers.

The parallel destinies of Charles IX and Jean-Claude Marschal suggest a political and historical subtext related to questions of individual powerlessness in a world governed by vast bureaucratic networks. Just as Charles IX was manipulated throughout his short reign by his mother, Catherine de Médicis, Marschal is so far removed from control of his destiny that he can be dispatched at will by the directors of his father's firm. As a result of the circumscription of his function by the Sopex, Jean-Claude is forced to question the value of his role and the purpose of his life, ultimately leading him to embark on a romantic episode with a young German girl. As Van der Valk puts it: "He was sick of planning and weighing consequences. He wanted to be free. His money could give him illusions of freedom, and this girl [Dagmar Schwiewelbein] would supply him with more. He had seen every pleasure there was in life, and found them all pretty thin. He was like the king of the rainy country" (KRC 125). In precisely the same fashion, Van der Valk recognizes that he, too, is little more than a pawn of the same multinational network as Marschal. If the younger Marschal's role has been reduced to one of "meeting, entertaining and communicating with the men all over the world with whom the company does business" (KRC 13), so, too, Van der Valk can be compelled to undertake an apparently extra-legal investigation by a company so powerful that it can interrupt normal police business by simply picking up the telephone and calling a minister (KRC 17). Given Van der Valk's empathy with Jean-Claude, as well as his own feelings of powerlessness, it is small wonder that he is led to blame himself for Marschal's death and to question his own ability to conduct a meaningful investigation: "I am just a plodding Dutch plainsman, he told himself; I was quite straightforwardly out of my depth" (KRC 128).

Van der Valk is thus forced to conclude that, given the power of the Sopexique to manipulate even the police, public servants like himself are virtual anachronisms. In a historical moment when only a multinational corporation and its technological elite can manage and account for events, the police are reduced to the level of pawns in an international chess game, and Van der Valk therefore finds himself functioning as an extra-legal private investigator with no more standing than Chandler's Philip Marlowe. As a result, after Marschal's death, Van der Valk pursues his investigation as if he were a hard-boiled importation from a quite different literary tradition. Through this transformation, initiated by the title intertext, Freeling implicitly asks whether the myth of the private investigator, as it is worked out in hard-boiled detective fiction, can adapt itself to a changed world that believes it requires the collective resources of the police, celebrated in the procedural. To elaborate a response, Freeling employs two levels of intertextuality: the first plays on superficial resemblances between *The King of the Rainy Country* and *The Big Sleep*;[16] the second deliberately reproduces Chandler's famous passage about the value of knights in a chess game. Together they open the novel to an investigation which foregrounds the archetypes of the hard-boiled genre.

Related images, like the similarities in the names of characters, channel the process of reading toward recalling *The Big Sleep* as a subtext to Van der Valk's investigation. In so doing, Freeling confronts the question of whether the individual or the group can finally restore order. Superficial resemblance thus begins to unleash the network of relations which will culminate in generic perturbation. The formulaic continuity of the procedural is deliberately disrupted through the central intertextual meeting between Freeling and Chandler: an almost perfect replication of the knight and chess game sequence that occurs shortly after Van der Valk finds Jean-Claude and Dagmar "sleeping the big sleep" of death in the cottage in the Vosges.[17] The sequence is one of the most well-known of Chandler's descriptions of the private investigator's work and has itself served as a focus of exegesis by many critics who have studied the hard-boiled genre.[18] It has come to define the romantic aspect of the detective's quest, foregrounding the importance of loyalty to the client and the case, the problem of the individual operating either legally or extra-legally in the face of stonewalling by higher or wealthier powers who protect the guilty, and the general decay of social morality which ultimately attacks even the investigator. Throughout *The King of the Rainy Country* Freeling raises these issues in much the same way that Chandler does.

In *The Big Sleep*, when Marlowe returns to his apartment after unsuccessfully attempting to figure out the link between Vivian Sternwood and Eddie Mars, he finds Carmen Sternwood naked in his bed:

> I went over to a floor lamp and pulled the switch, went back to put off the ceiling light, and went across the room again to the chessboard on a card table under the lamp. There was a problem laid out on the board, a six-mover. I couldn't solve it, like a lot of my problems. I reached down and moved a knight, then pulled my hat and coat off and threw them somewhere. (TBS 144)

Freeling uses virtually identical language to replay a situationally analogous scene.[19] When Van der Valk takes Anne-Marie back to the cottage where he discovered the bodies of her husband and his young lover, she recounts that she has, in the past, tried unsuccessfully both to seduce him and buy him off, just as Vivian had done with Marlowe: "Van der Valk sat down. On the dusty window-seat the stones on their socles glimmered: a little dust did not affect them. [One] looked a little like the knight in a set of chessmen. He picked it up: he hoped this was a good move for a knight" (KRC 121).[20] Both situational and verbal similarities are triggered by Freeling's need to show that Van der Valk's frustrations when he reaches an impasse in his investigation parallel Marlowe's when he is faced with Vivian's refusal to enlighten him.

In *The Big Sleep*, Chandler returns almost immediately to the chess game image as Marlowe rejects Carmen's advances: "I looked down at the chessboard. The move with the knight was wrong. I put it back where I had moved it from. Knights had no meaning in this game. It wasn't a game for knights" (TBS 146). Similarly, after rejecting Anne-Marie's fabricated explanations for her husband's behavior, Van der Valk dismisses her and meditates upon his actions in virtually the same terms: "The knight's move was wrong; there was too much of a bold sortie into unknown country about it. Anyway, this wasn't a game for knights; he should have moved a pawn, very cautiously and gradually" (KRC 126).[21] Freeling's formulation here supplies the key term which is missing from Chandler's game. Were Van der Valk a circumspect, obedient, and unimaginative policeman, he would play the pawn's role, working within the fixed bureaucracy of Holland's criminal justice system. Because Freeling is questioning the police procedural's adequacy, however, Van der Valk *must* undertake the "knight's move," the "bold sortie into unknown country" – he must enter the intertextual space between one sub-genre and its successor.

Marlowe's rejection of Carmen and his realization that "the move with the knight was wrong" both grow out of his loyalty to his client and his case. As he tells Carmen, "It's a question of professional pride. You know – professional pride. I'm working for your father. He's a sick man, very frail, very helpless. He sort of trusts me not to pull any stunts" (TBS 146). Van der Valk, too, realizes at this point that he must remain loyal, that is, act as his professional pride guides him. Although he can simply go home now and file a report that will not be read (KRC 127), he chooses instead to follow Anne-Marie and the case to Biarritz in order to prevent her assassination of Canisius. Van der Valk does so because "He was a professional. It is only in books that one finds the brilliant amateur detective X; real policemen are obstinate and hardheaded, are slow and literal-minded, are frequently mean and nearly always narrow: they have to be" (KRC 132). Of course, readers of Freeling's series know that this unflattering self-description is in fact false to Van der Valk. Were it true, the detective would not immediately launch into a long passage of self-examination which functions as a meditation on the history of detective fiction as a genre.

This meditational intertext must be seen as continuing the dialogue triggered by the knight sequence. Thus, Freeling uses Van der Valk's contemplation of his role and his subsequent actions as a vehicle to extend his interrogation of the formula and the society whose complexities it purports to articulate. In this respect, he elaborates not only an intertextual exploration of *The Big Sleep*, but also, through his detective, a commentary on Chandler's own aesthetic meditation, "The Simple Art of Murder." This undertaking is an appropriate one; the latter essay is itself a product of Chandler's own dissatisfaction with the inadequacies of Golden Age myths.

By the time Jean Claude-Marschal has died in *The King of the Rainy Country*, Van der Valk's thinking about the Sopexique and his role has become troubled. He has been caught in a game of someone else's devising, has reached the end of his "official" investigation, but he also knows that he must go on. He must follow Anne-Marie to Biarritz because he has helped bring about Jean-Claude's demise. Van der Valk's meditation thus revolves around the bureaucratic bind in which he finds himself as a policeman with no official standing in the case. He has no direct evidence that either Canisius or Anne-Marie is directly involved in the double deaths, so he cannot employ standard police methods to stop Anne-Marie. What he must do, then, is act the knight, employ his professional training in an amateur mode, and free himself from the rigid bureaucracy in order to serve the true ends of detection: uncovering the "hidden truth" which Chandler identifies as the goal of detective fiction ("Simple Art" 21).[22] As Van der Valk asks himself, "What could a professional policeman do in these circumstances? His famous rules and procedures were all meaningless – nobody had broken any laws. A professional policeman, if he had any sense, would have washed his hands of it at once, turned his back resolutely" (KRC 133). Freeling's detective, though, cannot be merely "sensible" because he is more than a simple cog in Holland's bureaucratic machine which, in its rigidity, "was far too good. It was so detailed, so perfected, so rigidly armoured against attack or pressure, that if it did break down it took a year to get it back on the rails. There is nobody that can improvise, nobody that can imagine, nobody capable of independent effort" (KRC 132). This transcendent and creative role is, of course, precisely that of the private investigator of detective fiction's earlier manifestations, and it is the part which Freeling asks his displaced professional to play in order to assess its adequacy. Thus, just as the narrative is structured as a flashback which returns Van der Valk to an earlier period (the beginning of the case), so, too, this return to a previous formula invokes an earlier and apparently less threatening time.

Van der Valk's sense of personal honor is the crucial factor in his decision, just as it is for Philip Marlowe in *The Big Sleep*. There, Marlowe realizes that he is a "part of the nastiness" (TBS 216) and that his only consolation is "twenty-five bucks a day – and maybe just a little to protect what little pride a broken and sick old man has left in his blood . . . " (TBS 213). Van der Valk, too, finds himself a "part of the nastiness," "the chain of reactions" that has led to Jean-Claude and Dagmar's deaths: "He himself was among those links, in actions he had made or provoked" (KRC 127). As a result, he continues his "absurd chase": "For the sake of the shaky old man in Paris, for the sake of an innocent girl's parents, for the sake of Jean-Claude, who had made an effort for a scrap of peace and happiness, and yes, for the sake of Anne-Marie herself – he had liked her . . . " (KRC 137).

Van der Valk aspires, then, to replicate Chandler's definition of the detective hero: "He must be a complete man and a common man and yet an unusual man. He must be . . . a man of honor – by instinct, by inevitability, without thought of it, and certainly without saying it. He must be the best man in his world and a good enough man for any world" ("Simple Art" 20). It is no accident, then, that the final scene of his pursuit of Anne-Marie recalls a crucial set-piece from the opening page of *The Big Sleep*, the "broad stained-glass panel showing a knight in dark armor rescuing a lady" (TBS 1). Much as Marlowe repeatedly bails out Carmen Sternwood despite herself, Van der Valk pursues Anne-Marie. He intends, clearly, to "rescue" her against her will by preventing her from killing Canisius. Freeling, however, recognizes the futility of trying to return to an earlier code and in fact dooms Van der Valk's mission from the beginning.[23]

Even as Van der Valk drives all night to Biarritz, he realizes that he is "a fool and an amateur, but this had to be done in an amateurish way" (KRC 137). To emphasize this point, Freeling ironically recreates Marlowe's vow to climb into the stained-glass panel when he has his detective slowly climb the hill where Anne-Marie has hidden in order to shoot Canisius. While Marlowe at least has the good sense to unload Carmen's gun before she tries to kill him and can at least ensure that Vivian Sternwood will institutionalize her sister before she can kill again, Van der Valk is, as he says, "not clever enough, being much too Dutch, to be an amateur" (KRC 134). When he finally does find Anne-Marie, she simply shoots him and then herself. Freeling thus ends Van der Valk's investigation in a tableau which recreates the beginning of Marlowe's case, and, as Van der Valk himself recognizes, he has in fact accomplished virtually nothing: "'The world we live in, it's the types like Canisius who win'" (KRC 155). Just as Marlowe cannot return to an earlier, pre-capitalist code of honor to eliminate evil from his society, so, too, Van der Valk cannot resolve the problems of his case by retreating to individualist methods that cannot apply to a corporate world.

For Freeling, then, the mode of the private investigator provides no solution to the problematic of the contemporary detective novel. Like the critics who have variously interpreted Chandler's lonely knight image, Freeling himself seems unable to decide between two readings. While Chandler recognized the limits of his detective's ability to "solve" a crime, he nevertheless created his hard-boiled dick as a morally positive response to both the generalized and official corruption which dominated his America. Marlowe is thus seen as an individual powerless to reverse the course of social decay, yet the reader obstinately comes to applaud his anachronistic attempts to clean up the world, even temporarily, and his nostalgic effort to revive a simple medieval purity. Neither interpretation seems to work for Freeling, however, because Van der Valk's position among the competing conglomerates of late capitalism is even more complicated. As a result Freeling's effort to hark back to an earlier, more romantic myth, however interpreted, nearly costs the life of his police detective. Van der Valk is, after all, by no means normally a lonely knight; he is part of a national police force that is charged by society with the duty to protect it. By choosing to write police procedurals, Freeling has thus ostensibly rejected a previous sub-genre in favor of one that should theoretically respond more adequately to contemporary social anxieties. Why, then, does the Van der Valk series inevitably focus on the individual rather than the force? Indeed, why does Freeling take such pains to create a protagonist so clearly at odds with his ostensible role?

Van der Valk is distinguished from others of his rank largely in terms which recall his class background. He grew up in the Pijp district of Amsterdam, the son of an "artisan carpenter" who died during World War II (AB 129). His father was "a wonderful craftsman" who "used to copy Empire and even eighteenth-century pieces in old wood" (AB 247) and whose primary legacy to his son seems to have been an appreciation for craftsmanship. The father's artistry in wood has been transformed in the son into an investigative artistry: "police investigation is a work of art. Attempt to impose form on immaterial" (AB 157). Van der Valk retains his aggressiveness "about being 'working class'" (AB 129). Even as a child, he had been ridiculed by his petit bourgeois schoolmates "for his accent and his street manners" (AB 12). Throughout the series Van der Valk's artisan background is contrasted with the bourgeois snobbery of conformist Holland. For this reason, his investigative specialty is the "queer jobs. Anybody with a funny name or a funny business. Or who talked other languages . . . . Aliens. Cranks. Artists. Anything the others found difficult to understand" (GB 7–8).

Van der Valk therefore challenges both Dutch social conformism (he dares, for example, to marry a Frenchwoman) and bureaucratic identity (he refuses to work with a team and often carries out unofficial investigations by unsanctioned methods). Although the detective is constantly assigned to the "marginal" cases, Freeling can employ this very "marginality" to explore what should be the central social question, the place of the individual in a world increasingly dominated by the corporate.[24] It is not surprising, therefore, that Freeling's murderers and their victims, like the detective who pursues them, are often in flight from the pressures to accept the structures and the categories of modern life. They are frequently romantics who celebrate their "idiosyncratic" values, no longer prized by the society that rejects them.

Just as Jean-Claude Marschal broke through the constraints of life in the Sopexique when he fled with Dagmar Schwiewelbein, so, too, for example, Lucienne Englebert and de Winter/Stam reject the roles which society demands they play. De Winter, the Belgian hotelier, becomes Stam the gallant smuggler, doubly romanticized by Lucienne who herself rejects a bourgeois heritage of "woman's work." To be a secretary or a hostess is, to her mind, simply to engage in "polite prostitution" (GB 33), so she asserts her independence first by working as an attendant in a gas station and later by joining Stam in what she believes to be a romantic battle against Dutch bourgeois values.[25] Stasie Martinez and Denis Lynch in *The Lovely Ladies* are locked in an affair that arises from Stasie's inability to accept her "dull life" as a Dublin housewife; she longs to "create excitement, thrills, risks – she wants to be on the trapeze all the time . . . " (218). In this respect, she resembles her murdered father "whose life was full, too, of fantasies and pretenses, little intrigues and theatrical gestures . . . " (218). Abetted by her sisters, Stasie exploits the men around her who have this same failing, like Malachai MacManus, with his "restless" or "reckless" streak (238–39).

The case of Esther Marx is itself a particularly striking example of the price to be paid for romanticism in a world which can no longer accommodate the quixotic; her death is specifically linked to the youthful ideals that sent her to Indochina as a combat nurse. Here, a personal or literary nostalgia for an obsolete code of values is elevated to the level of the political. Esther Marx refuses to speak of the loyalty that drove her first to join the soldiers at Dienbienphu and then to shoot her dishonored lover, but she cannot obliterate either the history of her personal involvement or that of the equally romantic French national mission in Indochina. She thus serves as an emblem of one of Freeling's larger questions in the series: can the state apparatuses of Europe cope with the complexities of a transitional society?

Esther Marx is precisely the sort of person who is incomprehensible to the bureaucracy officially charged with investigating her murder,[26] and in Freeling's world, the bureaucracy has taken on a life of its own. Rather than serve the needs of an evolving community, it has severed its ties to the people and works to maintain itself, conferring the label of deviance on those who oppose or question it. From Van der Valk's position within the bureaucracy, it is clear to him that, rather than maintaining community, the bureaucracy subverts it by compartmentalizing knowledge about human character and denying its relevance to criminal investigations:

> "What's paradoxical about this job is that we've got to be interested in character, since otherwise we'd never understand anything at all. At the same time it's not our work, as you learned in training school, to worry about whys and wherefores. That is usurping the function of the magistrate. What we are given is a form, which we get people to fill in, just like every other godforsaken functionary. . . .

It's exactly like the form for filling in your income tax, for applying for a passport, for soliciting a job. One of these forms, we are supposed to pick the one that adds up to a criminal. But the really interesting things, the things that make up a character – they are too complex, too illogical, too inconsequent. Décousu. . . . they follow no laws. We have to go up against people as though they were characters in a book – oversimplified." (SO 173)

In bureaucratic terms, then, human beings are simply a list of characteristics whose relations to one another are beyond the purview of the police. As Carol Shloss puts it, Freeling "has led us to understand bureaucracy to be incapable of generating a mode of understanding continuous with, and thus adequate to, its object," the victim (169) or the "criminal." He is thus "more interested in dramatizing the tension between the methods of bureaucratic inquiry and the realities of Dutch bourgeois life than with criminal discovery *per se*" (160). Such a conclusion focuses attention on a crucial element which runs throughout the series: the possibility of justice in a bureaucratically defined world.

By creating a participant-critic like Van der Valk, Freeling invites attention to that very issue. A primary vehicle for exploring this question is the ongoing dialogue over the complementary functions of the police and the judiciary. That is, he insists on examining the relationship between law and order on the one hand and justice on the other, a task made easier by the checks and balances that structure the Dutch legal system. In *Death in Amsterdam* Freeling articulates the relationship between the police and the judiciary, a relationship which is characterized at least in part by tension and suspicion. The role of the police is to adhere strictly to "established methods of interrogation" (59); they are, however, to gather only factual evidence, but to draw no conclusions and to make no judgments, since this is the prescribed role of the "examining magistrate" (131; 134). This means in turn that morality may conflict with legality; while a detective like Van der Valk may believe that there is insufficient evidence to charge Martin with a crime, a magistrate like de Bruin must hold anyone who is suspected of involvement in the guise of protecting them from further depredations by the police (138).

While Martin is resident in the House of Keeping, he is kept at the beck and call of the magistrate whose insistent questioning Martin likens to an inquisition (141) and is examined by a court-appointed psychologist, Cominius, whose rapid-fire questions suggest a form of physical torture (153–54). Martin's only hope, then, is to agree to serve as bait in a trap of Van der Valk's devising, the "'Mousetrap. Police technique from time of Noah, modernized by Gestapo'" (167). The murderer of Elsa de Charmoy is finally killed in a shootout with the police, and Martin himself is wounded. The rights of the victim, Elsa, are thus protected in the sense that her murderer is punished, but Freeling's point seems to be that the elaborate system of checks and balances designed to safeguard the rights of the suspect, Martin, serves only to jeopardize him and to cast the protagonist of the novel in the role of a modern Gestapo agent.

The same sort of problematic "solution" to a crime continues in the second novel of the series, *Because of the Cats*. Once again, Van der Valk's methods are linked to those of the Gestapo (95; 125). His "chansonnette" techniques with both "the Ravens" and "the Cats" are directly responsible for the death of Kees van Sonneveld who is not even involved in the rape and robbery of which the Ravens are accused. Sonneveld dies when Van der Valk attempts to protect him from a judicial inquiry which will be "too slow and unwieldy"; the "elaborate machinery of magistrates and judges" is theoretically off-limits to the police officer, yet Van der Valk reasons that the "experienced" policeman should transgress the boundaries of his mandate to "settle minor misdeeds himself, and even in serious cases . . . use his sense and training to simplify and disentangle and when possible adjudge . . . " (94). Because of his dissatisfaction with a likely verdict of manslaughter that will be handed down in the case of Hjalmar Jansen, the person responsible for the initial rape and robbery as well as Sonneveld's death, Van der Valk takes justice into his own hands and drives him to suicide (180–90). Once again, then, Freeling undercuts the very system which serves as the basis of his procedural precisely because it implicates his detective protagonist in a series of miscarriages of justice.

In the third novel, *Gun Before Butter*, Van der Valk again takes justice into his own hands, allowing Lucienne Englebert, the murderer of de Winter/Stam, to go free, placating his superiors with Stam's ill-gotten gains. In *Double Barrel*, Van der Valk succeeds in arresting Miss Burger, the author of the anonymous letters which have led to several suicides, but this successful conclusion to his investigation pales next to his accidental discovery that Besançon is really the S.S. Lieutenant General Müller. By having Van der Valk explicitly question whether or not bureaucratic justice is adequate to the case of Müller and by leading him to the brink of resignation from the force, Freeling brings to a head earlier critiques of the Dutch legal system embedded throughout the text and locates them in his protagonist, a participant-critic whose investigations become explicit vehicles to interrogate the legal system itself. In so doing, Freeling goes beyond his predecessors in the police procedural.

As George Dove points out, police procedurals as a group highlight two sorts of subversions of "the System." In the first instance, the cop strikes back at the authoritarian police establishment in a kind of game rather than a rebellion (77). In the second, cops sanction a "sub-rosa system of justice," composed of "officially unrecognized methods and procedures . . . for the propagation of justice and the maintenance of order" (107). In both these cases, Dove notes "subversion of laws and regulations is the result of a group consensus and is universally applied" (109). Dove argues as well that the sub-rosa system, while unsanctioned, generally supports officially recognized law enforcement (110). Dove's use of the term "subversion" is, however, problematic. Both the earlier "game" and the "sub-rosa system" in fact are arrived at by consensus and finally serve to reinforce the established aims which society has embodied in its "code." Freeling shows that, in the case of Van der Valk, his petty rebellions and his extra-legal actions derive from a fundamental disagreement with society's definitions of deviance and justice.[27]

For Freeling, then, the question is not *how* can one be a good policeman, but *whether* it is possible at all. At the end of *Double Barrel*, for example, Van der Valk offers to resign because he believes that his ambivalence towards Besançon/Müller makes him "a bad policeman"; his resignation is not only refused, but he is actually promoted. He is told that "The State of the Netherlands . . . will not accept the loss of a responsible public servant," even though he feels powerless in the face of such monstrous evil (246). That is, Van der Valk is told that his own moral sense has no bearing on his effectiveness as an agent of the State since only the bureaucracy, which the reader must understand to be amoral itself, is allowed to articulate "the" social consensus and effect a moral judgment.

While Van der Valk remains an official in the police bureaucracy, Freeling nonetheless rejects that institution's moral primacy. He does so by reproducing his own outsider perspective in two ways: in the figure of Van der Valk himself and in that of Arlette. She provides a kind of "unofficial" lens through which the quotidian details of family life and social interaction can be scrutinized; Van der Valk functions as the vehicle through which Freeling can study both the "official" structures manifested in the multitude of bureaucracies which comprise the political landscape of Holland and, as we have seen, some of those which are beyond the pale of official surveillance. In the course of several investigations Freeling takes great pains to integrate these two perspectives when Arlette serves as a sounding board, almost as a consulting detective versed in the idiom of personal relationships. She thus complements Van der Valk's expertise in institutions,[28] and the two of them constitute one of Freeling's reformulations of the traditional police squad.

Arlette's role both within the series and within Dutch society itself can be clearly seen as early as *Double Barrel*. Van der Valk is "exiled" to Drente to investigate the source of anonymous letters that have led to a series of suicides among the townspeople. Because the police have decided that the investigation can best be conducted by an outsider to Drente who will not be identified as a police officer, Van der Valk is assigned to the task and given the cover of "an official – a responsible official – of the Ministry of the Interior": "'Suppose we were to say that you were conducting ethnographic research? That means nothing and will cover everything'" (11–12). His investigation does, in fact, become an ethnographic survey of the town of Zwinderen, and Arlette furnishes the skills she possesses as a *femme au foyer* to complement those of Van der Valk who wanders the streets of Zwinderen "feeling like an anthropologist among the Papuans" (26). Despite Arlette's "usefulness" in the case, however, she is also a burden; her foreign qualities provoke suspicion among the Dutch in general, whether she is in Drente or in supposedly cosmopolitan Amsterdam, and she is at least partially responsible for Van der Valk's inability to advance through the ranks since her presence suggests something vaguely dangerous in Van der Valk himself (TB 55–57).

The combined skills of Arlette and Van der Valk are necessary because of the apparently open, but actually closed nature of Drente society. Because the burgomaster knows Van der Valk is a policeman, the detective can gain access to all official records. In the guise of the functionary he is able to penetrate "such sanctums as the local bureau of the Income Tax Inspectorate, the Ministry of Social Affairs, and the adjutant of the local police force" who are "delighted to find that a superior official from the Ministry of the Interior had little to do, too, that he liked nothing better than a quiet natter, and that he had not, apparently, come to disturb their repose. They were all friendly bureaucrats together . . . " (DB 93). When Van der Valk wants information on the truly personal, that which escapes the official channels of surveillance, however, his bureaucratic compatriots cannot help him.

The nature of a Dutch provincial town is such that "Everything was known, and nothing": "Everything could be seen. The Dutch, especially the more provincial Dutch, do not draw their curtains even at night. There are many explanations of this. Van der Valk had always thought it was due to anxiety – the Dutch neurosis. The anxiety lest anyone think them not normal, not conforming, not respectable" (DB 34). This apparent openness to surveillance actually constitutes "a favorite Dutch pastime that is called 'shadow watching'" (DB 34), and this is precisely what Van der Valk asks his wife to do.

Arlette is, however, loath to intrude into the lives of others; her French background makes it difficult for her to adapt to the "terrifying nakedness of Dutch life," where houses are not surrounded by walls and where "Every home has huge windows, front and back" (DB 34).[29] Her discomfort at being the subject of inspection in turn makes her uncomfortable at being asked to inspect others: " . . . out of loyalty to him, she was trying to teach herself to gaze. It was a kind of treachery; it was painful to her" (DB 107). Since the "criminal" turns out to be the burgomaster's hyperefficient secretary, the person who actually controls the flow of information through bureaucratic channels, it is only through the sort of "outside" investigation embodied in Arlette's "ethnographic study" that Van der Valk can finally solve the mystery.[30]

The "treachery" that Arlette feels at engaging in the sort of surveillance demanded by police work is justified in a particularly striking sequence late in *Double Barrel*. Van der Valk stations himself in a house under construction across the street from Miss Burger's flat and watches her "solitary seduction": "Watching a person through binoculars . . . is a strong emotion. You are ashamed and excited. . . . With binoculars you are the submarine commander, the assassin, the preacher in the pulpit, God. As well as, always, the pornographer" (208–9). Van der Valk's reflections here build on the strong streak of Calvinist repression which runs throughout Drente, and they also call into question the entire process of undercover surveillance which the detective has endorsed from the beginning of the case. Van der Valk's own "arrest" for being a Peeping Tom reaffirms that he, and all policemen, are in fact distorted mirror images of Miss Burger. They, too, are driven by a "Compulsion toward public service, resentment of governmental inflexibility. Meticulous, perfectionist neurosis" (DB 216).

The point that Freeling seems to be making, then, is that the investigator, the criminal, and the victim are all united – in the face of the system. He does so by first establishing the bond between the "perpetrator and the victim," what is called a "penal marriage" (TB 123). As early as *Death in Amsterdam*, for example, Freeling demonstrates that Elsa de Charmoy is somehow responsible for her death at the hands of the nameless young photographer who, terrified by and jealous of her other lovers, kills her without premeditation (171–72). These two, then, are forever bound by their "complicity" in the crime. As Van der Valk investigates the crime, he, too, is linked to both Elsa and her killer as he attempts to reconstruct the crime, a process made especially clear in this novel since the "mousetrap" he employs to capture the killer results in an unplanned shootout in which the young man himself dies by Van der Valk's hand. In choosing to "mousetrap" his victim, Van der Valk places himself outside bureaucratic methods – and thus outside his world – just as surely as Elsa's life of lies and mystification and her murderer's violence remove them from bourgeois Dutch community values. Even as early as the first novel in the series, then, Van der Valk is driven from his bureaucratic community to uphold the values of the larger society. If he is to discover the murderer's identity, he must contravene police regulations; if he is to remain "within bounds," he must content himself with failing the community as a whole. Thus, Freeling's detective's true kinship is with the "outsiders" who prompt and commit crimes against the social order, and readers come necessarily to see him as alienated from the very agency which should give definition and meaning to his life.

Shloss argues that "Freeling sees in unofficial life the grounds for reclaiming a public world increasingly alienated from itself, imprisoned by ossified procedures, unable to know itself fully and thus unable to generate a viable and holistic culture" (172).[31] While the political and social programs of post-war European reconstruction were designed to remedy the dislocation and uncertainty that followed the war, Freeling's police procedurals suggest that any remedy to post-war Europe's malaise is quite simply beyond the capacity of his discredited bureaucracy or his heavily qualified version of the lonely knight:

> Society . . . was a fermenting mass, like a huge farmer's-pot of pig-swill, boiling on fires of hatred and envy, of bad education and war and outrage, of poverty and starvation, homelessness, joblessness. The scum rose to the top, where he was supposed to skim it off with a ridiculous tiny spoon. He could never reach the ferments and instabilities inside, let alone the fires below. He too was part of that sinister boiling in the pot. (BC 73)

Like Van der Valk, Freeling arms himself with the "tiny spoon" of his fiction; like Van der Valk, he knows that he can never finally reach the "fires below," though he also insists that to stop trying is simply to acquiesce in the social decay which is the embodiment of the latest stage of capitalist development. He therefore compels his readers to return to a new version of the same problematic articulated in *The King of the Rainy Country* in the final novel of the series, *Auprès de ma Blonde,* where he recapitulates the ideological possibilities of earlier forms of detective fiction and proposes a radical, though ultimately unsatisfactory, solution to their shortcomings.[32]

Van der Valk's shocking death at the end of the first part of *Auprès de ma Blonde* divides the novel into a diptych whose linking episode is an "I"-narrative transition in which Freeling adopts the persona of a friend of the dead detective to announce yet another generic transformation.[33] With the individual as cop now out of the picture entirely, an amateur police squad (a "committee" of friends and neighbors assembled by Arlette) undertakes to solve his murder. A neat reversal is thus accomplished on many levels: Van der Valk's wide-ranging European investigations are reduced to the Amsterdam quarter where he lived for so many years, his free-wheeling jaunts through the annals of history are limited to a very specific moment in time, and the professional police are converted to an amateur collective. These changes all occur within a text which the reader assumes will follow the formula of the police procedural. Those expectations are challenged even in the first half of the novel, however, when Van der Valk undertakes a purely private investigation which he specifically keeps from his superiors, and the failure of his individual quest provides the starting point for Freeling's final generic question: whether the collective efforts of Arlette and her cohorts, an "amateur procedural," can accomplish what Freeling has shown to be beyond the capacity of either the private operative or the "traditional" police squad.

The generic transformations which mark *Auprès de ma Blonde* do not, of course, obliterate the issues which have confronted Van der Valk throughout the series. Instead, Freeling chooses to emphasize the very questions which have come to be central to his procedurals: how best to explore the social myths that embody conflicting attitudes on issues of law, order, and justice. The novel immediately focuses the reader's attention on these issues by opening with Van der Valk serving on "The Commission for Inquiry into Law Reform (subcommittee criminal code, studying the replacement of repressive elements by educative mechanisms)" (AB 13).

As Freeling's readers know when they turn to *Auprès de ma Blonde*, Van der Valk has come to find himself increasingly frustrated, with "No further promotional prospect and precious little of real interest" (AB 13) since he is "hampered by a crippling physical injury [inflicted by Anne-Marie in KRC], and a built-in reputation for being both indiscreet and irresponsible" (AB 13). His appointment to the government's Commission and his simultaneous promotion to Principal Commissaire, for what Freeling ironically identifies as "literary reasons" (AB 16), occur at a time when Van der Valk's detective work has come to seem essentially meaningless:

> Especially in the last five years, in a society breaking up and becoming continually more fluid under the pressure of fermentations not understood yet, and least of all by government functionaries, his work had come to appear increasingly trivial and irrelevant. Not much interest or pride to be found in the identification and sequestration of criminals in ever-growing numbers, most of them either not really criminals at all or defined as such for the wrong reason. (AB 13–14)

Because Van der Valk's creativity and imagination are at odds with the utterly inflexible criminal justice bureaucracy which he decried in *The King of the Rainy Country*, and because bureaucrats never expect meaningful reform, Van der Valk is kicked upstairs to the Commission in order to allow the governmental machine to go on unhindered. Rather than merely acquiesce, however, he undertakes a personal inquiry as a means to do field research on the effectiveness of private investigative methods for police squads.

In language which clearly points to Freeling's concern with the alienation of the individual in the third stage of capitalism, Van der Valk concerns himself initially with

> "The relearning of sensitivity. The professional detective has none because he is (a) over-worked; (b) overspecialized, i.e., deals only with fragments of an inquiry; (c) blunted by repetition; (d) same as (b), he is part of a clumsy machine, a cog, with no interest or understanding of other cogs.
>
> Contrast now the attitude of the classical fictional 'private detective' – he is one man, with all the elements in his possession. Invariably his time and leisure are used in contemplative and imaginative work, aided by pipes, violins, dope, as S. Holmes, or chess and whisky, as P. Marlowe. Quite unreal, because such type does not/cannot possess all elements. Consequently author cheats – imputes far more knowledge and skill than one man possesses . . . which is legitimate and necessary in fiction, but in life . . . ." (AB 29)

Van der Valk's thoughts once again become the vehicle for Freeling's intertextual interrogation of previous sub-genres of the detective novel in which the adequacy of their responses to the social, economic and political questions which underlie them is rehearsed. Both classic and hard-boiled detectives bring a sensitivity and imagination which are impossible in the context of the police procedural, but they fail precisely because authors must "cheat," must resort to detectives who are "quite unreal." While Freeling is clearly not proposing some simplistic standard of "realism" as the primary criterion of detective fiction, he is obviously centrally concerned with the social and cultural context in which such fiction is produced, and he recognizes here, as he did in *The King of the Rainy Country*, that merely returning to earlier forms can provide no answer to the questions raised by his own generic investigations.

He does, however, propose a possible solution through a test case: a version of the police procedural adumbrated in *Strike Out Where Not Applicable*, where Van der Valk assembles a distinctly unofficial squad composed of two retirees from the force, two former colleagues from Amsterdam, and two young sub-inspectors (130). Such a squad will supply the "sensitivity, the skills at analysis and synthesis [that] are indispensable and not easily acquired by police school training":

> "Conclusion: a criminal investigation unit should perhaps consist of no more than four or five men, each with specially sensitized skills. . . . [However], the 'private detective' element cannot be eliminated. Take for example this boy Richard, which is perfect fictional 'private' example. A Marlowe/Archer might be interested because he had nothing better at the time to do. Existing police structure would have no interest and no ability anyway. Since no complaint has been made, no administrative machinery has even been set in motion. Said ad/mach. hopelessly lumbering and cumbersome." (AB 29–30)

On the surface, at least, Freeling's first generic "solution" is clearly doomed to failure in *Auprès de ma Blonde*. Van der Valk decides to investigate the case of Richard Oddinga on his own, spurning police machinery and asking no help whatsoever. His experiment is unsuccessful on at least two counts. He is gunned down, and Oddinga, hounded by the policeman and driven by Larry Saint, becomes the criminal he never was.[34] Van der Valk's investigative failure then becomes the starting point for yet another literary experiment: the second panel of the novel's diptych approaches the test case from a radically different angle, foregrounding Arlette and her "committee" of neighbors and friends.

Freeling creates a set of characters who effectively reproduce Van der Valk's own ideal police squad, and they do what the police have been unable to do – discover the identities of the detective's killers. They do so because they incorporate Van der Valk's own primary investigative method, the study of character. That is, they return human elements like creativity and imagination to an enterprise that, as Freeling has shown throughout the Van der Valk series, has become as alienating as the bureaucracy which drives it. Even here, though, Freeling cannot rest content with a "final solution" to his generic questions. At the end of the novel the committee is left with the knowledge of the killers' identities and no way to bring them to justice. Although they initially decide to execute Larry Saint, to replace the criminal justice system with private vengeance (AB 220–30), they are in fact too clearly creatures of their society. Ultimately, then, and perhaps inevitably, they come to the same conclusions that Van der Valk might have: the police are the only authority to carry out the law. They can only call on the police, bring them the evidence they have collected, and hope that the very machinery they have circumvented can bring Larry Saint to the bar of justice.

This ending, of course, supplies no real escape from the formula of the police procedural, and this is precisely the trap in which Freeling finds himself.[35] His interweaving of political and historical allusions as well as literary intertexts throughout the Van der Valk series indicates that he is aware that he is writing in a new stage of capitalism in which the cultural myths of the thirties and forties persist but have been invalidated by new historical conditions.[36] While focusing constantly on the return of History, he has, ironically, remained interned in his own aesthetic House of Keeping, a prisoner of the very generic history he has interrogated. Nonetheless, Freeling's challenges to the formulaic structures of the sub-genres of detective fiction mark his mission as a crime writer.

Although Freeling has not been a best-seller among contemporary detective novelists, his works, especially the novels of the Van der Valk series, have generally been acclaimed by reviewers and peers as superior examples of popular literature.[37] The praise his novels have earned has presumably justified Freeling's "youthful enthusiasm," though his infrequent appearance on best-seller lists confirms that he has indeed challenged a formula-conscious audience. Even Freeling's reviewers have often drawn attention to the fact that his work is not easy to categorize, and they have been quite inconsistent in identifying the precise genre in which he writes. Anatole Broyard, for example, simply places Freeling's work in the broad field of suspense fiction (35). An earlier reviewer, describing *The King of the Rainy Country* in *The Times Literary Supplement*, wrote that "It would be fair to say that from a melange of existing ingredients he has remade and extended the thriller" ("One Man's Mote" 37). This sort of imprecision is perhaps best exemplified by the same writer's claim that "Mr. Freeling is at the moment the educated man's Ian Fleming, an excellent writer of Gothico-psychologico-detective-thrillers . . . " (37). Surely such a formulation is one mark of an author's ability to challenge received conventions.

One of the most common tactics employed by reviewers who nonetheless insist on pigeonholing Freeling definitively has been to identify Inspector Van der Valk as a reincarnation of Georges Simenon's Inspector Jules Maigret (Boucher 64; Foote 59). This association with Simenon has come to be commonplace even among academic critics who have reflected more substantially on the genre of detective fiction. For example, George Dove, in *The Police Procedural*, writes that "In at least half of the stories, particularly those in which he pursues suspects and clues across national frontiers, Van der Valk belongs unquestionably to the Great Policeman school, . . . but he works enough with other policemen and follows customary police routines to put the series into the procedural class" (211). Dove goes on to point out that "Van der Valk is a great reader of George [sic] Simenon, and he constantly compares his methods with those of Maigret, imitates Maigret's habits of walking and drinking, even tries to think like him" (213). While Dove's conflation of Freeling and Van der Valk raises its own problems, what interests us here is, rather, the generic question upon which Dove touches.

The figure of Maigret does, in fact, surface early in the Van der Valk series, but it is first applied to the character of Martin in *Death in Amsterdam*; in *Because of the Cats*, Van der Valk is accused by his superior of transgressing police procedure in the anti-bureaucratic manner of his fictional predecessor (146). Maigret undergoes a further transformation in *Gun Before Butter* where he is a foil for Commissaris Samson (54), one of Van der Valk's superiors. By the time of *Tsing-Boom!*, Van der Valk has come to be specifically likened to Maigret in his physical mannerisms (92; 104).[38] Merely to note these references to Simenon is, however, to overlook the fact that Freeling peoples his texts with the characters of the entire pantheon of detective and thriller writers, ranging from Conan Doyle through Ian Fleming, and compares Van der Valk to Philip Marlowe almost as often as he invokes Maigret.[39] This generic matrix in the novels seems to bear out Eisenzweig's judgment that detective fiction, by its nature, measures itself against previous texts in the genre (163–64). While Eisenzweig's analysis directs the critic's attention to specific "qualitative" aspects of the form, such as the "superiority" of a particular surprise ending (171), in the case of Freeling the measurement is ideological rather than aesthetic in the sense that he critiques the validity of the myths which inform the genre. It would therefore be a mistake to conclude, with Dove, that Van der Valk is essentially Maigret's double, or to concur with Eisenzweig that purely formal conventions govern references to prior detectives.

Defining the genre in which Freeling writes is therefore not merely a simple exercise in classification because Freeling deliberately and self-consciously blurs generic categories at various points in the Van der Valk series. He is clearly aware of the development and evolution of the various sub-genres of detective fiction, and he understands that these transformations are integrally connected to changing socioeconomic myths. His decision to write in the mode of the police procedural indicates that he recognizes that a narrative dependent upon the single investigative heroes who populate Golden Age and hard-boiled detective fiction can no longer even begin to portray the complex socioeconomic reality of contemporary capitalism. Thus, it should come as no surprise that Freeling has continued to explore the possibilities of the police procedural in his Henri Castang series.

5
A Family Affair

> It has become an essential ritual of our societies to scrutinize the countenance of the family at regular intervals in order to decipher our destiny, glimpsing in the death of the family an impending return to barbarism, the letting go of our reasons for living; or indeed, in order to reassure ourselves at the sight of its inexhaustible capacity for survival. Far removed from the immediate rationality of political discourse, it appears to constitute the other pole of our societies, their darker side, an enigmatic figure to which oracles are drawn in order to peer into the depths where it moves and read the inflections of our collective unconscious, the encoded message of our civilization.
>
> Jacques Donzelot

As we have seen, Nicolas Freeling's Van der Valk series uses a police detective's investigations to conduct a sophisticated literary interrogation of the ideological constraints of the three major sub-genres of detective fiction; his Castang series constitutes a more pointedly social inquiry in which Freeling explores more fully the nature of policing as it is distributed throughout French society. Unlike Van der Valk, Henri Castang is thoroughly integrated into the *police judiciaire*; because he is less the independent operative within the state structure than his predecessor, Castang's cases establish the official domain of the traditional control mechanisms of the State as the starting point for an examination of the broader modes of collective social discipline.

Through a change in venue from Holland to France, with its tradition of centralized authority, its apparently more narrowly defined legal code and its more rigid social structures, Freeling directs his attention to the interaction of the different – family-based, class-based, government-based – spheres of discipline throughout French society in order to show that every aspect of "policing" is currently undergoing a crisis. The musings of Van der Valk in *Auprès de ma Blonde* with regard to the Dutch legal system and the place of the detective in the maintenance of public and private order constitute a bridge to the Castang series' full-blown, though finally inconclusive, investigation of social responsibility for criminality. Neither the official nor the unofficial agencies of control can effectively combat what Freeling perceives to be the devolution of a disciplined society.[1]

What makes France such fertile ground for Freeling's work is an inherent contradiction in French life identified by Alain Peyrefitte as the struggles of a "decomposing Caesarean society": "France is too liberal for her hierarchy, too authoritarian for her democracy. . . . authority acts as an emetic; democracy as a solvent; it is as if both have lost their positive principles" (217).[2] The nation is thus constantly trapped between the poles of consensus and coercion, unable to achieve the former and unwilling to accept the latter. As a result, the French bureaucracy is simultaneously an object of hatred (it intrudes on every aspect of individual lives) and a convenient excuse for citizens to avoid individual responsibility (it provides a version of cradle-to-grave security). All too often polarized, theoretical discussions of this tension replace concrete efforts at reform, and commentators on French culture find themselves prisoners of the abstract level, unable to address practical reality. Because this conflict between theory and practice permeates French society from top to bottom, it provides one perspective from which every facet of French life can be analyzed.

Freeling himself is well aware of this state of affairs.[3] For example, he contends that French social engineering, as it is embodied in various Codes, shares the same benefits and shortcomings that characterize its industrial counterpart: "an engineer . . . receives a very strong schooling in theory, but the practical realization of his acknowledged brilliance is flawed or faulty with disturbing frequency" (NL 267).[4] It comes as no surprise, then, that an English jurist can argue that France has "been gifted with legal institutions the theory of which seems superior to our own. Yet all too often the result – the decision laid down by the court – appears as confused and confusing" (NL 268). As the author of a series of police procedurals, Freeling necessarily concentrates on the domain of the law, attempting to work out the practical ramifications of French legal theory. However, because the *Code Napoléon* is absolutely and integrally tied to every other "code" which governs French life, his novels inevitably exceed narrowly defined legal issues. From the first novels of the new series, Freeling carefully outlines the nature of the hierarchies which, in concert, enact the power embodied in the codes.

In *Dressing of Diamond* and in *The Bugles Blowing*, these hierarchies are laid out in encyclopedic detail; Freeling insists particularly on the separation of powers that should ensure the smooth running and equitable results of the system. Each arm of the law (police, prosecutor [*procureur*], examining magistrate [*juge d'instruction*], court) operates within clearly defined boundaries to guarantee, in theory, that the law will be interpreted "without fear or favour" (DD 22). Despite the Anglo-Saxon misconception that "under the Code a man is presumed guilty until he can prove himself innocent," the exact opposite is true and "unless the judge is convinced, after exhaustive inquiries, that there is a strong case for the accused to answer, he will never go to trial at all." A suspect's rights are further guaranteed by the presence of defense lawyers at every interrogation and the access they have to all documents and witnesses in the case. Moreover, the examining magistrate who directs the investigation "does not appear in the trial court, where he has no function, and no status. He merely forwards his recommendations. All pressure upon the accused person is thus removed" (BB 78). The role of the examining magistrate, that of shedding "light upon the personality" of the criminal (BB 185), thus resembles the role that Freeling has created for himself as he inquires into the social dysfunctions which produce crime.

If the Van der Valk series constitutes a pan-European House of Keeping in which Freeling scrutinizes the relationship between History (the public past) and crime, the Castang series takes a different tack. It begins with a narrowly French focus because the highly codified French legal system provides a textbook example of the workings of a social inquiry. Thus, each novel in the Castang series becomes the record of an "instruction," an attempt to construct a dossier theoretically so complete that criminal responsibility, and the reasons for it, will be firmly established. In later novels, the plots are broadened as they are multiplied, and the supra-national investigations enable Freeling to demonstrate that what is popularly thought to be a peculiarly French mania for knowledge and classification is in fact generalized throughout the parliamentary democracies of Western Europe.

Each of the "instructions" of the series, then, becomes an inquiry into a specific breakdown in discipline which inevitably has broader social implications. In France, where the *Code Napoléon* proposes an even more rigid classificatory system than that which Freeling outlined for the Netherlands, the responsibility for maintaining order ought to be less problematic. However, the edges of the Code have been "riddled by termites: these impossible social-sciences people" (CC 170). That is, it is no longer interpreted solely by jurists but is instead the province of a new network of voices who interpose themselves between the Law and the accused: they represent "the invisible jurisdiction of the normalizing agencies grouped together in a single tutelary complex" (Donzelot 115). Thus, Foucault recognizes that current penality has a two-fold object: "the offender" who is punished for "his act," and "the delinquent" whose "sum total existence," his life, is the object of "punitive technique." The *Code Napoléon* is therefore directed toward the offender, who has transgressed its articles, while the discourse surrounding the Code focuses on the biography of the delinquent. The interaction of the two produces the "'criminological' labyrinth" (Foucault 251–52) which is the heart of the police procedural as Freeling practices it here, and these novels frequently record the difficulty of assigning clear-cut blame within this labyrinth.

The first novel of the Castang series, *Dressing of Diamond*, explicitly opens Freeling's discussion of the interrelationship of the public and the private through the image of the family as a site of state intervention. The novel centers on the kidnapping of Rachel, the young daughter of Colette Delavigne, herself a *juge d'instruction* in the Children's Court. By choosing to put a crime against the family at the heart of this first book, Freeling once again affirms his interest in his literary predecessors – here, the novelists of the Golden Age. As we noted in our introduction, John Cawelti has demonstrated that a primary, though perhaps unconscious, focus of classic detective fiction is the dysfunctional bourgeois family and the crimes arising from its repressive nature. In the late Victorian and Edwardian Ages, however, with their conservative emphasis on a fundamentally stable social order, the doubts of the middle class could be dealt with only by indirection. Because Golden Age novelists insisted upon villains who were guilty of individual evil, villains who were emphatically not the products of their society but instead of their own twisted natures, family tensions were concealed in heavily encoded texts. Freeling, however, strips away the veneer of gentility that marked these earlier texts and lays bare the repressive mechanisms of the contemporary bourgeois family.

It is, as Commissaire Richard tells Bernard Delavigne, the mission of the police "'to ask some questions that may strike you as unpleasantly personal and indiscreet upon occasion'" when they are probing "'as difficult an affair as this – a family affair'" (DD 92). When the police investigate "'a serious crime against the person,'" they necessarily shine an "'unpleasantly bright'" searchlight on private lives. As Castang tells his wife Vera,

> "You have to go trampling in on people's privacy. All sorts of little details that aren't necessarily damaging but that they'd rather keep to themselves or that they wouldn't mind telling a doctor inside his professional secrecy, but having it typed out and read back to them makes them wriggle . . . . We get pretty depersonalized about this, even brutalized. But it still comes as a shock when it happens to oneself, or to one's friends." (DD 148)

It is no wonder that Castang later describes policemen, "'as the little joke goes,'" as dentists and "'upon occasion . . . gynaecologists. We ask intimate questions, without embarrassment'" (BNW 80). Whereas Freeling's Golden Age counterparts never violated the "doctor-patient" privilege of their characters, largely so as to avoid distracting the reader from the Great Detective's powers of ratiocination, here those confidences are the focus of the novelist's examination.

The Delavigne case is complicated by the fact that Colette is herself responsible for the destiny of wayward children and the adjudication of family crime. First, because she knows the cost to private lives of an official investigation, she is necessarily wary of setting in motion the investigatory process that has heretofore made her own job possible. She is well aware of the tripartite technique utilized by the investigative network that surrounds the accused in a juvenile case. As Donzelot describes the "police-like" inquiry, it involves a "circular approach to the family" by means of those with peripheral knowledge (neighbors and teachers, for example); "separate and contradictory questioning" of family members in order to "obtain a maximum of confidential disclosures"; and the "practical verification of the family's way of life," in which the investigator carries out "a relatively painless and systematic collection of information" (122–24). The point that Freeling stresses in *Dressing of Diamond* is that the inquiry directed at the family of the accused is inevitably duplicated as the police question the family and acquaintances of the victim. The "criminological labyrinth" which creates both "an object of intervention" and "an object of knowledge" (Donzelot 97) draws into its maze the biography of the victim as well as that of the "delinquent."

Second, because Colette is a female judge, she is doubly vulnerable. Not only does a crime against her daughter strike at her maternal role, but she is also liable to accusations that her feminine nature will disable her in the exercise of her official duties: "Little Madame Delavigne does not pester us with untimely displays of knee and bosom, does not spend interminable hours in the lavatory, leaves us mercifully free of boring involvements in her menstruations and fornications and lactations, has a good little head screwed on her shoulders, and still manages to be pleasantly feminine. But now there's a drama about a child throwing the whole place in an uproar: somehow one always knew this would happen" (DD 100). To confirm that private and public lives are thoroughly intertwined, Freeling adds another complication. Both Colette and Castang fear the possibility that official channels will misconstrue their friendship as an adulterous affair, and Castang surmises that he might be accused of aiding Colette because she is his mistress (DD 147, 201). For this reason, Castang tells Bernard Delavigne, "'You and I are both condemned to the possibility that at any moment our private life might not exist any more'" (DD 106).

The "drama about a child" thus becomes public evidence of Colette's private "failure" as a bourgeois mother whose monitoring of her latch-key child has been inadequate. In fact, Colette's investment in her daughter is even more precious because Rachel is an only child. Recognizing this, Colette has endeavored to counter the danger of spoiling her daughter by including her in the philanthropic network meant to forestall delinquency; Rachel has been encouraged to devote time to charitable activities involving Vietnamese babies and other disadvantaged children. Rachel's "education," then, is meant to prevent her from straying from the bourgeois values of her parents. However, despite the efforts of the Delavignes, Rachel has escaped the *cordon sanitaire* of surveillance (Donzelot 47) which they have constructed to enclose her. As a result, Rachel's real "reeducation" comes at the hands of her kidnappers, a peasant family whose "primitive" existence in the rural Aube supplies another model – repressive in its own way – for family behavior: anomic, brutal and "warped by misery" (DD 138).

The "family affair" is thus at least two-fold: on the one hand, Freeling can anatomize the smug bourgeois family by intruding a public eye upon its apparently smooth functioning; on the other, he can deflate the nineteenth-century notion of the close-knit and harmonious peasant clan through the innocent eyes of a proper bourgeois child.[5] Moreover, because the kidnapping is motivated by ancient inter-family rivalries over the peasants' right to pick fruit on the gentry's land, the family affair here is inevitably connected to the relations among the various hierarchical levels of the "national" family. While one of Freeling's larger goals in *Dressing of Diamond* is to point to the almost literal class warfare between the French peasantry and the bourgeoisie, his initial emphasis on family crime establishes an early – and important – conflict between private and public lives which runs throughout the entire Castang series.

Subsequent novels in the series expand upon Freeling's interest in familial crime. *The Bugles Blowing* moves up the social ladder to foreground the moral breakdown of a high bourgeois family. When Gilbert La Touche murders his wife and daughter as well as their mutual lover, he both avenges a blow to his private values and reasserts his patriarchal control. That is, he attempts to re-establish the "discretionary power" which he would have had over the destiny – and definition – of his family in earlier times but which has now become the province of the State's own powers.[6] For this reason, La Touche's need to regain his authority is ironically seen by the Public Prosecutor as a "grievous and insidious attack" on the "essential basic unit" of society, the family (BB 227). In addition, because La Touche is a senior civil servant, responsible for the probity of government finance, the corruption and adultery of the La Touche women can be read as a vehicle by which Freeling continues to explore both a crisis in "the smallest political organization possible" (Donzelot 48) and, by extension, the disintegration of the "national" family as the embodiment of responsibility and moral probity.

The image of the wife and daughter of an Inspector of Finance engaging in sex with an illicit lover is such a threat to traditional values that it motivates the search for a suitable scapegoat. Rather than face the "social anxieties" provoked by such a scandal, unable to believe that a family of such "standing" could be the symbolic seat of disintegration, representatives of the media and the police seek desperately to superimpose a conspiracy involving Arabs and Israeli intelligence agents. Such an explanation would at least deflect attention away from the promiscuous behavior of the La Touche women and locate the "real" problem beyond the borders of France.[7] When the fiction of political espionage is no longer tenable, the forces of law and order opt to protect the traditonal values of the family by ascribing La Touche's actions to temporary insanity. The fact that La Touche refuses to go along with the unspoken legal plan to declare him insane and therefore not responsible for his act suggests that he, too, recognizes that the earlier alliance between private fathers and the public Father (the King) has been finally dissolved in the new bourgeois State. That he goes quietly to the guillotine, inviting members of the police force, the carceral system and the government to witness his death, underlines his ties to the *ancien régime* and its spectacular punishments. There, the head of the family and the head of State worked cooperatively to establish the central values of both the nuclear and the national families; in contemporary France, La Touche is a dangerous throwback whose actions directly challenge the power of the State to shape every level of "the family."

While the analysis of society as family is finally overshadowed in *The Bugles Blowing* by Freeling's concomitant interest in capital punishment, he returns directly to the issue in *Sabine*. Here his task is made easier by the geographical limitations which he imposes upon his investigation; although he continues to compare a single family to a larger community, he narrows his focus to the town of Soulay and suggests that the familial passions of the Lipschitz clan are directly analogous to those which drive village affairs. Soulay is properly a citadel, a walled town once instrumental in the defense of Louis XIV's realm, now in a transitional stage that will carry it from sleepy pre-war village to bustling post-war suburb within the Hexagon. Behind the walls of Soulay there are passions linked to patrimony in a dual sense: family inheritance and the preservation of national culture.[8] Just as Monsieur Lipschitz's efforts to protect the national treasures entrusted to him run counter to the mania for development which marks most of Soulay, so, too, Sabine's efforts to preserve her home, and thus to continue her hold over her son, are overwhelmed by outside interests intent on profit at the expense of "family."

Sabine's house, the origin of the hostility which results in murder, lies behind a locked grille, surrounded by a garden that has turned to jungle through neglect. The house itself is a fortified sanctuary against the outside world, a repository of antique furniture that evokes past centuries of French culture (S 18–21). This is one of the few clearly metaphoric descriptions Freeling employs in the series; the "decaying" garden behind the "high stone wall" suggests both the decline of the Lipschitz family and the dense thicket of passions which culminate in Sabine's death (S 18). Sabine has herself overprotected her adopted son, confining him behind the walls of her house and the village of Soulay with the promise of the money he will derive from the sale of the increasingly valuable family property. Sabine's protection cannot, however, guarantee a secure future for the family since outsiders interested in land development come to manipulate her discontented son. Her daughter-in-law, Janet, conspires with Monsieur Barde, a gentleman farmer whose apparently solid standing within the community masks financial weakness, to seize the Lipschitz wealth and "free" themselves of the social and monetary constraints of the village. The stability of the family which depends on its internal, hierarchical organization – and of Soulay itself which also depends upon the carefully differentiated "standing" of its citizens – is thus threatened by the forces of social change which Freeling associates with a grasping bourgeoisie, and it is the role of the *police judiciaire* to penetrate the walls which conceal both personal and social conspiracies. Once again, the State is called upon to defend and preserve the family.

In *The Night Lords*, Freeling employs parallel plots for the first time in the series to reaffirm that families can undercut rather than promote the greater good of society. In both the Armitage and the Goltz plots, families conceal the identities of murderers, justifying their actions by a "higher" loyalty.[9] Since this is also the first novel in the series in which Freeling describes in detail the PJ squad which investigates the Armitage and Goltz crimes, the novel pits a representative "public family," the police, against the private family, and Freeling seems to come down squarely on the side of the larger community. His ultimate conclusion, though, is more problematic than a simple public versus private confrontation suggests, since Monsieur Bianchi, the "outsider" in the local PJ, and Vera, the Czech refugee, actually identify the criminals. While the police hunt through the "dustbins" of bourgeois society (NL 74, 178) for their material clues, Vera and Bianchi, echoing the earlier Van der Valk, concentrate on probing the human heart.

Bianchi is specifically linked with "a vanishing race ... of police officers" who have come up through the ranks, with no diplomas, and who have served for more than thirty years (NL 93). The pride he takes in his status as a "Companion of the Liberation" indicates his continuing distance from official channels, since his association with the Resistance suggests his devotion to a higher ideal at the same time that it implies his suspicion of state-sponsored policing: it is Bianchi, after all, who explains to Vera that the realm of the police is the realm of night and darkness (NL 136). Bianchi's use of geological terms to describe Goltz, the dealer in semi-precious stones (182–85), marks his ability to attune himself to the character of his suspect rather than relying on the technical capacities of the police: "Adolescents who run away from home, respectable businessmen who go suddenly haywire, wives who take to the bottle, shoplifting or unsuitable lovers; and all enquiries in the interests of families (still a surprising proportion of PJ business) – all this is meat and drink to Monsieur Bianchi" (94). Bianchi's ability to establish confidential relationships is precisely what leads him into danger in *The Night Lords*, and he, like the earlier Van der Valk, is shot when he comes too close to his quarry.

By virtue of her marriage to Castang, Vera, likewise, occupies a position on the margins of the official police, and her status as a Czech refugee endows her with a thoroughgoing suspicion of governmental surveillance. Vera's success in identifying Armitage as Laetitia Toth's murderer comes about because she operates outside the official investigation, understands the character of the victim, and thus is not blinded by the PJ's desire to arrest Armitage's son, Colin, in order to avoid unpleasant political complications. Vera establishes a confessional relationship with the elder Armitage in a Jesuit garden which is remarkable as a landscape "Trained, modified, patterned by man in an essentially simple way – it's only a surface sophistication" (NL 293). Within the rigid order imposed upon nature, Armitage is convinced to confess to the murder of Laetitia Toth; just as "wild" nature has been tamed in the garden, so, too, Armitage's passions will finally be circumscribed by his submission to the Law. The paradoxical use to which the Jesuit garden in *The Night Lords* is put suggests the complicated position of policing in French society. Under the *ancien régime*, the garden would have been a site of meditation and prayer under the watchful eye of God and his earthly representatives. There, both priests and students would have contemplated their own sinfulness as preparation for confession and, thus, submission to divine law; Vera, the unofficial "confessor," brings Armitage, a representative of secular law, to see the "evil" of his actions and to confess.

The irony which governs the solution is that she urges Armitage to confess to Castang and Richard, themselves official and secular agents but committed, according to Vera, to a concept of justice which is more than mere adherence to a legal code (297). Vera's suggestion thus re-humanizes Castang and Richard and elevates them above the average run of policemen; such a formulation is itself problematic, however, since it confirms the heroic status of Castang (and Richard) but implicitly denigrates the state apparatus which is the *raison d'être* for the police procedural as a form. In this sense, Freeling here echoes many of the same doubts he expressed in his earlier series where Van der Valk is carefully distinguished from official, bureaucratic authority and successful because of his insistence on understanding the private, usually with the aid of Arlette.[10] Once again, the ability of the public sphere to monitor the private as well as the tension between private and public roles is at the heart of his procedurals.

The French desire for privacy which manifests itself in high walls and shuttered windows also reveals itself in the constant attempt to compartmentalize one's private and public lives. Etienne Marcel, the adjunct mayor of *Castang's City*, is an apparent master of this mode, yet the novel ultimately demonstrates that his ostensibly public assassination is in fact rooted in the alienation of his family life. The Marcel family lives in the rue des Carmélites, a reference to church property expropriated by the bourgeoisie during the French Revolution. This expropriation suggests that the power of the Church under the *ancien régime* to discipline and order its members into a harmonious community intent on serving God has been displaced by a secularized and increasingly fragmented power.[11] Although Castang notes that the houses on the street demonstrate no "order, regulation, or discipline" (CC 52), he nevertheless believes himself capable of solving the case rapidly (CC 80). His inability to do so marks the breakdown of orderly relationships that once allowed the combination of church and state power to regulate relations between their subjects.

If the Carmelite nuns' lives in their cells and lives within the convent were a seamless whole under the watchful eyes of God, Marcel's desire to separate his life into "watertight compartments" (CC 80) is a misuse of the cellular model. He attempts to avoid public surveillance of his private life (in contrast to the Carmelites) because he sees no connection between his two roles – private father and public "father." Although Castang is initially impressed by the Marcel family's apparent unity and affection (CC 77), the segmentation which marks the lives of the Marcels leads them to seek relief in a sub-rosa world of secret associations which answer their need for wholeness but where, ironically, tangential relations provoke murder. In Freeling's France, therefore, one cannot wholly separate one's private life from one's public associations since to do so is to produce a life in which one is alienated from both spheres.[12]

At the same time that *Castang's City* details the disintegration of the Marcel family, it compensates for this image of loss through the birth of Castang's daughter, Lydia, and the consequent enrichment of the protagonist's family. To this point in the series, Castang, too, has attempted to compartmentalize his own life: "His habit of taking a shower directly he got [home] was in a way symbolic. It wasn't just sweat that had to be scrubbed off" (BB 101–02). Lydia's arrival opens up Castang and Vera's private life to the friendship of Commissaire Richard and his wife Judith; at the same time, though, that very friendship with figures from Castang's public world increases his family's vulnerability. It is the ambiguity of this interaction which becomes the theme of the next novel in the series, *Wolfnight*.

Here the public world that intrudes upon the family circle extends beyond the confines of the Hexagon. Freeling details the operations of a multinational political "family" whose mission is to create a "Committee of Public Safety" (W 118) to return France and other European states to the glory days of nationalism and to reject "'The most abject and pusillanimous flight from reality, from decision, from manhood'" (W 149). The Committee is a conspiracy among members of "the bourgeois clans" who have come to believe that they are losing control over the technocratic world they have helped to create: they are "'Not part of the mandarinate; nomenklatura as it's now fashionable to call it'" (W 61–62). While the high bourgeoisie may seem to have been reduced to foxhunting, in reality "'They're in directorships in everything from nuclear power stations to banking. And they're especially thick with the Elysée'" (W 62). The members of this extended bourgeois family, then, are responding to a perceived threat to their status: they attempt to establish an alternative order in which they will recapture their position in the devolutionary liberal state, where family discipline has broken down.[13] In other words, the Terror of the Revolution is ironically invoked to restore the hegemonic rights of the bourgeoisie in the face of what Stanley Kranitz calls "'this claptrap about social justice for the poor: mean to say, the poor are bloody awful; they're not just invincibly ignorant, they're disgusting. You can't do anything for them and they wouldn't want it if you did. . . . Keep the order and the law will take care of itself, right?'" (W 175–76). The privileged "family," threatened rather than protected by the State's new welfare systems, themselves vehicles of social discipline, proposes what amounts to a divorce.

Implicit in the birth of this alternative political family is a "crisis of hegemony" in western capitalism. From the point of view of Alberthe de Rubempré and Stanley Kranitz, "*the whole basis of political leadership and cultural authority* [has become] *exposed and contested.*" While one might well expect the state to intervene directly to shore up the rights of the dominant classes by moving "the operation of the state away from consent towards the pole of coercion" (Hall *et al.* 217), Freeling suggests that such a perceived crisis can generate an equally dangerous private response if the state moves too slowly.[14] The bourgeoisie itself can embrace its own brand of extremism and thus become a threat to both the public and the private spheres. On the overtly political level, a fraction of the "reforms" endorsed by Alberthe de Rubempré and her cohorts would lead inevitably to civil war (W 150). On the personal level, the creation of this super-family inevitably endangers the nuclear one. Stanley Kranitz, for example, is willing to kill his wife Viviane in order to drive Vibert and their movement further to the right, and this willingness to attack within the family threatens all who oppose the new order – especially representatives of the old, like the police. Thus, when Castang is called upon to investigate the disappearance of Viviane Kranitz, his own family becomes the object of violence; his apartment is machine-gunned and Vera is kidnapped. To suggest the depths of the threat embodied by Rubempré, Kranitz, and their co-conspirators, Freeling requires his police to indulge in extra-legal methods in order to expose the plot, and no network of relations, from nuclear family to bourgeois clan, escapes unscathed.

In all these novels, then, Freeling uses the traditional family as the starting point for his social investigation. In the novels before *Wolfnight*, the cases revolve around children who fail to internalize the social values of their families or whose lack of family has made them social misfits.[15] Freeling recognizes that the family control that was obscurely threatened in the Golden Age detective novel has predictably succumbed both to the fragmenting power of contemporary capitalism and the extension of state intervention in the socialization of family members (Donzelot 199). While the classic detective novel could only critique the family indirectly, within an ultimately reassuring framework, Freeling is able to penetrate the disciplinary breakdown within the family in a more sophisticated fashion by linking it to broader questions of political unease. As Hall *et al.* have shown, crucial definitions of social values are rooted in the image of the family since, "In the traditionalist lexicon, the sphere of the *family* is of course where moral-social compulsions and inner controls are generated, as well as the sphere where the primary socialisation of the young is first tellingly and intimately carried through." While the family provides an important "refuge" from the anxieties of the "outside" world of work, it is more centrally concerned with "the construction of social identities, and in transmitting, at an extremely deep level, the basic ideological grid of society." This is why discipline outweighs release in the dominant conception of the family and why "fears and panics about the breakdown of social discipline – of which crime is one of the most powerful indices – centre on the indiscipline of 'youth', 'the young' . . . " (144–45).[16]

In the world of Freeling's novels, then, the private world inevitably touches the public, and each provides a commentary on the other. *Wolfnight* sums up what has been established as a pattern of intricate relationships between family and state since the first novels of the series. Every case includes in its cast of central characters a member of the civil service who is part of the national "family" hierarchy, theoretically contributing to the socialization of members of the national clan. However, as Peyrefitte demonstrates, the highly centralized and compartmentalized bureaucratic structures that characterize French life lead to "the absence of direct responsibility," a lack of rootedness in the "realities of powers" and, finally, a "profound feeling of everyone's impotence" (416). Peyrefitte thus argues that the absence of personal responsibility within the state system provides an unintended model of irresponsibility for the citizenry in general, leading to the periodic, explosive "revolutions or rebellions" that have shaken France for hundreds of years (304). Paradoxically, this in turn requires that the private family be an even more crucial site of discipline and socialization in France than in a less centralized state.

When Freeling locates social disorder (crime) in family relations, and insists upon including bureaucrats in his representative families, he clearly intends to link the failures of both spheres in order to present a society wracked by a crisis of responsibility and order. Thus, when Rosemary Armitage nostalgically recalls an earlier civil service tradition of "'devotion to the public weal'" as "'an ideal of responsibility: a dedication almost religious,'" Castang responds that "'it's general police thinking'" that we "'deplore the decay of individual responsibility. Everything now gets shoved on to the shoulders of the State . . . . But the more the State does the more we want it to do, somehow. It can't take over all a family's duties'" (NL 258–59).[17] Freeling does not – indeed, cannot – propose a progressive solution to the microcosmic and macrocosmic unrest which he uncovers through the family. Instead, despite the constant invasion of the private by the public, he retains an almost patriarchal fondness for the essential validity of the traditional family unit which flies in the face of the social realities he catalogs. As Castang puts it, in confronting apparent social breakdown, "'There isn't a lot we can do . . . except love our children'" (BNW 96).

It would seem, then, that Jameson's vision of mass culture "as a transformational work on social and political anxieties and fantasies which must . . . be 'managed' or repressed" applies to Freeling's treatment of the family within his Castang series. Even as the family is threatened by various public assaults, Freeling's novels detail the attacks only to undercut their real power by offering a series of "imaginary resolutions" and "an optical illusion of social harmony" ("Reification" 141). The portrait of Vera, Castang, Judith and Richard clustered around baby Lydia at the end of *Wolfnight* blurs the spectre of attacks by a "terrorist family," proposing instead an impossibly utopian rehabilitation of both the private and the public spheres embodied in the tripartite restoration of the order of the father: Castang as papa; Richard as father/mentor to Castang, and Castang and Richard both as patriarchs of republican authority.[18] Freeling thus "naturalizes" the police by constituting them in a familial form which in turn defines the nation as family, subject to the benevolent, paternal discipline of the guardians of order.[19]

Freeling's rehabilitation of the family would appear, on the surface, to qualify him as an exponent of a very conservative ideological strain in the detective novel. In fact, he comes uncomfortably close to reproducing the Vichy model of *"travail, famille, patrie."* Yet in the three later novels, Freeling attributes attacks on order to right-wing zealots intent upon reinforcing a rigid nationalism, itself dependent upon class distinction and the resanctification of the private. Curiously, then, the destabilizing forces against which the police must act are precisely those which conspire against the nation in the name of law and order. The Charlemagne society, another Committee of Safety envisioned by Aldo de Biron in *The Back of the North Wind*, infiltrates even the police in its attempt to reestablish the Holy Roman Empire on French soil.[20] The seriousness of the threat is underlined by two acts: the burning of Richard's house and the "duel" between Castang and Maltaverne, a Principal Commissaire who has been recruited by Biron. The attack on Richard's home, which ought to be the bastion of those values endorsed by Biron, suggests that Biron and his co-conspirators are indeed "'not dazzled by ideologies'" (BNW 109); that is, Freeling implies that Biron's society is not really an attempt to enact a "legitimate" restoration of a decaying liberal state, but is instead nothing more than a grab for raw power. In a similar fashion, the plot engineered by Agatha Martindale and Sevenhampton in *No Part in Your Death* pays lip service to authoritarian solutions – the creation of a private militia to remedy "'the craven-hearted gutlessness of [the police]. Pack of fucking socialists no doubt . . . '" (NPD 219). Like Biron, Miss Martindale is seen to have no identifiable "ideology"; rather, she is dismissed as a "Boer War relic, nostalgic" for the days when the different classes knew their place (NPD 213).[21]

Biron and Martindale thus exemplify the most dangerous aspects of the "secret societies" which Freeling sees both contemporary capitalism and state intervention producing to compensate for the loss of personal identity and secure families. Before the political "clubs" of *Wolfnight, The Back of the North Wind* and *No Part in Your Death*, Freeling had already established other varieties of private havens to combat alienation: "The modern structures of society, intensely fragmented, with their ever-narrower appeal to small areas of specialized knowledge and limited responsibility . . . yes, sure. Creating numerous areas of solitude – yes, sure. Mankind went about thus inventing pretexts for obscure types of togetherness – right, mate. Hence the amazing proliferation of little groups." According to Castang, such creations are "normal" and "even a basic ingredient in the fabric of social intercourse" because they counter the "mighty flood of Outsiders" who have broken "all the old bonds" (CC 176–77). While these groups can, to some extent, remedy dislocation and destabilization at the family level, they also may become the nexus of personal and political crime.

On another level, Freeling is intent upon showing that, just as these compensatory "families" do not address the fundamental fragmentation which produces them, so, too, society offers no new vision of class relations to defuse traditional hostilities. *Dressing of Diamond* introduces this warfare early on, focusing on the clash between the inhabitants of Colette Delavigne's *nouveau riche* residence and the living relics of the older villages transformed by the spread of suburbia (DD 58–59). The central plot is, as we have seen, a class-related one, pitting the "cunning" peasants of the Moustier-Gaboriau clan against the formidable resources of a married couple who unite the forces of the State (an examining magistrate) and capital (a yogurt merchant). While Freeling's portrait of the anomic peasants in their home, watching television, staring at their dirty fingernails and swigging beer (DD 175), is perhaps not calculated to gain the reader's sympathy, he does raise the question of the role of the police as defenders of the rights of the rich (DD 213).[22] He also queries the effectiveness of the juvenile justice system since Pierrot Gaboriau has become a recidivist; that is, he has escaped the normalizing techniques of bourgeois institutions and strikes out once again at the network of oppressors figured in Colette Delavigne. The ending of the novel, which "draws a veil" over the motives of virtually everyone involved (DD 221–22), leaves unresolved the validity of the peasants' complaints which prompted their kidnapping of Rachel; on a larger scale, Freeling thus leaves unresolved the possibility of any end to the class and caste compartmentalization that has historically provoked "suspicion, intolerance and aggression" between the peasantry and the bourgeoisie, the country and the city (Peyrefitte 486).

If the ending of *Dressing of Diamond* suggests that the *Procureur de la République* is going to prosecute the peasant clan despite the flimsy evidence and "inconvenient facts" (DD 221) precisely because they have dared to attack the family property (both child and land) of an examining magistrate, the same sort of class clannishness dominates *The Bugles Blowing*. Here, La Touche's own standing as a higher civil servant, as well as his wife's links to the aristocracy, make it more difficult for the State to accept La Touche's claim that he has committed premeditated murder. Instead, the entire judicial system conspires to generate a verdict of insanity and thus excuse a fellow member of the civil service. The novel demonstrates that apparently personal, apparently "moral" issues, rooted in family relations and questions of patriarchal authority, are necessarily political despite the Code's designation of them as "private" actions. It is La Touche himself, however, who refuses to take the easy way out and who welcomes the prospect of the guillotine; by rejecting the protection of his class and its politics, La Touche simultaneously refuses to be classified as insane and to be treated as a cipher rather than as an individual. His personal rebellion thwarts the efforts of his class to shield him; it also, ironically, forces the government's hand, since the President of the Republic cannot take the obvious political risk of granting clemency to one of its own, while others, of lesser classes, die unpardoned (BB 257).

Once again, however, Freeling's own attitude seems to be ambiguous: through Vera we come to respect La Touche's intellect and "rebellion" against the conspiracy to "normalize" his act, yet it is clear that La Touche has not completely transcended the system but merely succeeded in manipulating it for his own ends. Thus, his rejection of the protections afforded him by his position "within" the Code can only be effected within limits imposed by the object of his rebellion. Whether he wishes to be or not, he is still an object of discipline within the established order, as is his family, and in revealing this "powerlessness" before the law Freeling creates a plot which uncovers the penetration of the bourgeois family – and its class – by the State in ways which were unavailable to his Golden Age predecessors.

By the time of *The Night Lords* Freeling complicates the issue of class conflict even further by placing it in the international context of European politics. The investigation of the murder of Laetitia Toth enmeshes Castang and the PJ cops in a diplomatic web in which the family of the English judge Armitage is removed from the normal channels of police work by both his nationality and his status. Whereas La Touche manipulates the judicial system from within, Armitage need only acquiesce in the protection automatically afforded by the diplomatic niceties of inter-European relations. Moreover, when he finally admits to having murdered Toth, it is clear that his case will be given "the widest and most liberal view" (NL 309), and his punishment will be little more than removal from the English bench and, perhaps, eight months in "a nice clean airy room, plenty of library books and no low company" (NL 312).[23] While Castang is unhappy about the predicted outcome, Freeling

A Family Affair 145

makes it clear that only figures like Goltz, the "legal thief" and slum landlord (NL 188), will bear the full weight of French justice.

Driven by greed and foolish enough to shoot a policeman, Goltz has no one to intervene on his behalf except a brother who will hide him momentarily. Here Freeling reveals his scorn for those who, like Goltz, have "the morals of a stoat," but he insists that there are far worse criminals whom the legal system cannot touch: "'What are politicians?'" (NL 311). They are those who believe, as Foucault says, that "Law and justice do not hesitate to proclaim their necessary class dissymmetry" (276). Goltz has transgressed the "rules" which protect him as a member of the petty bourgeoisie; his "legal thievery" in real estate would go unchallenged as he adds to the wealth of the middle class, but his attack against the very state agents whose task is primarily to protect property threatens the embedded "class dissymmetry" and opens him to the discipline normally reserved for the members of the working classes. Once again, then, the *Code Napoléon* theoretically proposes an egalitarian treatment under the law, but its complex system of classification and discipline cannot transcend the subtle distinctions of privilege inherent in a class-based society. In fact, it secures dominant class interests *"as a 'general interest'"* (Hall *et al.* 199), and in order to keep underlying traditional class hostilities in check it depends upon minute classifications of behavior for its operation.

As Foucault argues, the "Napoleonic character" marks "the point of junction of the monarchical, ritual exercise of sovereignty and the hierarchical, permanent exercise of indefinite discipline. He is the individual who looms over everything with a single gaze which no detail, however minute, can escape" (217). In Freeling's France, surveillance remains the cornerstone of the disciplinary system which has called it into being. In fact, the notion of a "cornerstone" is literally invoked by Freeling in his constant recurrence to the physical sites of police headquarters and *palais de justice*.

These buildings are either nineteenth-century conversions of earlier disciplinary facilities such as military hospitals, which themselves resemble lunatic asylums (NL 28), or their architecture recalls such facilities: "The building where [Castang] worked was a massive and dreary block of the previous century, in the ponderous rectilinear architecture then thought suitable for schools, orphanages or madhouses; and suitably it housed some hundreds of functionaries supporting state bureaucracies of the sort whose purpose nobody can guess and whose meaning if they have one is carefully concealed" (NPD 5–6).[24] The physical engineering of the site of bureaucratic labor doubles as an emblem of the social engineering proposed by the Code itself, to be enacted by the "technicians of discipline . . . for the individual and collective coercion of bodies" (Foucault 169). Thus, the particular function of a particular bureaucracy may be "concealed," but the building in which it is housed proclaims the generalized power of the Code and the State over the citizenry who pass by, reminding them of the various agencies which can and will be called to action in moments of "crisis."

Castang's investigation of motive in the Gilbert La Touche case provides an opportunity for Freeling to detail the profusion of policing mechanisms that officially maintain order in the Hexagon: the urban police (*sûreté urbaine*), responsible for municipal police brigades; the P.J. (*police judiciaire*), an extended regional counterpart of the urban police; the D.S.T. (*surveillance du territoire*), linked to counterespionage; and the R.G. (*renseignements généraux*), "translatable vaguely as 'Spying on Everybody'" (BB 174–77). These entities are complemented by the C.R.S. (*Compagnie républicaine de sécurité*), responsible for duties as diverse as lifeguarding and riot control, and the gendarmerie, "a military body organized in a military hierarchy": "The gendarme is pretty well everything his municipal colleague is, as well as handyman in the fire and ambulance services, public works and rural engineering, but he is also an officer of judicial police. . . . The extremely elaborate separation of powers, with subtle distinctions between legislative and executive, which prevails in the city, and ensures that no Gestapos arise upon the territory of the republic, is in the country fused" (DD 205–06).[25] The network of public surveillance generalized throughout the Republic is thus reinforced by overlapping responsibilities; in theory, no citizen's crime ought to be able to escape detection, nor should the motives for that crime go unexplained. Yet, as Castang reflects, there is a difference "between knowing a thing and being aware of it" (BB 177). Police work itself is merely a technical response to an "infringement of a formal code" (S 30), but it builds upon the ubiquitous impulse to knowledge that characterizes communities.

The systems of surveillance in the Castang series therefore range from the internalized to the externalized; that is, the police can rely on the panoptic networks which operate within families, clubs, and villages before they must call upon their own resources, both human and technological, to maintain order. For example, Castang interviews Magali in *Castang's City* in order to ascertain her impressions of "'Character – mentalities'": "'In talking to members of your family I didn't want my big feet getting obtrusive'" (70). In the same novel the police interview the secretary of the Bridge Circle who refers to himself as having "'an eye and an ear everywhere,'" although he is not allowed to be "'intrusive'" (241). In *Sabine* in particular, Castang exploits village gossip and neighborly opinions in order to find important clues: "A small town, where everybody gossiped. A place where nothing ever happened, where the scandal of the year was the mayor's trafficking in influence to get his parking lot built! Where anonymous denunciations flew, where nobody could really live in peace. Poor old Barde couldn't even enjoy his maids in peace, an estate agent had to slip about furtively at night, and even Sabine, quite respectable widow of a cultural-affairs civil servant, spun strange webs and dark suspicions" (121–22). Thus, the system of surveillance necessitated by the Code is already inherent in the everyday functioning of society in spite of the walls constructed to protect privacy, and even the moments of intimacy spent with the village call girl become sources of information to be exploited (S 141).[26]

Occasionally, the police find a happy coincidence between local gossip and the official investigator. In *No Part in Your Death*, for example, Noel Arnaud, the village constable, is "a busy local grapevine; that's one phone line that is never down . . . " (105). In the provinces, it is at times the case that the representatives of the entire system of surveillance and discipline "'are all cousins and in the clan. "*Maqués ensemble*" . . . '" (DD 81). In such cases, the family literally doubles as an agent of unofficial and official surveillance; it forms the primary "concentric circle" which Donzelot points to as part of the network that surrounds the accused.[27]

In large measure, then, the ability of the State to insist upon discipline through surveillance necessarily depends upon the internalization of such values and techniques by the population as a whole: "Conventional people – which most people are – live in strange discomfort forced upon them by the rigidity of their notion of what an interior ought to look like" (W 43). Convention, in other words, is little more than an acquiescence in a prior pattern of discipline which is reinforced by the surveillance of every visitor to a home. What Freeling is intent upon showing is that the power of conventional patterning is so deeply embedded in Western society that it has quite literally been naturalized.

Even this process, however, cannot wholly prevent delinquency. When internalized mechanisms of surveillance are inadequate, the police are authorized to bring to bear the full force of the Panopticon upon the private lives of the citzenry. The increasingly complex techniques of police surveillance are displayed in Freeling's explanations of the various modes of shadowing suspects. *Castang's City*, for example, is a virtual textbook on the techniques of both "light surveillance" (141–43, 161) and the "classic 'open watch'" (211). While this sort of material is, at a superficial level, "necessary" to the requirements of procedural realism, it is also calculated to expose the extent of the growing intrusion of the public into the private sphere. Liliane, after tailing Bertrand and Magali, notices even the smallest changes in their routine: "'B's style of driving the car, habitually relaxed, has changed: more jerky and hurried. M. likewise: e.g. on a perfectly easy piece of road (traffic light) suddenly swerved over to midway line & nearly touched oncoming car which cursed her'" (227).[28]

The camera eye which surveys the railroad station in *The Back of the North Wind* is perhaps the most egregious emblem of state panopticism; only the lavatories escape its gaze because "'snooping in the shithouse is unconstitutional'" (121). The camera replaces eight men and localizes not only Thérèse Martin as well as an assortment of drug dealers, but it also tracks the movements of every weary traveller who passes by. Castang rightly compares his position to that of "King Louis XIV with the whole of Versailles under personal control" (122), but with a most important difference. As a member of the *police judiciaire*, Castang cannot employ his power in a spectacular way in order to exercise "the vengeance of the sovereign"; rather, he exercises a hidden power in "the defence of society" (Foucault 90). The link between the Sun King and Castang is, of course, well-founded, since both are potentially dangerous, and Freeling's attitude is duly ambivalent towards this Orwellian development. On the one hand, he defuses the danger by turning to comedy, recounting Castang's fear that if he does not uncover some narcotics traffic, the PJ will be sent an "enormous bill for Labour" by the Narcotics Squad from whom he has borrowed the equipment (123). On the other, he points to the spectre of utterly dehumanized control when Castang reflects that "The Sony Corporation will shortly abolish policemen altogether . . . . Wonderful. Roll on this splendid dawn" (122).

The camera sequence is an apt way to sum up a series of small panoptic exercises which the police undertake. Their techniques can involve a simple phone tap manned by a "slave" in the basement (DD 121). On the one hand, this is relatively ineffective since "'Tracing a call is a thing only done in detective stories . . . . And a recording isn't evidence, [although] what it leads to is'" (DD 182); on the other, it allows the police to localize and classify Marie-Thérèse's *parigot*/peasant accent and thereby to crack the case (DD 180–85). This same "'localisation of individuals'" takes on a more sinister cast in *No Part in Your Death*, where representatives of the Pan-European Panopticon discuss the invention of an Individual Genetic Badge in reponse to the requirements of security enforcement (NPD 25–26).

This prying into the routines of personal lives is not without its cost to the integrity of the agents themselves. When Castang is detailed to rummage through Viviane Kranitz's apartment, he feels "both like a burglar and a voyeur: he had been both, upon occasion. A crime-detail cop has learned that there is a dreary similarity about the ways people hide their valuables (burglars become skillful at the rapid recognition of patterns) while there is a multiplicity and variety to what goes on behind the bedroom door which will stretch even the older cop's eyes" (W 42–43). Castang as burglar adumbrates the extra-legal activity in which he and Richard conspire later in the novel, while Castang as voyeur recalls the police intrusion into the orgy organized by Jacques Maresq in *Castang's City*, where the police feel a "nasty kind of excitement . . . and something mean. Like picking a dead man's pocket" (274).[29]

A similar kind of excitement is generated in the sequences in which the police are obliged to adopt disguises in order to break down resistance to their search for information.[30] Inevitably, these scenes are described as a "comic operetta" (BNW 142) or a "kindergarten performance" (W 103); in *Wolfnight* in particular, Castang's impersonation of an "Attaché de Direction. The Bank of Nova Scotia, Paris" (82) reveals how ridiculous he feels at having to misrepresent himself. Yet, at the same time, there is a sense of Carnival that pervades the assumption of a mask, especially when that disguise forms part of an extra-legal activity. When Richard, Castang and Orthez, "giggling, like three children on New Year's Eve" (W 103), alter their appearances (W 102) in order to pass as French counter-espionage agents intent on foiling a plot against Alberthe, they are themselves seduced by the reversal of their official status, by the titillating prospect of "one tiny detail" going wrong and ending up in "Paraguay: three jobs as male nurses in Doctor Mengele's clinic" (W 103). Here, the disguise is not generated by the need to defuse hostility on the part of their target but is rather a function of the squad's operating without the sanction of the State. The disguise, in this sense, represents an attempt at divorcing the person of the cop from the consequences of his own extra-legality; it is no longer Richard, for example, but "Commissaire Machecoul" who kidnaps Alberthe (W 100–1). This same "divorce" also serves to reassure the reader that, however illegal the squad's actions may be, Richard's team is acting in the best interest of "the People."

Alan Clarke argues that the presence of extra-legal procedures in current British police television series reflects a contemporary interest in "the tensions between the policeman's role as a policeman and as an individual . . . ": "A dedicated detective risks putting his job in jeopardy – threatening his future and his life outside the force – to protect the individual rights of other members of society" (51). Because such extra-legal actions are generally successful, they call into question the "bureaucratic restrictions which tie the policeman's hand," and they thus serve as springboards for a developing "anti-statist ideology" (50–51). While those detectives who operate outside the law might be portrayed as heroic in Clarke's series, in Freeling's novels, any sense of the heroization of the extra-legal is undercut by Castang's nagging sense that "All three . . . thought that what they had done was mad, wrong, silly, and they'd live to regret it . . . " (W 108). Later, Castang tells Alberthe that Richard's "'total illegality'" was limited to her kidnapping because, "'like most cops he has nothing but his pension to live on. He has to get back into legality and stay there'" (W 145). Through the reactions of the cops themselves, then, Freeling problematizes the whole issue of extra-legal methods in the service of some "higher" cause, focusing on the conflict between the desire for personal security and allegiance to one's principles. Indeed, Castang himself is later a victim of illegal acts by both Maltaverne (BNW) and Rennemann (NPD), renegade agents of the legal system who claim the same type of "higher" authorization for their actions.

The introduction of the theme of political intrigue into *Wolfnight* and its continuation in the more recent books in the series suggest that Freeling is transposing into the police procedural elements of the thriller. While he interrogated the police procedural formula in the Van der Valk series by introducing the conventions of prior detective fiction, here Freeling is less interested in a specifically intertextual relationship than in the incorporation of the conspiracy model that characterizes thriller fiction.[31] In one version of this mystery genre, "'high tech paranoia'" literature, "a distorted figuration of . . . the whole world system of present-day multinational capitalism" is embodied in a conspiracy "in which the circuits and networks of some putative global computer hook-up are narratively mobilized by labyrinthine conspiracies of autonomous but deadly interlocking and competing information agencies in a complexity often beyond the capacity of the normal reading mind" (Jameson, "Postmodernism" 79–80).[32] In the Castang series, this material appears in greatly reduced form, as a part of the general network of surveillance which Freeling establishes. For example, when "Commissaire Machecoul" tells Staff-Captain Ailleret that he needn't inform his superiors of the extra-legal action they are about to undertake, Castang can hardly believe that Ailleret will swallow the story: "Why not? We are living in a world . . . where staggering quantities of information are stored in a silicon chip, instantly retrievable to every Jones or Schmitt who troubles to breathe on the button" (W 104). By the time of *No Part in Your Death*, Freeling has come to see that such informational capabilities are part and parcel of the methods of European police forces generally: "'How far can we extend data storage without threatening liberties? Put it another way: access to this information is strictly limited. Is that the best safeguard we can invent, towards the preservation of these liberties?'" (18). These questions, posed by a police officer from the Federal Republic of Germany, define the depth and breadth of state intrusion into private lives.

If the earliest novels of the series demonstrate the painstaking construction of what is quite literally a paper dossier, the later novels, with their diffuse triple plots, reproduce the rapid pace of contemporary data collection. The absolute, plodding linearity of plot in *The Bugles Blowing*, for example, leads to a certain, if unsatisfactory, conclusion. By contrast, the multiple investigations in the later novels seem almost breathless; the solution of the first crime only brings Castang face to face with a new dossier, which is even more difficult. This spiralling complexity would seem to invite a high-tech reaction on the part of the police, overwhelmed by criminality even among children; yet Freeling offers the invitation only to pull back from the Orwellian brink and redeem the police by insisting that the focal point of the novel must remain a human enterprise. For this reason, Richard himself undertakes to break the Biron case (BNW), and Castang places himself at risk while investigating his friend Roger Riderhood (NPD).

Freeling's *police judiciaire* do, of course, rely on computers for information, but the author's real interest in conspiracy takes a different turn. The forms of surveillance which the Castang series addresses cause Freeling to focus his attention not on the high-tech world of informational networks but on the relatively low-tech world of home-grown political plots generated by self-interested conspirators. As a result, the generalized fears of a police conspiracy against the rights of citizens are displaced onto shadow "policing" entities like Alberthe de Rubempré's nationalist guerrilla fighters, Biron's Charlemagne squad, and Martindale's army of gunrunners. That is, Freeling, too, asks the question, "*Quis custodiet ipsos custodes?*," but he extends the definition of "guardians" to include the self-appointed unofficial forces who seek to create alternate orders and substitute them for those ratified by social contracts. As a result, the various secret societies and Committees of Safety which pervade the latter books of the series transform the obliquely political questions of the earlier family crimes into overt inquiries. Likewise, the shortcomings of the bureaucracy explored in the early books become the *raisons d'être* of the organizations of Rubempré, Biron, and Martindale.

Such transformations have two sorts of consequences. On the one hand, Freeling's plots seem to become ideologically conservative: even though the conspiracies in the novels come from the right, and thus one might be tempted to see their downfall as somehow "progressive," the fact that it is the agents of the state apparatus who prevent their success reproduces the reassuring myths of harmony and security to which Jameson has pointed in mass culture. On the other hand, the actions of those agents raise troubling questions because their work forces even them to question the actions of and their loyalty to the State as well as to resort to extra-legal methods of control, and their unease remains unresolved.[33]

In this context, it is important to remember that Freeling begins his series by situating police routine metaphorically within society. Early in *Dressing of Diamond*, for example, Castang describes himself as "Sorting out the discards in a great mound of evil-smelling waste – it formed by far the greatest body of police work. Garbage miners we are . . . " (51).[34] The effect of such a description is to create narrative distance between criminals and readers, reassuring the latter that "delinquency [belongs] to an entirely different world," that "delinquency appears both as very close and quite alien, a perpetual threat to everyday life, but extremely distant in its origin and motives, both everyday and exotic in the milieu in which it takes place" (Foucault 286). Such a formulation thus enables the reader to penetrate the "exotic" world of crime without risk, "mine" society's "waste," but at a safe remove. In this sense, the novels contain the reader's fears by evoking the world of criminality while simultaneously presenting the police as a barrier between the criminal and the reader. This in turn means that the police function as the rhetorical "line" which circumscribes delinquency and "sets it apart" from the everyday world of the bourgeois reader (Foucault 286). Thus, the reader "visits" the universe of the Gaboriau family, but the exotic and alien world presented through Rachel's eyes is eventually circumscribed by the *police judiciaire*, the gendarmerie, and the courts.

Were Freeling to rest content with such a formulation, he would merely reproduce, though in a contemporary form, the same myths of reassurance created earlier by Golden Age detective novelists. He is, however, unwilling to do so, and he forces the reader to confront the "reality" of crime by shifting his descriptions of police work from the metaphoric to the literal as early as *The Night Lords*. Here, the "dustbins" that the police sift through for clues to the murders in both plots are real; the key to Laetitia's disappearance and to the deaths of Auguste and the *clochard* are literally to be found in trashcans, containers for the detritus of bourgeois civilization. The yoking of a relatively exotic figure like Armitage and an utterly banal one like the petty Goltz in the two murder plots suggests that the earlier, careful "circumscription" of the criminal is beginning to break down; the passions erupting in a rural milieu in *Dressing of Diamond*, the threat to patriarchy concealed behind the aristocratic facade of *The Bugles Blowing*, and the conflicts hidden behind *Sabine*'s citadel and garden walls are here naturalized and begin to come into public view. By the time of *Castang's City*, what is essentially a family dispute is "settled" by a very public assassination.

To this point the police have continued to serve as the barrier or line between the delinquent and society. However, the distance between the delinquent and the reader has slowly diminished. The exotic and alien character of crime in detective novels underlined by Foucault begins to erode so that the reader is increasingly threatened by the "return of the repressed": what have heretofore been seemingly parochial crimes which indicate widespread social crises only by indirection, as in the novels of the Golden Age, assume the form of crimes which directly and overtly threaten the State in the person of Castang. The crucial turning point in the series is *Wolfnight*. Here, the *cordon sanitaire* between society and criminal is breached when Castang's family is twice the victim of violence: his apartment is machine-gunned, and his wife is kidnapped. The logic of Freeling's plot suggests that if the guardians, those who both "protect" the reader and with whom the reader identifies, can be attacked, criminality has become so general throughout society that it can no longer be seen merely as something to be "enjoyed" safely and at aesthetic remove.[35] The destabilizing purposes of Alberthe de Rubempré's conspiracy thus become the first vehicle by which Freeling can begin to destabilize the conventionally "safe" world of detective fiction.

This breakdown of defenses is explicit not only in the physical threats to the protagonists of the series (Castang's family; Richard's home), but in the spiralling self-doubt which Freeling's cops are forced to confront. In the earlier novels, the police must deal with "typical" characterizations of their work coming from external sources: "The public, even when treated with quite exaggerated politeness, always feels guilty of something or other, and takes refuge in feeling browbeaten" (S 57). By the time of *Castang's City*, however, these charges begin to come from within the force itself and, more significantly, from the divisional commissaire:

> "We're the agents and slaves of a centralised apparatus. The Nation. Which doesn't deserve to exist, and doesn't in fact exist. We're nobody. Hated by the people, as we deserve, treated with contempt by Paris, as we deserve, underpaid little informers, dressed in shoddy clothes, armed with shoddy guns, with shoddy little minds. We do nothing, Castang, but keep in power a crew that isn't worth powder and shot.
>
> "We're the Guardia Civil, and that's just our speed. We're – just barely possibly – less bad than we were.
>
> "Keep that in mind, boy. That's your job. Try to leave things less bad than they were." (CC 133)

It would be simple to dismiss this self-characterization as an ironic reprise of the litany of hostility to the cops that is formulaic in the police procedural, where police work is described by Dove as "The

Thankless Profession" (*Procedural* 113). Yet in those conventional gripes there is no serious doubt as to the validity of the policing enterprise; to conventional cops, the public simply does not appreciate the difficult and dangerous work they do. Thus, in fact, Freeling is much closer here to Sjöwall and Wahlöö's lament on "the rats of fascism," which led Lennart Kollberg to resign from the force.

To see such a connection is not to insert Freeling into the same sort of concrete political critique which shapes Sjöwall and Wahlöö's analysis of "the People's Home," but it is certainly to reaffirm the ideological dimension of a popular form like the police procedural. In Freeling's hands, the entire policing enterprise is problematized in order to question the value of the police *cordon sanitaire* in contemporary France and, by extension, in Western nations generally. *The Night Lords* itself, for example, refers directly to "Les Seigneurs de la Nuit," the "worst kind of political police" in Venice (136). While Vera's account to Castang of her discussion of the police with Monsieur Bianchi immediately becomes "a bit theological" in its thrust (136), the net effect of the scene is to insist that the metaphysical and the political remain inseparable. Bianchi's putative memoirs, "'Forty Years of Police Malpractice,'" becomes the starting point for a theory of policing which suggests that the police must be "'Elastic . . . between good and evil. The law is more evil, and criminality less, than the law is able to accept, because "hard cases make bad law," and the police function is to absorb as much of the creaking as possible'" (134–35). If "'night was an ancient spirit of evil. Night is the cholera . . . ,'" the best of the police are "an influence, a *rayonnement*," against it (135–36). The important question which Freeling develops after *The Night Lords* is the role of the "best" of the police in a world in which the State itself comes to be associated with the night.[36]

The next novel in the series, *Castang's City*, brings to the fore precisely the nocturnal qualities of the police, citing, for example, the rape of a fourteen-year-old Algerian girl by three drunk, off-duty cops (22). The crucial point Freeling makes, however, is not contained within the litany of examples of individual policemen straying from the straight and narrow. Instead, he focuses on the institutional level when he introduces Castang's musings on the fact that "His detestation for the State grew year by year but he had not allowed it to become cynicism. The State paid him; he was a servant. There was much he disliked about that, but he had to keep things simple" (10). This initial disengagement is chipped away over the course of the novel as Castang is forced to confront the reality of his involvement in the "shady part . . . of local power-structures" (69). Though he may reject the petty dishonesty that characterizes much government functioning (127–28), he comes to recognize that he is trapped within the system which gives him his identity: "Sewerage, dustbins and cops remain, and will go on remaining major municipal preoccupations . . . . The PJ could become a powerful instrument of oppression, and was certainly unpleasantly pliable in the hands of its masters in Paris. But believe me, it's necessary to any semblance of civilisation" (152–53). Thus, the theme of the "endless war" evoked by the constant references to Kipling's "Boots-boots-boots-boots-movin' up an' down again!/There's no discharge in the war" leads Castang to see that, at least in this case, both he and his work transcend the "masters" in Paris because he "belongs" to the city, owes it a loyalty that transcends the merely personal (285–86). While this expression of duty is finally positive in *Castang's City*, by the time of *Wolfnight* Freeling has begun to explore the problematic ramifications of fidelity to the "higher" authority of a personal code.

Wolfnight raises this issue through the analogy of 1940: "In the Vichy time, the Resistance time . . . it was as Richard said, you were freed from your oath. The existing government was too cowardly for anything but compromise, spent all its energies in searching for formulae to save its face. Legal, illegal; moral, immoral: good God, it meant nothing any more" (130). In the new "wolf-time" Castang cannot be comforted by the notion that he is simply a "servant" of the State responsible to his "masters" in Paris, however reassuring that idea may be, since he believes that the State itself has abandoned its own authority in order to avoid political discomfort. Worse yet, by its inaction, the State itself becomes a co-conspirator with Alberthe de Rubempré and her band, as it did in 1940 with another right-wing army. Much of the novel is thus devoted to Richard's attempts to convince Castang to abandon his morally neutral stance and to embrace Richard's dictum that "If the government to whom your allegiance is sworn acts in both an illegal and immoral fashion" (89) one must remain true to a personal and transcendent vision of the State (118).

This is clearly difficult terrain for Freeling to negotiate, as the repeated debates about kidnapping Alberthe show. The dangers are obvious, as history demonstrates. Superimposing a personal vision on a political map can lead to the abuses of power embodied in the kidnapping and shooting of the Duc d'Enghien by Napoleon's minions and the kidnapping of the OAS's Colonel Godard by the "parallel police" (W 88–89). On the other hand, doing nothing is simply acquiescing in the government's own inability – or unwillingness – to cope with political complexity. Freeling never manages to get himself out of the bind which he has created. Instead, he retreats before the consequences of the actions of Richard, Castang, and Orthez, and he shifts the grounds of Castang's efforts to the purely personal. Ultimately, the fact that it is *his* flat that is machine-gunned, that it is *his* wife who is kidnapped, motivates him. *Wolfnight* thus raises troubling questions about the conflict between personal responsibility and submission to the Law, only to conclude conservatively with a family portrait which suggests that in restoring the family one begins to defend what is valuable about the State.

The novels which follow, *The Back of the North Wind* and *No Part in Your Death*, confirm both Freeling's interest in "transcendent" loyalty and his inability to articulate a coherent vision of the concept. In each novel, the plots are tripartite, and in each, attacks on the family precede an overtly political plot from the right. In the former, Lonny is killed while she is alone in Castang's city, having left her bourgeois Dutch family to continue her education in the theater. Thérèse Martin, the sociopathic adolescent who has escaped the "tutelary complex," is the obverse of Lonny, though both confirm a breakdown in family control. On the national level, as we have seen, Biron's invocation of Charlemagne suggests that his plan is to restore power to the ultimate father, the Holy Roman Emperor. Faced with the election of a socialist, "Uncle François, known to all as 'Tonton,'" Biron attempts to found his own alternative political family (BNW 177). In so doing, of course, he operates beyond the law and thus creates a political version of the archetypal criminal "Family": "It's just a Mafia, like any other. Political rather than financial but experience shows the two to be the same. Power, says the Mafia exactly like a bank, comes in the wake of a great deal of money. Acquire the power, reason politicians, and all the money you could wish for arrives in its train; a natural corollary" (BNW 117). In other words, Biron disguises his self-interest by seeking to offer the citizenry the same sort of utopian fantasy which contemporary critics have discovered in popular or mass culture.

No Part in Your Death shows Castang personally involved in the dissolution of two families. The first plot revolves around the manipulation of state power by Herr Rennemann in order to wrest custody of his grandchild from his daughter-in-law. The fact that Castang is seized and interrogated by German security forces at Rennemann's behest confirms the impossibility of separating the private life of the family from the political life of the state. The second plot, involving the death of a family friend, Marlene Riderhood, demonstrates that Castang cannot separate his private self from his public persona. If Castang is drawn by accident into the Rennemann case, through Vera, here his presence is prepared for by the ongoing friendship with the Riderhoods, a relationship which haunts Castang because he had failed to interpret the troubling signs of the marriage's breakdown. Just as Castang could not successfully intervene in the troubles of the Rennemann family, he cannot successfully solve Marlene's murder. In both cases, he comes to realize that his attempt to act in too many capacities (social worker, psychologist, marriage counselor, confessor, friend and policeman) has so diluted his power that he becomes an unwitting accomplice in the first case, and an ineffectual witness in the second. For these reasons, he must bear part of the responsibility for the deaths of two women.

In the Martindale plot, Freeling rescues Castang temporarily from the pitfalls of his earlier "private" involvement by again shifting his focus from the nuclear family to the national one. Once more, the proposed restoration of an earlier order is cloaked in the guise of patriotism, but here the conspirators are quite clearly mad. While Sevenhampton can rail against the cowardice of the police, and brand them as "Traitors!" (NPD 219), neither he nor Miss Martindale exercises any real political power that could be threatened by a perceived weakening in the surveillance powers of the police. Their creation of a private militia is thus an irrational version of Biron's earlier, equally dangerous defense of privilege.

The combined efforts of two national police forces achieve a partial solution in that the conspiracy is revealed and the murderers of Anne-Sophie and Daniel are identified, but Castang continues to feel an obscure sense of guilt because "today's Black Death," violence, persists in "rolling inexorably over Europe" (NPD 212–13). Both Anne-Sophie and Daniel have cast off their family bonds, rejecting the narrow conservatism and "fixed patterns" that both families shared (NPD 222). Their innocence, now unprotected by family authority, makes them vulnerable to manipulation by a putative political family. They become victims of "the real madness: Europe for the past ten years has been overrun by it. The ideologies appear loony, whether extreme left wing or extreme right (so incoherent that it is not easy to distinguish which is which) but all coherent in their extreme of hatred, brutality and violence" (NPD 212–13). It is the prospect of the continued spread of this "real madness" which reminds Castang that his part in maintaining law and order is a miniscule one; he can "tidy up" a murder (NPD 232), but he is helpless to prevent its causes.

The sense of impotence that Freeling creates in the fictional worlds of both *The Back of the North Wind* and *No Part in Your Death* is established by techniques analogous to the methods by which "moral panics" are created by the media. The press, for example, relies on what Hall *et al.* identify as a "signification spiral" in which events are conveyed so as to "intrinsically [escalate] their threat." In this sequence a specific concern is subsequently linked to other problems which, by their "convergence," lead to the crossing of a "threshold" that evokes a greater danger. The thresholds define "symbolically the limits of societal tolerance," so that the higher up the ladder of thresholds an event is placed, the greater its danger to society (223–25). The last two novels, in their tripartite plots, contain their own "signification spirals" because they create a direct link between family breakdown and political extremism. They thus recapitulate the movement of the Castang series as whole, since it, too, moves "up the ladder" from family crimes to transnational conspiracies.

In his Castang series, then, Freeling builds on his earlier work in the Van der Valk books where "His novels describe a world irretrievably polarised into public and private sectors, a world characterized by fundamental dissonance, a culture only superficially coherent. The official mechanisms of authority, as represented by the police, form a thin, ineffective superstructure which sits lamely over a block of civilian hostility and resentment" (Shloss 160). Shloss contends that in the Van der Valk series, Freeling records "civic privatism's successful resistance to state encroachment" (160). Such is clearly not the case in the later series, where the penetration of the private sphere by public power is absolute. As a result, the series documents the subversion of the nuclear family by a succession of dangerous, politicized replicas. Initially, the police are "caught" in the middle since they are the state agents required to probe the citizenry's most private relationships. They continue to be "caught," but in a quite different fashion in the last three novels. There, they are attacked both as private family members and as representatives of the public, national or trans-national, "family."

At the same time, the State itself has come to be seen as morally bankrupt and hardly worth saving. If Castang's efforts merely safeguard and advance the interests of his "masters" in Paris, then the whole policing enterprise is a corrupt one. While this is certainly the thrust of *Wolfnight* and *The Back of the North Wind*, *No Part in Your Death* seems to hold out the hope that the police can rise above the narrowly-defined interests of a given state to attempt the defense of a larger, European community from the "plague-struck madness" (NPD 212) that threatens to destabilize the inevitably related public order and private refuge. Freeling's hope is, however, qualified by the fact that his own police question the extra-legal methods they are obliged to use in order to counter both the bureaucracy they serve and those who seek to institute a new, repressive order.

The Castang series therefore seems to ask one overriding question: what is the real nature of personal moral responsibility in a public world which seeks to survey the private? As is to be expected in the procedural as a sub-genre of detective fiction, Freeling's most important explorations of this question revolve around the police themselves; their own "morality" is one of the crucial vehicles he can use to assess the honesty and integrity of the society they are sworn to uphold. Alan Clarke has shown that British television police series have had "a central role" in constructing the myths that the British bobby is "gentle, honest and faithful," a loyal retainer of the public he serves, but to do so those series have resorted to "the simplification of the moral questions" they highlight in order to reaffirm "the policeman as hero" ("Television Police Series" 57). It is a mark of Freeling's daring and sophistication that he refuses precisely the sort of "simplification" which characterizes the series Clarke examines; instead, he raises issues which call into question the entire enterprise of policing itself. Are cops ever justified in resorting to extra-legal methods to prevent assaults on the security of the citizenry or the State? What role must they play when the State itself fails to confront the social and political realities within its purview? Thus, if British television police series become vehicles by which the dominant culture responds to a crisis in its political authority, Freeling's Castang series helps to define just how deep and problematic such a crisis can be in a highly centralized state where the conflict between the citizen and power has been a source of tension for hundreds of years.

Such a view does not, however, necessarily imply a coherent ideological position on Freeling's part. Indeed, if his Van der Valk series is finally a study in generic irresolution, his Castang series ends in ideological irresolution. One can argue, for example, that Freeling's presentation of the breakdown of the traditional family unit and the consequent intervention of representatives of the public sphere is a conservative call for a return to individual responsibility. In this case, Freeling would be espousing a perspective similar to that of Peyrefitte who contends that France's lack of a "Puritan ethic" has led to crippling inertia in a citizenry that depends upon the State to meet its needs from the cradle to the grave (159–93). On the other hand, one could conclude that Freeling's concentration on the stricken family as an important source of crime leads to a sophisticated link between the "smallest essential unit of society" and the dysfunctioning of the nation and its bureaucratic manifestations. Such a "progressive" reading is supported by a character like Richard who, as Castang's mentor, leads him to see that a simplistic reliance on a conception of the State as "family," as the source of moral authority to which all individuals owe blind allegiance, leads to an unthinking acquiesence in "The all-too-notorious Reason of State" (W 118).

Clarke points out that the evolution of British television police series of the 1950s through the 1970s foregrounds two categories of response to perceived social threats, one which sees the policeman as a representative of the State detailed to support family relationships and one which rejects authoritarian solutions to the problem of maintaining law and order (54–55). Whether one chooses to endorse individual moral responsibility rooted in the family or to opt for the coercive power of the State, one is still moved to accept the dominant values of the culture which appear to be threatened. In the case of Freeling, both the decline of the family and the excesses of the State call into question the same sorts of values which Clarke's series serve to endorse. That is, the Castang series becomes a "voice" articulating the depth and breadth of the crisis rather than one which resolves it in favor of a particular ideological perspective. Thus, the reassurance which is fundamental to earlier forms of detective fiction, especially that of the Golden Age, is here the subject of the novels' "investigations."

Freeling does not, therefore, rely upon a traditional formulation of the "criminal class," since to do so would insulate his readers from the political realities upon which his series is based. As we have seen, the later novels insist on diminishing the "distance" between an aestheticized, "exotic" criminality and the underlying structures which lead to criminal acts. Instead, he suggests that criminality is endemic in society, that the "mound of evil-smelling waste" (DD 51) derives from the dissolution of the "consensus" embodied in the dominant ideology of a given culture. That the vast majority of crimes in Castang's city are committed by members of the upper classes intent upon protecting their privilege against the perceived attacks of both the "lower orders" *and* the State defines that collapse.

At the same time, Freeling's cops attempt to maintain the *cordon sanitaire* by utilizing methods that refer to an earlier, perhaps less complicated era. As Castang enters the grounds of Alberthe de Rubempré's chateau in *Wolfnight*, he feels a sense of dislocation when he is surrounded by trees which are "at once striking and puzzling." His initial confusion comes from the fact that the entire estate is arranged as an arboretum with trees "there to be studied, thought about for their character, majesty, port": "What had he come here for? To Botanise, my boy, he told himself, intelligence coming belatedly to the rescue. To classify" (W 53–55). This brief moment in *Wolfnight* aptly sums up the problematic heart of the entire Castang series. On the one hand, Castang's contemplation of the arboretum has important generic consequences. It suggests that, in Freeling's hands, the police procedural, precisely because it reproduces the policing mechanisms of the state itself, enacts a classificatory function: it becomes a "botanical" handbook for the culture that produces it, detailing different species and their distribution throughout the social environment. On the other hand, Castang's efforts to apply the techniques of Enlightenment philosophers to a contemporary society whose components are in crisis and thus escape neat categorization marks the failure of the State to impose its version of the "ideal," infinite penality described by Foucault.[37] As a representative of the Napoleonic Code, Castang may feel himself compelled to re-enact the "Napoleonic character," exercising "a single gaze which no detail, however minute, can escape" (Foucault 217). Freeling's novels are a testimony to the urge to survey, to "instruct" the reader in the complex moral issues that surround policing and criminality, at the same time that they articulate the ideological constraints on such an impulse.

6
Imperfect Invigilation

> *So Vice is beneficial found,*
> *When it's by Justice lopt, and bound;*
> *Nay, where the People would be great,*
> *As necessary to the State,*
> *As Hunger is to make 'em eat.*
> *Bare Vertue can't make Nations live*
> *In Splendour; they, that would revive*
> *A Golden Age, must be as free,*
> *For Acorns, as for Honesty.*
>
> Bernard de Mandeville

As we have noted, English Golden Age detective fiction presupposes a fundamentally sound society (embodied in the ubiquitous collection of guests at a country house weekend) whose secure and stable culture is temporarily shattered by a disruptive force from within. Early authors within this tradition are simultaneously smug about the achievements of their society yet fearful that some underlying flaw may jeopardize the structures that legitimize middle- and upper-class hegemony. That is, they fear that the social history they are ostensibly encoding in their texts may well be only a veneer of civilization masking a deeply disturbing atavism that at any moment will undo the progress upon which they so often congratulate themselves. A contemporary Dutch writer of police procedurals like Janwillem van de Wetering faces a similar problem since modern Dutch culture is predicated upon a comparable legacy of containment: the cultural verities of the Golden Age of Dutch Empire.

Van de Wetering, no less than his seventeenth-century predecessors, assumes an audience familiar with such crucial concepts as "Civility, [which] in its most 'ideal' and perfectly internalized form, includes not only good manners and a sense of decorum but also more personal qualities such as self-possession and a sense of duty and responsibility. . . . These tendencies are reinforced by the time-honored tradition of orderliness in Dutch society, a tradition that proceeds from its international power position and the unmilitaristic proclivities of its burgher elite" (Goudsblom 126). Similarly, the notion of order in Dutch society manifests itself in the concept of *verzuiling* (pillarization) which posits political cleavage among sub-cultures (Calvinist, Catholic, secular) but cohesion under the umbrella of the nation itself. Thus, social conflict is minimized through "the politics of accommodation" in order to avoid irreparable rents in the cultural fabric (Bagley 2–8; Lijphart, *Politics* 17–23, 103–04). If sub-groups with distinct and dearly-held values cannot find the means to achieve national consensus, waves of civil discord could quite literally erode the entire foundation of the political entity called the Netherlands just as surely as the North Sea could wash away its territory.

The seventeenth-century Dutchman feared, perhaps more than anything else, being swept away: either by the sea, which was only held back by a thin ribbon of ceaselessly rebuilt dikes, or, metaphorically, by a flood of material excess from the far reaches of the Empire. In fact, the real fear seems to have been that the gratification of desire through the seemingly limitless surfeit of exotic goods flooding Amsterdam and other Dutch ports would provoke a Calvinist God to unleash his angry waters. It is thus no surprise that in both early "vernacular history chronicles" and "shipwreck epics, . . . parables of a manifest national destiny . . . followed a standard moral formula in the narrative." "Crime and punishment" in these texts are articulated as sin and retribution, instances of "corruption or moral laxity that [invite] nemesis" (Schama 30–31). Van de Wetering's procedurals continue to reproduce these myths of his Golden Age (Dutch and English, mercantile and literary) ancestors when evoking the "primal Dutch experience," the "struggle to survive rising waters" sent to chastise (Schama 24).

Early in the series,[1] while on an investigation in Curaçao, the commissaris meditates on the destiny that awaits Holland if its citizens and their moral guardians, the police, fail to uphold their commitment to order:

> At home the sea was lapping at the dikes, waiting patiently for the day that it could flood the swamp and squeeze the life

out of its inhabitants, creating new living space for its own denizens, for the sharks, and the turtles, and the dolphins and the myriads of little creatures who would become the new citizens of Amsterdam, covering its streets and buildings and bridges with their shells and waving leaves and creepers and flitting in and out through broken windows. (T 114–15)

Later in the series, in *The Blond Baboon*, the apocalyptic vision of a threatened Holland is enacted in the narrative. The novel opens with the city authorities confronting a hurricane; the citizenry "knew that the authorities had been taken by surprise but that the emergency was being dealt with, and that the dikes were manned, and that heavy earth-moving machinery was on its way to the danger areas, where high seas were threatening man-made defenses and strengthening their attack methodically, repeating their onslaught every half-minute, raising roaring, foam-topped water mountains in deadly rushes, whipped by shrieking blasts of furious air" (1). While emergency crews rush to defend Holland's coast from the assault of nature, Grijpstra and de Gier are called to a police emergency in the Mierisstraat, an elegant upper-middle class neighborhood where families are "making their money in gentle leisurely ways" (8). Sheltered from the gale, the street is "unlikely . . . to be stalked by violent death" (8), yet the corpse of Elaine Carnet punctures the myth of security of the Mierisstraat just as the gale reminds the Dutch at large of their vulnerability.

By the time of *Hard Rain* nemesis has been simultaneously naturalized and parodied. That is, the novel's opening scene in which Amsterdam is subjected to "divine anger" in the form of a furious thunderstorm sets the stage for the investigation of the death of Martin Ijsbreker, a bank director who lives in a "luxurious, fully restored" home on the Binnenkant (1). This apocalyptic imagery is refracted through scenes of the commissaris creating his own version of Noah's Ark by sheltering his cohorts from the assaults of agents of the Society for Help Abroad; the commissaris' gesture is finally parodied in the comic deflation of Carl's sculpture of Noah's Ark in which the animals are copulating (266). In *Hard Rain* the vision of a submerged Amsterdam no longer has the same impact it would have had in the distant Calvinist past; instead it is "normalized" as a hallucinatory daily reality: "The commissaris, driving to Headquarters, felt as though he were in a one-man submarine, looking out on an aquatic world. Streetcars glided past his car like gleaming whales, and hundreds of cyclists in their shining plastic coats darting about everywhere could be a shoal of herring" (117). The streets of Amsterdam in these procedurals are described in language which evokes traditional myths in order to emphasize contemporary transformation. The streets thus become the site of a confrontation between the forces of the State that seek to preserve order and an orderly past, and more "primitive" forces, from both within and without, that seek to disrupt that order and challenge the contemporary "Dutch god, an old man living in a stuffy room, a powerful manifestation wearing slippers and interested in a wide range of phenomena, such as waterworks, the price of butter, theology, the right to argue, and Ajax, the national soccer team" (T 15). The results of that confrontation can be the death of one man, or the breakdown of the entire system.

Throughout the series the stuffy, controlled – and controlling – Dutch God who reigns over the mythic Amsterdam of the city fathers' tourist brochures is challenged by the quotidian social and physical transformations the city undergoes as well as by the quest of the tourist for the unusual and the illegal. In *Death of a Hawker*, van de Wetering writes:

> Amsterdam, by its tolerance for unconventional behavior, attracts crazy people. Holland is a conventional country; crazy people have to go somewhere. They go to the capital, where the lovely canals, thousands and thousands of gable houses, hundreds of bridges of every shape and form, lines of old trees, clusters of offbeat bars and cafes, dozens of small cinemas and theaters encourage and protect the odd. (DH 14–15)

Van de Wetering here plays on a combination of the colorful, the exotic, the aristocratic and the anarchic in order to stress the conception of Amsterdam already familiar to the adventurous tourist – not the city of the stuffy patriarch, but rather that of the eccentric and the free.

By the same token, however, van de Wetering is not unaware of the seamy reality that lies behind the facade of the tourist brochure. As a kind of counterpoint, he refers constantly to the vast quantity of architectural, social and cultural change that daily transforms the face of Amsterdam: the city builds a subway; contractors raise bleak housing blocks in Ams'erdam South; the number of squatters increases constantly, and they explode into riot; pollution transforms canals and rivers into "hellish sewers"; pimps, drug addicts and prostitutes congregate in the city center, haunting the Dam Square and fanning out into the Newmarket; patrician houses are turned into brothels and sex shops facing the few remaining lovely canals; "long cramped streets of soot-soaked grayness lining up houses that [are] an insult to humanity" (BB 37) replace sixteenth- and seventeenth-century neighborhoods; and the Seadike quarter becomes "gray and smelly, a sewer . . . through which the lower lusts slide along by night and dribble by day" (S 45).[2] Inevitably, it would seem, the legacy of the Dutch Golden Age has been defiled by what its moralists continually warned against: overindulgence has taken its toll on Amsterdam's soul.

Although van de Wetering eventually reconfigures many of the images of surfeit, nemesis and apocalypse as parody, in his treatment of the police as the antithesis of disorder and vice he nevertheless anchors his texts in earlier Dutch images of penality and virtue. For example, in seventeenth-century Amsterdam, the model reformatories contained a "drowning cell" for, among others, the "incorrigibly idle." This cellar room filled slowly with water and, unless the prisoner literally pumped for his life, he would eventually drown (Schama 22). In the world of van de Wetering's police procedurals, Amsterdam itself seems "incorrigibly idle," sinking into the swamp from which it sprang as its inhabitants are distracted from their industrious civic pursuits by the temptations of drugs, sex, and greed. Although Grijpstra concedes that "'Anarchy is not yet complete. The citizens keep up appearances'" (HR 47), he nonetheless believes that "'It's still shit . . . . The whole thing is shit. We're losing.'"[3] Even were the scene to shift to another planet, he claims, "'It'll still be the same horror, endlessly repeated, with types like me running about forever, hopelessly trying to restore order'" (HR 43). While the single cop may attempt to generalize his own frustrations, it is significant that van de Wetering leaves it to the novel's villain, Fernandus, to articulate the decline of the entire social organization: "'Whatever energy you may think you can apply, you'll have to draw from the State. The State is out of energy these days. The police, like any other corrective office that represents the ailing government now, malfunctions'" (HR 96). The drowning cell that is contemporary Amsterdam fills inexorably; the citizens no longer care to pump, and the police cannot pump fast enough.

Are there, then, any constants which van de Wetering can oppose to the entropy that characterizes Dutch society? The answer is quite literally embodied in the figure of the commissaris who is consistently linked to his forebears among the guardians of State and Empire and, as we have seen, meditates upon the dangers of the flood retaking Amsterdam. His office, we learn in *The Corpse on the Dike*, is decorated in an antique style; it is an oasis of seventeenth-century furnishings in a sterile modern building. It contains, in *The Blond Baboon*, portraits of earlier city-builders, "men of past authority" (30). He wanders Bickers Island in the same novel, and in *Hard Rain* seeks refuge on Prince's Island; these remnants of the Dutch Golden Age are his favorite haunts. He wears suits designed by "a very old tailor who, in his young days, had designed suits for the great merchants who made their wealth in what was once called the Dutch East Indies" (DH 190). He is described as "the image of a kind but exact person of authority, a headmaster, a miniature patriarch even" (BB 19). What van de Wetering seems to be suggesting is that an unbroken thread links the commissaris to the civic-minded merchant princes of the Golden Age.[4] While the commissaris is thus the mythic guardian brought to the present, his adversaries partake of the dark side of the Dutch inheritance – the degenerate lust for wealth warned against by seventeenth-century moralists.

In *The Corpse on the Dike* van de Wetering defines the commissaris in opposition to two figures linked to the growth of contemporary greed and a consequent decline in *civitas*. The Cat is a latter-day incarnation of Holland's mercantile past: "'I'm a buyer and seller.... I often go away – I'll go anywhere and usually I manage to buy there as well. The world is full of merchandise; it's amazing it's still turning with all that weight attached to it'" (CD 71).[5] In fact, under the guise of restoring the self-esteem of the poor citizens of the Landsburger dike, the Cat has organized them into a theft ring, masterminding crimes in order to take a percentage of the profits. He deals as well with the Arab Sharif who operates an entire chain of stores dedicated to offloading stolen goods and who thus provides a twisted twentieth-century version of the exploitative practices of seventeenth-century Dutch mercantilism. Confirming this connection, the brothel which Sharif visits once a week to conduct business as well as pleasure is a restored seventeenth-century villa, originally designed as a merchant's summer home which, according to de Gier, "'hasn't changed its purpose .... The merchants of the Golden Age liked to have their parties where they wouldn't be disturbed'" (CD 166). Here Sharif distributes free cigars "big enough for the large toadmouths of bankowners and shipbuilders" (CD 168); here too, however, the commissaris sets his trap for the merchants who bilk rather than build contemporary Amsterdam.

By the middle of the series, in a novel like *The Blond Baboon*, virtually everyone even remotely connected with villainy is associated with the merchant class.[6] The putative victim, Elaine Carnet, owner of a company specializing in imported furniture, is killed by her stepson, Francesco Pullini. He has been simultaneously extorting bribes from her firm and siphoning off profits from his father, Elaine's former lover, for whom he acts as agent. These complicated relationships are even more closely linked to the business of buying and selling when we learn that Giovanni Pullini essentially "bought off" Elaine rather than admit to his illegitimate family, just as he attempts to buy off the commissaris who is investigating Elaine's death. As the elder Pullini puts it, describing himself in the third person as if the linguistic device will somehow confer objectivity and thus authority to his narrative, "'Marry a nightclub singer? A foreigner? When he had just invested his entire capital in a furniture factory? He needed connections in those days. He needed textiles to upholster his furniture, didn't he? And the young lady he married was the daughter of a textile manufacturer'" (BB 163). Even those who have taken the Hippocratic oath are implicated in fraudulent practices; thus Dr. Havink creates false test results in order to generate even more tests, all in the name of using expensive "gadgets" which merely duplicate existing services and mislead the general populace (BB 191). While love, commerce, and justice are essentially identical commodities to those engaged in trade, the commissaris insists throughout *The Blond Baboon* on moral distinctions. It is only appropriate, then, that he solve the murder of Elaine Carnet and bring down Dr. Havink single-handedly, thus reaffirming his role as moral center of the series.[7]

In *Hard Rain*, van de Wetering even creates a *doppelgänger* for the commissaris in order to map the moral boundaries of Amsterdam. The opening scene in which a bank director is shot in his renovated "medieval gable house" (1) pulls together earlier aspects of degeneration like drug-dealing, the corruption of the merchant class, and the amorality of the rich. All these aspects of villainy are finally embodied in the figure of Willem Fernandus, President of the Banque du Credit and founder of the Society for Help Abroad, an organization which specializes in illegal gambling clubs, brothels, and drug dens for the young (15). Fernandus is described by the commissaris as "the archetype of organized crime" who could be "cast as the boss in . . . gangster movies," a "false father image" replacing the Golden Age icon, the civic-minded patriarch (93).[8] It is no accident that van de Wetering takes a nominally benevolent society, ironically designed to help precisely those people his ancestors had enslaved, and perverts it, since Fernandus himself presents to the commissaris as his guiding creed the notion that "Our forefathers didn't enjoy the smell of slave ships, . . . but a lot of the money that went into the splendid architecture that makes up our town today was made from the slave trade. The helpless will be exploited . . . . Only the elite lives well. I'm part of the elite. So are you, in a small way. If you hadn't been so wishy-washy, you would have stayed with me and done a lot better" (HR 101–2). The crucial point here, of course, is that the commissaris has not "stayed" with Fernandus and the "ruling party" (HR 235) he represents; he has left the world of private business for that of civic affairs. Thus, van de Wetering's use of the *doppelgänger* enacts the bifurcation he finds in contemporary Dutch society. Although the commissaris is often linked by means of a series of portraits to representatives of the sixteenth- and seventeenth-century city militias composed of the merchant elite, he must distance himself from the descendants of these earlier figures. In van de Wetering's Amsterdam the public and the private are mutually exclusive rather than mutually supportive, and *civitas* seems to be the sole province of the commissaris' squad; both these features mark out the devolution from the Golden Age of Amsterdam's past.

For these reasons, the series of portraits hanging in the commissaris' office undergoes a metamorphosis. As we suggested above, early in the series the paintings connect him to the public-spirited merchant elite of seventeenth-century Amsterdam. Even as late as the ninth novel of the series, *The Streetbird*, when the commissaris assembles his team to plot the downfall of Lenny, they can convene beneath "gold-framed portraits of ancient Civic Guard officers" with swords drawn "indicating their readiness to guard the peace" (188). Later on in the same book the validity of this relationship is underlined with specific reference to the role of the commissaris: he "sat by himself and smiled at the framed Civic Guard officers. The officers looked grim but not altogether unsympathetic because the little old man was their successor and carried their prestige;

they forgave him his lack of plumed hat and sword" (214). But the allusions, here and elsewhere, to "the little old man" as well as to his frail health and rheumatic body no doubt suggest the fragility of the "new guard," and this is precisely the point that Willem Fernandus makes when he confronts the commissaris in a key scene in *Hard Rain*. As they sit beneath an "oil portrait of a seventeenth-century constabulary officer," Fernandus notes the superficial similarity between the two policemen but contends that "'maybe that captain wielded more power with that muzzle-loading handpiece of his than you do now, I don't care how much modern might you may be able to command. It won't take much to bring you down'" (97).

In fact it is Fernandus himself who is brought down by a squad of police officers acting in unofficial capacities. Though they are relieved of duty in close succession as a result of Fernandus' pressure on superior officers, they reconstitute themselves as a team free to work on the case outside the confines of the law. As the commissaris puts it, "There was always the State before, but she has left me now" (228). It is at this juncture, then, that van de Wetering's thinking seems to have come virtually full circle. Rather than an image of anarchy, this squad, with its loyalty to a higher Law, in fact replicates the responsible behavior embodied in the portraits of the *schutterijen*, the militia guilds of the sixteenth and seventeenth centuries immortalized in paintings like Rembrandt's *The Night Watch*.

The militia guilds assisted in the defense of the Netherlands and in freeing the country from Spanish domination. They were, in addition, responsible for guarding Amsterdam and its gates at night as well as for maintaining public order (Haverkamp-Begemann 48–49). Membership in the militia originally constituted an honor, a distinction reserved for those whose sense of civic duty had been responsible for the growth of Amsterdam into a city-republic which held "a veritable world empire of trade in her own right" (Haverkamp-Begemann 35–36). Even by the end of the Dutch Golden Age, however, the militia's guard duties had become largely ceremonial, and the *schutterijen*'s role was limited to participation in city festivals (Haverkamp-Begemann 41). Thus, it has been suggested that the familiar heroic portrait by Rembrandt of "The Officers and Men of the Company of Captain Frans Banning Cocq and Lieutenant Wilhem van Ruytenburgh" is in fact anachronistic because the *schutterijen* would not have been engaged in the sort of warlike activity the artist depicts. In other words, Rembrandt's use of action is nostalgic, deliberately designed to evoke Amsterdam's glorious heritage and its ambitions of empire at a point at which the Golden Age was coming to an end (Haverkamp-Begemann 113).[9] The yearning for past order found in Rembrandt's *The Night Watch* implies that the police squads of van de Wetering's later novels can be read as reproducing the *schutterijen* at several removes.

If the frail yet dapper commissaris resembles his ancestors in *The Night Watch*, if his squad of detectives brings to mind the officers and men of Captain Banning Cocq, it may well be because the details which van de Wetering uses to particularize his policemen are those used by Rembrandt to distinguish "his" *schutters*. Rembrandt isolates the leaders and emphasizes the most important figures in the company as van de Wetering foregrounds the commissaris, Adjutant Grijpstra, and Sergeant de Gier. Rembrandt's action pose enables him to highlight the company drummer, a title that might just as aptly be applied to Grijpstra.[10] Most civic guards had several pipers as well, and de Gier's omnipresent flute echoes this detail. Even the murder squad's precinct house is located in precisely that precinct of Amsterdam which produced the company of Banning Cocq (Haverkamp-Begemann 72–83). This is not, of course, to insist that van de Wetering's novels are an explicit, albeit ironic, version of a single Rembrandt painting. It is certainly clear, however, that through his policemen van de Wetering does insist on the importance of a central tradition in Dutch life: "the militiamen stood for ideas of civic virtues of the past and present" (Haverkamp-Begemann 4), precisely those virtues which are all too often threatened by the villains of the series.

The Night Watch seems to represent both the memory of order and the precariousness of that order in a society whose standards of behavior persist under the form of "bourgeois civility" (Bagley 12) but the power of which has diminished.[11] This realization takes the form, in van de Wetering's novels, of the tension between the law enforced by the police and the Law from which the State's code of conduct is derived. The commissaris is the figure in the series who consistently draws attention to the widening gulf between theory and practice. It is no doubt for this reason that he is described in *The Streetbird* as "'Our patriarch . . . our admired archetype'" (252), because his thinking on the Law necessitates the evocation of its archetypal principles. In *Tumbleweed* the issue is still embryonic; the commissaris doubts his commitment to "justice":

Holy mother, who cares for the sailor and for me, an old weasel sworn to catch the murdering rabbit. For the murderer would be caught, there was no doubt in his mind. Maria van Buren, the fashionable whore in Amsterdam, the dead woman whose death was to be revenged. Order had been disturbed, order would be restored. We cannot allow a man to throw a knife into the living back of a fellow-citizen. He sighed, and stirred his coffee, mechanically patting his pocket to find his tin of cigars. Did he really care? Perhaps he did, perhaps part of his mind cared. (T 114)

Over the course of the novel, however, the commissaris comes to realize that revenge – "to hurt" – is a "perversion . . . so the real thing would be to cure, to restore" (T 144). Thus, the novel closes with the commissaris teaching Drachtsma to see, on his deathbed, that by having Maria killed he had simply given in to his own childish pride and broken the Law as well as the law.

This line of reasoning continues in *The Corpse on the Dike* when the commissaris distinguishes between "'the law of our law books . . . the shadow of the law, the law as we can understand it'" and "'the Law [which] is very beautiful'" (104). The recipient of this pearl of wisdom is both an informant and a petty thief known as the Mouse who has taken public monies but has then refused to turn over crucial information to his paymasters in the police. According to van de Wetering, what is at stake here is not just the failure of an employee to fulfill a contract, but something far larger. While the Mouse argues that he is "'an informer . . . but . . . not *obliged* to inform'" (CD 103), the commissaris claims that the "'taxpayer's money is holy money. To me it is. And to many others. More others than you expect. This is a decent city. If something is given, something is expected'" (CD 104). Here the commissaris harks back to earlier standards of behavior, linking contemporary "bourgeois civility" to the norms of the Golden Age and the State's code of law to its Judaeo-Christian roots.[12] That a discussion of the highest civic ideals is directed at a petty informer is no accident, for it is precisely the necessity of creating this ironically diminished exchange which lies at the heart of van de Wetering's argument.

Just as the law is a diminished version of its original Ideal, so, too, the Cat's program of social reform on the dike, which involves an organized theft ring but which at the same time restores the self-respect of the dike's inhabitants, is a degraded version of *civitas*.

Thus, it is important to recall that the entire conversation between the Mouse and the police is deliberately located in a bar on Bickers Island, "a forgotten corner" of sixteenth-century Amsterdam where "the city had come to life again and cared about itself" (CD 100) under the aegis of "official" restoration agencies. The distance between the nostalgia for the earlier age which Bickers Island evokes and the *sub rosa* activities of the denizens of the Landsburger dike indicates precisely the problematic nature of the contemporary sense of community.

The most interesting discussion of the relationship between the law and the Law, insofar as it concerns the maintenance of the ideals of civic virtue, occurs in *The Mind-Murders*. The commissaris interrogates Borry Beelema, who has been indirectly responsible for the death of Boronski. He is unable to prove Beelema guilty, since the law, which is "primitive," requires that he demonstrate Beelema's "intent to kill" (211). Beelema thus feels free to "confess" to the commissaris the reasons that have led him to indulge in subtle psychological vigilantism. He views himself as a more efficient provider of justice: "'In a way I also police this area; I restore order'" (MI 212). Beelema believes that his self-proclaimed "talent" gives him the "right" (MI 216) to take charge of the daily lives of those who inhabit his neighborhood. Ironically, then, it is his perverted sense of civic virtue that leads him to manipulate others: "'This area is all I care for, I hardly ever move outside it. . . . I listen to my friends, I observe them, I see what goes wrong with them, I also see ways to right the wrong'" (MI 211–12). The commissaris at first approves of Beelema's impulse to do good, noting that the police themselves often arrive too late to restore order: "'*Optima civi cives*. The highest value of a citizen is the citizenry. We'll let them muddle through as best they can and only interfere when they break the law'" (MI 212). Beelema, though, cannot allow people simply to "muddle through." Rather, his attitude is a betrayal of both "civility" and the Calvinist doctrine which lies behind it – the notion that if one is granted a talent, one is thereby obligated to employ that talent for the common good.

For van de Wetering, then, Beelema has clearly stepped beyond the bounds of propriety: his manipulation of others has become mere self-indulgence. Whereas Calvinism suggested that a talent implied a responsibility, for Borry Beelema talent implies gratification; he claims that he is "entitled" to "'interfere with the patterns of others'" because he has "'both the talent and [therefore] the right'"

(MI 215–16). The discussion of the subject ends, however, with the claim that:

> "There is the law," the commissaris whispered so that Beelema had to lean over to hear him. "I don't mean the law in our books, that's no more than a projection. The true law is in all of us, in our center, in the core of our being, where we are all connected and where the illusion of identity no longer obscures our insight. If you have, as you say, the talent, you are misusing it. Reflect, sir, and take care." (MI 216)

This lesson is confirmed by Beelema's death in the final chapter of the novel, a death which is explicitly labeled as the "'one right'" which all humans have – "'the right to face the consequences of our deeds'" (MI 222). That this is meant to be "the moral" of the novel is evident from Beelema's sphere of influence, which includes his tavern and that area of the city immediately surrounding it. These "tavern scenes," in other words, have a dual function: they simultaneously amuse and warn the reader of the excesses which may lure them to their downfall. In this respect they seem to follow the tradition of Dutch genre painting of the Golden Age. For example, Jan Steen's tavern paintings, many of which seem to convey merely a jolly portrait of the Dutch involved in leisure pursuits, in fact alert the viewer to the dangers and evils of the abuse of tobacco and alcohol: vanity, lethargy, and stupefaction (Schama 211). The tavern scenes in *The Mind-Murders* raise serious questions about the relationship between the ideal Law and the laws enacted and encoded by human beings, but they do so within a comic framework. It is only logical, then, that this relationship should be scrutinized further in later novels, where van de Wetering turns his attention to the great agency of the law, the State, which projects its code into the lives of its subjects.

In *The Streetbird* van de Wetering harks back to the Golden Age when areas of the city were officially set aside as "zones of . . . impurity" to accommodate the maritime population. This was a form of "civic hygiene" tolerated by the magistracy and the constabulary, the latter of whom were bribed by brothel-owners even as late as the eighteenth century (Schama 467). In a discussion with Grijpstra, Karate, a uniformed policeman occasionally given undercover jobs, outlines the nature of the Quarter today: "'This is another type of district, different from the rest of the city'" (S 142).

He cites illegal activities by prostitutes, gamblers, bar owners, drug dealers and junkies. Grijpstra responds by pointing out that all of these activities fall between a purist's definitions of legal and illegal because "'Those who govern us know that not only we, but that they themselves are not what humanity pretends to be. They therefore allow the unpermitted under special circumstances and they do so at our own request, for this is a free country and we choose the executors of our own laws ourselves and whisper into their ears how we would like the rules to be applied'" (S 142–43). That the conversation about the nature of the Quarter takes place in the Hotel Hadde is no accident; no longer a hostelry but rather a "'dilapidated and dirty'" relic of the Golden Age, a "'festering hole of the netherworld wherein evil leers nastily'" (S 136), it provides an apt background for the team's plotting of the arrest of Gustav, a pimp and drug-dealer. He will be seized not because drug-dealing itself is a high-priority crime in the Quarter, but rather because he has quite simply "'gone too far'" (S 143) even for the most permissive area of the city.[13]

As Schama points out, citing Bernard de Mandeville, the concept of "imperfect invigilation" allowed the authorities of Amsterdam to tolerate in the Quarter behavior which they would find offensive elsewhere. Thus, they "upheld the normative code of the city without ever making it so absolute as to jeopardize prudent administration" (468) because Golden Age burghers understood the function of vice in much the same way that van de Wetering does: "Virtue needed vice as a civic prophylactic, a sponge that could soak up all the loathsomeness that would otherwise seep into the purer body of their community. And virtue needed vice to mark off borders just because its own frontiers were so uncomfortably indefinite" (Schama 480). Even today, according to Maurice Punch, "the city-centre of Amsterdam can be viewed as a testing ground for . . . tolerance because norms are pushed to their limits" (*Policing* 21–22). In this view, deviance can function positively by forecasting "potential future developments," but the "specific ecological problems" of the "mixed population" of inner-city Amsterdam mean that the police are "estranged" from the residents. They are "forced into repressive enforcement, and are perceived as critical gatekeepers maintaining the existing social system of rich and powerful citizens cloistered in their suburban enclaves against the poor, the weak and the newcomer in the urban ghetto" (*Policing* 22). Ironically, then, Amsterdam's latter-day *schutterijen* have become "gatekeepers" in a different sense; instead of guarding the city against military invasions by foreign powers, they guard the society against "un-Dutch" incursions from within.

The tenuous border between vice and virtue is ultimately the subject of a serious discussion in *The Streetbird* between the commissaris and Grijpstra after the station-commander, Jurriaans, banishes himself to South America. While the commissaris, Grijpstra, and de Gier all know from the beginning of the investigation into Obrian's murder that Jurriaans is the killer, none of them is willing (or able) to accuse a fellow-officer. Instead they consciously allow themselves to be manipulated into participating in the "spring cleaning" of the Quarter (S 243). In so doing they serve the State rather than the Law, the law rather than the higher moral calling which van de Wetering has celebrated earlier in the series.[14] As Grijpstra notes, defending himself against the commissaris' "accusation" of dereliction of duty, "'Jurriaans may judge himself . . . . I refuse the choice. We serve the law, but the law may be wrong. Jurriaans chose to ignore the rules we made ourselves, didn't he, sir?'" (S 244). That is, Jurriaans has essentially replicated the criminal behavior of Luku Obrian, Gustav, and Lenny; he has, quite simply, "gone too far" in his misguided attempt to defend "his" state, the precinct which he runs as a miniature monarchy.[15]

While the conversations about the nature of the State in *The Streetbird* evolve from the glib to the substantive, the next novel in the series, *The Rattle-Rat,* provides a consistently parodic treatment in which discussions of the putative purity of the Frisian state within a state are juxtaposed to Frisian claims about the "lower regions" of Holland, the Gomorrah that is Amsterdam (42–43).[16] Moreover, just as there is a discussion of a state within a state, van de Wetering inserts a text within a text, the "bundle of Frisian stories called . . . *We're Out of Condiments at Home, and Other Stories*" (RR 61). As de Gier discovers when he (more or less) translates the story "Optimal Functioning," "'The author is telling me, the intelligent reader, that here in Friesland, where true goodness reigns, evil is active under pressure'" (RR 83).

The pressure which can be brought to bear upon evil in Friesland, though, is pressure of a rather peculiar sort, consonant with the rather peculiar relationship between Friesland and Amsterdam which, in Frisian terms, is characterized by the "semiliquid filth of [the] damned city's waterways" (RR 7). In a novel like *The Rattle-Rat,* then, van de Wetering invokes the Golden Age fear of the wild men of the swamps, here either conveniently cordoned off above the Great Dike in Friesland or wallowing in filth in Amsterdam, depending on one's point of view. This generalized (i.e., national) anxiety is made clear throughout the novel in a series of pseudo-military confrontations between the forces of the State and the criminal elements both above and below the Dike. What could be more unlike the celebration of national values embodied in *The Night Watch* than the absurd shoot-out between two groups of Chinese "gangsters" on the Great Dike that protects the nation from the flood?

The end of the battle – a massacre engineered by one of the State's technological marvels, an Arrest Team – is horrifically funny. The Team, "kenneled and trained in the south of the country, dressed in combat fatigues," was originally sent out to "exterminate or, if possible, to arrest two dangerous criminals, Bald Ary and Fritz with the Tuft." The result of the "battle" with the Chinese is the laconic report, "'They're all dead, sir, will that be all right?'" to which their commander replies "'Very nice'" (RR 147–48). That we are meant to understand this entire strand of the novel as emblematic of the breakdown of myths like those embodied in *The Night Watch* is made clear through a meeting between the commissaris and his "colleagues" in the chapter that precedes the massacre:

> I'm a minority, the commissaris thought, looking down the long conference table headed by the lofty figure of Chief Constable Lasius of Burmania, flanked by the equally tall Colonel Kopinie of the State Police and the even taller Lieutenant Colonel Singelsma of the Military Police. He ignored the other participants, but they were tall too, upright and all in complete agreement. It isn't that their combined forces are *against* me, the commissaris thought. Maybe it looks that way, but that can't be the case at all.
> "Hello?" the commissaris said.
> The conversation flowed on, in Frisian. (RR 138)

The fact that the commissaris, a repository of all positive aspects of the police and, thus, the State, cannot even understand the conversation clearly demonstrates just how far from "traditional values" current policing practices are. Because the meeting superficially resembles a gathering of Golden Age *schutters*, it deliberately reinforces the connection with the past; however, the devolution from the heroic to the absurd is made clear by the fact that the threats the forces of the State now face come from the Other based in Amsterdam and the Hague rather than the Other from beyond national boundaries. If the hyper-invigilation and technological absurdities of the Arrest Teams are the best answer to criminality the State can devise, suggests *The Rattle-Rat*, the nation is indeed once again on the brink of destruction.

Other sequences concerning current police and military practices underline the parodic intentions of *The Rattle-Rat*. The computer at headquarters, ostensibly programmed to know "everything," crashes when it is requested to supply information concerning "Friesland" and "crime" (RR 38); it will continue to malfunction throughout the novel, unable even to produce information about Ary and Fritz despite the fact that the pair are well-known criminals with a reputation for violence who have only recently been released from prison (RR 64). When the commissaris asks Chief Inspector Sigma what information he can provide to help in the investigation of Scherjoen's murder, he is told, "'Nothing at all. I state my information simply, as is the custom in this province. My computer is connected to yours at Amsterdam Headquarters, and the machine malfunctions. When I switch it on, I see only a small green square, trembling a little'" (RR 140). The leitmotif of the computer is reinforced by the inability of virtually everyone to find his way about Friesland: the commissaris and Grijpstra are continually lost as they cruise about in their silver Citroën, and towards the end of the novel even the local State Policemen find it necessary to circle the ring road a few times in order to find their way back to the municipal police cube.

The armed forces are no better organized than the police, and to an outsider their bureaucracies are even more arcane. While pursuing a deserter on Ameland, de Gier encounters representatives of several branches of the military, all of whom blithely insist that appearance has absolutely nothing to do with reality. As they sail toward the island, for example, Private Sudema of the military police points to the branches and buoys which mark the channel and says "'A service tendered by Water Inspection ... or rather by Forestry. They have their own boat too, but registered in the name of Water Inspection .... No, let's see now, maybe the Pilot Service plants those branches, in a boat that belongs to the Port'" (RR 170). The deserter on Ameland is accused of stealing used shell casings which the military recycles. Air Force jets use the islands as a shooting range:

"The Air Force sends a vessel for the casings."
"An Air Force vessel?" de Gier asked.
"No, Marines. They ride their armored vehicles on the islands' beaches, and one of their ferries will be lent to the Air Force, but the ferry is really Army."
"The Wet Engineers?"
"The Dry Engineers." (RR 169)

The chapter ends with a description of maneuvers over the channel. As de Gier leaves the island for the mainland, he notices two helicopters above the jetty: "'CIA . . . cooperating with our Security Service. There's an East German fishing boat offshore, loaded with electronics, to snoop on the NATO exercises that are going on again. The helicopters will be Army, I guess, but they could be Navy, too. Air Force pilots probably'" (RR 180). The proliferation of security forces, their nonsensical supply system, and their insistence upon completing all their "leisure activities" (tennis-playing, for example) on duty so that they do not jeopardize their "free time" (RR 173) all combine to undercut the myth of the *schutterijen* in much the same fashion as the high-tech havoc wreaked by the Arrest Teams.

The breakdown in electronic and interservice communication thus becomes emblematic of the far more general breakdown within Dutch culture that van de Wetering chronicles. In a society which comes to depend on the gently trembling green square of the computer screen to understand itself, civility, which necessarily implies face-to-face contact, has already lost its place to the forces of anonymity and bureaucracy. Once again it is the commissaris who articulates the nostalgia for the old order: "'In the old days . . . we'd just follow a robber. We'd tap him on the shoulder. We'd address him in a polite way. Then we'd take him along. . . . in the past we were quite peaceful. The idea was not to disturb the peace even further'" (RR 65). The novel enacts both traditional and contemporary police methods, significantly at the cattle market of Leeuwarden, itself a vestige of an older order. In a scene which quite deliberately evokes the stereotypes of the American western film, the Frisian policeman, Eldor, stares down Ary and takes him prisoner without firing a shot. Fritz, on the other hand, is "captured" by the members of an Arrest Team whose combined firepower decapitates him in the heart of the city (RR 221–22).[17]

The ending of the novel apparently confronts the question of whether Dutch society is still self-policing. Although the police know that Oppenhuyzen, an adjutant in the police force who has dealt primarily with the problems associated with Chinese immigrants, is guilty of murdering Douwe Scherjoen as a favor to Wo Hop who has supplied him with heroin to combat the pain of his neuralgia, the police likewise know that they cannot touch him. Nor, according to Oppenhuyzen, can they touch Wo Hop since they would have "'to work in high places'" (RR 283).[18] Ultimately, however, some sort of justice prevails. Wo Hop is murdered by rival Chinese gangsters, and Oppenhuyzen falls to his death while repairing the roof of his house. Or does he? When the commissaris and de Gier discuss what will become of Oppenhuyzen, the commissaris suggests that he will commit suicide (RR 290) precisely because he is such a good Dutchman that he will not be able to live day in and day out with a killer. Thus, the novel seems to suggest that, although Chinese immigrants may settle their scores by public violence, and for the wrong reasons, somehow the notion of Dutch civility and *civitas* will protect the culture come what may. In reaching such a conclusion, however, van de Wetering has for all intents and purposes returned to another Golden Age, that of the classic detective novel.

As Uri Eisenzweig notes, Golden Age detective fiction ostensibly directs our suspicions to the criminal "Other," the stranger, the foreigner. In the early texts which lie behind the genre, the heroic adventure stories of the late nineteenth century, the criminal is often literally from one of the host nation's colonies. As detective fiction evolves, this Otherness becomes interiorized and normalized. By the time of Golden Age detective fiction the specifically colonial dimension disappears and a new phenomenon occurs. The foreigner is present; he is suspicious; but he is not guilty (237–46). What van de Wetering does in his novels is to combine elements from these two earlier phases of detective fiction to show that the Oriental Other continues to be an object of suspicion because he has a different social, biological, and territorial identity and he therefore disturbs the homogeneous and continuous space of the nation/family.[19] Still, though, the Oriental figures in the novels are never the "true" criminals (see Eisenzweig 247–48). In *The Rattle-Rat*, they may be heroin dealers, but they function to reveal what is ultimately a "deeper" criminality, the betrayal of *civitas* and civility embodied in a figure like Oppenhuyzen who will trade favors for heroin to control his personal pain. The betrayal from within the nation/family is therefore clearly the root of "the problem" with which Dutch society must come to grips. When the foreigner does figure in the universe of the novel, he does so either as a parodic figure or as a disquieting presence who forces the police, and thus the reader, to look beyond the superficially "strange" to the deeper criminality from which attention has been displaced (Eisenzweig 250).

In a novel like *The Rattle-Rat*, van de Wetering consciously invokes the parodic Other in two forms, Frisian and Chinese. The Golden Age fear of the wild men of the swamps is transposed to Friesland, that area viewed by the rest of the Netherlands quite simply as the "sticks," a suitable spot for a rustic vacation but certainly no place to live. The tax collector Verhulst takes an even more cynical perspective: "'We used to have our colonies in the Far East and exploit our plantations. Now we still have Friesland, same thing again. Reclaimed wastelands that supply us with crops. The backward tribes supply us with labor. I'm from The Hague, myself'" (RR 184). Verhulst is an especially apt commentator on Friesland since he is an experienced hand at exploiting native peoples: "'I did have a problem . . . . Aboriginal-related. It comes back to me when the government sends me here. I've always served the State. I majored in colonial law, but when I was given my papers, our only foreign colony was New Guinea, populated by wild men'" (RR 184).

The distance between colonizers and colonized is articulated by Grijpstra in his frustration at the slow progress of the investigation into the murder of Douwe Scherjoen; he describes the Frisians as "'human sheep . . . [whose] shit is never wiped and dries out in their ass hairs. Yellow-eyed, brainless throwbacks, happily hiding in their inbred stupidity'" (RR 192). That Grijpstra (and the commissaris) both claim Frisian roots but are incapable of interacting with the populace suggests that van de Wetering's depiction of deracination is a satiric re-creation of the sorts of discussions of "multiculturalism" that are found in literature on the successive waves of immigrants and their "problems" and which are treated more seriously in earlier novels in the series.

The Chinese in *The Rattle-Rat* are also consistently visualized in stereotypical terms. Early in the novel, Cardozo reflects on Wo Hop, the heroin-dealing owner of a restaurant: "What more could the Chinese be than a bit player in gray clothes, vertically adorned by old-fashioned suspenders like those worn by laborers in antique pictures? The owner of a small-time eating place, a retreat of footsore junkies and Chinese sailors, a hardly exotic migrant like so many, chained to their marginal establishments, saving hard-earned guilders that might, one faraway day, buy them a return ticket to Hong Kong or Singapore, home cities that their spirits had never left" (RR 53). This rather sensitive portrayal of the hard-working Chinese immigrant (no doubt because Cardozo is Jewish, and his own family had experienced persecution in Holland) is gradually transformed into a more racist vision of the relationship between Netherlanders and the Chinese. Karate and Ketchup, seeking ways to occupy their time, enjoy hauling in Chinese without proper papers, who are then "caged" at Headquarters and eventually flown back to the Far East (RR 115). Those that escape their vigilance "slide up the dike and hang out in Friesland" (RR 117).

By the end of *The Rattle-Rat*, it seems that the only two interests of each and every Chinese male residing in the Netherlands are dealing drugs and frustrating the course of justice. While the commissaris continues to try to empathize with the Other ("'See through their eyes,'" he tells Cardozo [RR 154]), he admits his own inability to master the Chinese puzzle: "'The Chinese like to complicate simplicity. Ever interrogated a Chinese? They even change their names every two minutes. They expect the enemy, us, to like complications too'" (RR 154). The current which runs throughout *The Rattle-Rat*, however, suggests that both van de Wetering and the Netherlands have had their fill of "complications" and once more yearn for the mythic stability of the Golden Age.

If *The Rattle-Rat* parodies the return of the Other, other novels in the series foreground the "disquieting presence" of the colonial past which intrudes upon contemporary Amsterdam and contests the traditional values of the Netherlands. Immigrants from both the Dutch East and West Indies call into question the validity of the cultural inheritance of the seventeenth century. Thus, van de Wetering explores the "return of the repressed" by examining both the ways in which Dutch society continues to enact the legacy of the Golden Age burgher and the ways in which that legacy is tested by those who come to the Netherlands from overseas.[20]

As early as the first of the Grijpstra and de Gier novels, *Outsider in Amsterdam*, the colonial legacy is central. The novel centers on the murder of Piet Verboom, founder and high priest of the Hindist Society, an essentially fraudulent cultural society designed by Piet to make money by offering his own brand of "enlightenment," expropriated from the East and debased in the Netherlands. Significantly, the Hindist Society's headquarters itself is a legacy of earlier colonial adventures:

> The porch was old, and magnificent in its Golden Age splendor. It had been designed in the seventeenth century for a gentleman-merchant who specialized in expensive timber, imported from Africa and the Far East and stored in the first three stories of the tall house, while the merchant himself would have lived in the top three stories from which he could see the harbor and his vast stocks of cheaper timber, stacked in an area of perhaps a square mile. But that was long ago and the stones of the porch were cracked now and the beams supporting the gable house sagged a little. But the well-built house still retained a good deal of its original stately beauty and the present owner had kept it in reasonable repair. (OA 4)

Thus, the Hindist society maintains a facade of respectability and spirituality even though the subsequent police investigation reveals that its appearance masks the moral turpitude of personal exploitation and drug-dealing; its structural elements, in other words, are crumbling beneath Piet's avarice, and its cultural "product" is only a debased version of "enlightenment."

Nonetheless, while Grijpstra and de Gier expect to find a disorderly if not filthy interior, basing their expectations on the affinity for things Eastern of the ubiquitous drug-takers they find wandering Amsterdam's streets, they in fact find cleanliness, neatness, and discipline, presided over by Piet's corpse, seeming hauntingly familiar:

> After a while [de Gier] knew that he hadn't seen the man before but that the strong chin, the long hair and the heavy mustache reminded him of a portrait he had seen in a museum in The Hague. A portrait of a Dutch statesman of the sixteenth century, a statesman and a warrior, on his way to do battle. The warrior had been sitting on a horse and had a sword in his hand. A leader. Very likely this man had also been a leader, a boss. A little boss in charge of a small society. Discipline, de Gier thought. That's it. (OA 11–12)

The discipline of the sixteenth-century statesman, though, can no longer be effective in this "small society," as the earlier description of the house and its "cracked" stones and "sagging" beams had predicted. As a result, the Hindist Society's scheme of enlightenment-for-profit can only be a diminished version of the grand capitalist enterprise of the seventeenth-century gentleman-merchant who had constructed the house to broadcast his business acumen and status in the community.

Although Piet Verboom has been killed as a result of his attempt to move into large-scale heroin distribution, he has not been killed by a rival in the drug trade. His killer is actually Jan Karel van Meteren, a Papuan resident in Amsterdam after the independence of the Dutch East Indies who finally claims that Piet's death was really only a continuation of service to the Crown begun during his days as a colonial policeman.

Grandson of a minor Dutch official and a Papuan chief's daughter, van Meteren had to choose in 1965 whether he "'wanted to be an Indonesian or Dutch,'" and he chose the latter. In his case such a choice was perfectly logical, since in New Guinea he had been a loyal servant of the queen as "'a real policeman, constable first class because I could read and write and my name was Dutch,'" a field commander of thirty men who intercepted Indonesian commandos and paratroopers (OA 27). In the Netherlands, though, he is thought fit only to be a traffic warden. As Grijpstra and de Gier study van Meteren's New Guinea identification badge, they realize that they are looking at "a memento of the past" which shows "A strong young face, proud of his rank and his responsibility and of his Corps, the Corps State Police of Dutch New Guinea, part of the Kingdom of the Netherlands" (OA 28). Thus, van Meteren, speaking impeccable Dutch and perfectly familiar with the nation's culture and values, is simultaneously insider and outsider, nominally accepted into Dutch society but not as a "real" policeman: "'... nobody wanted me when I came to The Hague to ask for the queen's orders'" (OA 246). The irony, of course, is that van Meteren is, to his mind, still working for the good of the queen's State in eliminating Verboom, in preventing Piet from enslaving the youth of Amsterdam just as Piet's forebears enslaved the youth of the colonies in both the East and West Indies.

It is useful here to recall, albeit briefly, the trauma undergone as a result of the Dutch "loss" of their colonies in the East Indies. The Dutch were clearly taken by surprise by the power of Indonesian nationalism at the end of World War II, an attitude even more disturbing to the Dutch because their policy of tolerating and protecting (at least in some spheres) indigenous cultures actually allowed the growth of a coherent anti-Dutch movement (Lijphart, *Trauma* 107; Bagley 48–49). In their settlement of the East Indies, the Dutch had always had a relatively positive attitude towards intermarriage with indigenous peoples. Moreover, the offspring of these marriages ("Eurasians") were accorded the status of Europeans both in the East Indies and in the Netherlands (Bagley 66). As a result, "Many Eurasians lived, more or less permanently, in the Netherlands. In 1930, there were an estimated 30,000 of them in the Netherlands, not including the Moslem community of seamen and domestic servants from Indonesia. . . . In Indonesia there was no taboo (although there were some barriers) on Eurasians reaching the highest positions, and some of the wealthiest families in Indonesia were Eurasian. Many Eurasians sent their children to be educated in the Netherlands, and some went to retire in The Hague like their European counterparts in the Civil Service" (Bagley 44–45). Nonetheless, it must also be said that "The Dutchman in Indonesia retained a firm belief in the superiority of his own way of life. The brown children he begot had to become Dutchmen" (Bagley 48). That is, while the Dutch, in Bagley's view, do not discriminate on the basis of color alone, they actively discriminate against those who fail to live up to the norms of Dutch society:

> . . . the Dutch tend to be extremely tolerant and generous towards ethnic groups who are familiar with, and loyal to, Dutch institutions. At the same time they can be extremely suspicious of, and initially hostile towards, groups . . . who are not familiar with Dutch linguistic and cultural norms. (Bagley 144)

There were several particularly painful points of contention in the process of granting Indonesia independence. The Dutch had attempted to ensure that Indonesia would continue the Dutch policy of tolerating – indeed, respecting – the plurality of cultures included in its former colonies in the East Indies, thus insisting upon a federal United States of Indonesia; in 1950, however, Indonesia transformed itself into the unitary Republic of Indonesia, and the Dutch felt betrayed. Among other concerns, they were especially obligated to, and desirous of protecting, the Ambonese who lived in the South Moluccas. The attempt in 1950 by the Ambonese to establish the independent Republic of the South Moluccas led to years of unrest and suppression (Lijphart, *Trauma* 126–27). As a result, a large number of Ambonese emigrated to the Netherlands, but they have tended to live apart and avoid being assimilated into the dominant culture. They were a high-status group in the East Indies, but they lost status in the Netherlands, especially after they were dismissed en masse from the Dutch Army, their primary source of identity within Dutch culture: "Their political status was uncertain; they did not regard themselves as immigrants; they retained Indonesian nationality, but did not regard themselves as merely visitors. They felt themselves rejected by both Indonesia and the Netherlands . . . ," especially as primary values like Moluccan nationalism were clearly alien to the values of their host society. As a result, there has been increasing friction between Moluccan nationalists and the Dutch (Bagley 98–112).

A second, even more troubling aspect of the end of the Dutch East Indies involved the loss of West New Guinea, now known as West Irian, the homeland of the Papuans. The Dutch insisted on retaining control of this area of the former colonies primarily for two reasons. First, the large Eurasian population, mistrusted by the Indonesian nationalists for their close relationship with the ruling Dutch, sought "a Eurasian fatherland. The impending liquidation of Dutch colonial rule in the Indies and the strong desire of the Eurasians to remain outside of the control of an independent Indonesian government gave a special urgency to their appeal" (Lijphart, *Trauma* 69). Not only were the Eurasians distrusted by the nationalists, but Papuan leaders of West New Guinea, trained by the Dutch, were also viewed with suspicion. Thus, the ultimately futile attempt to retain Dutch West New Guinea well into the 1960s, a move which necessitated further armed conflict with Indonesia and brought international condemnation from Western allies as well as developing nations, was especially painful. As Arend Lijphart puts it, "The agonies of the decolonization process are well exemplified by the painful and reluctant withdrawal of the Netherlands from its colonies. It did not grant independence to Indonesia until after more than four years of bitter conflict. Then another twelve and a half years were spent in a vain attempt to hold on to West New Guinea, the last remnant of its colonial empire. These experiences were extremely traumatic. Holland acted with an intense emotional commitment, manifested in pathological feelings of self-righteousness, resentment, and pseudo-moral convictions" (*Trauma* 285). Within two years of the loss of West New Guinea, however, the issue was essentially dead in Holland; diplomatic relations with Indonesia had been restored, and overt concern for the Papuans, "unfortunates" being "protected" by the caring Dutch, had disappeared (Lijphart, *Trauma* 286).

Thus, the history of Dutch decolonization, and the reactions to it by both native peoples and the Dutch themselves, goes a long way toward explaining the status of van Meteren in *Outsider In Amsterdam*. As Constanze Verboom explains, it must have been hard for the Papuan to live in Amsterdam since "'He could never forget New Guinea, of course, and here he would never be accepted. People were nice to him, I think. But nice is not enough. They stared at him. Perhaps it would have been all right if he could have been a regular policeman. He would have had his self respect'" (OA 127). "Nice" is indeed "not enough" since it provides van Meteren with no compensatory status for that which he lost upon coming to Amsterdam. The much-vaunted Dutch acceptance of its colonial peoples apparently founders on the realities of Amsterdam society, and van Meteren therefore encounters much of the same dislocation he discovered among former Ambonese paratroopers whom he met in the Netherlands: "'But there was a difference. They had each other. I was alone'" (OA 247).

Although he had actually lived at the Hindist Society and worked as Piet's bodyguard during hashish transactions, van Meteren reached the moral limits of his complicity when Piet switched to heroin dealing. Instead of continuing in the criminal enterprise, he resumed his role as an agent of the law, a role he had previously played as a policeman in Dutch New Guinea. That is, the Papuan attempts to replicate the disciplinary function of that seventeenth-century statesman whom Piet had merely parodied. In so doing, though, van Meteren finds that he is doubly "outside." He cannot give up his "Dutchness" just as he cannot deny his Papuan tribal legacy:

> "I had to kill him, but it had to be a good kill."
> "*Had* to kill him?" Grijpstra asked.
> Van Meteren nodded.
> "Perhaps your people in The Hague were right when they refused to accept me into the Dutch police. Perhaps I am still wild. You see, a Papuan chief is killed when his policy of government is wrong. Nobody can judge a chief, he is too powerful. So he is killed at the right moment. The killing is hardly discussed. The tribe decides, but quietly. A certain atmosphere

forms itself and everyone agrees. Then one or two men kill the chief, the men who are closest to him. But, it's hard to explain that to you perhaps, those men aren't the killers. The *tribe* kills.

". . . A Papuan has no individual face, you see. He has a name and people know him by that name, but that name is only for convenience. In reality he has no name, no face, no individuality. He belongs to the tribe, and that's all. He is part of the whole." (OA 253-4)

In Amsterdam, of course, van Meteren is singled out; he is "'a rare specimen'" even in so cosmopolitan a city as Amsterdam where "'You can find anything . . . when you look for it'" (OA 48). Thus, deprived of connection to his own tribe, van Meteren attempts to merge with the Dutch "tribe," to act on its behalf though in a method sanctioned by his past. In so doing, he claims that he is freer than Grijpstra and de Gier, since they can only jail Piet "for a bit" because "'The police can't change the law. I could, but no judge will believe me when I say that I killed him to stop him'" (OA 257). He thus claims that he has transcended the law to enforce the Law, eliminating the scourge of the degenerate merchant-prince, the depraved and wrong-headed chief, because the official agents of the State are powerless to do so.

That van de Wetering feels some sympathy with this position is obvious from the fact that van Meteren ultimately escapes back to New Guinea after he has helped the police capture two other heroin dealers, though van de Wetering is careful to excuse the police for van Meteren's escape. The commissaris argues, for example, that van Meteren "'is a policeman, a real policeman. I kept on having the idea that he was one of us, even after he had been arrested and was facing us as a suspect'" (OA 288). His escape can, in the final words of the book, only be attributed to "force majeure," an act of God (OA 290). Such a claim legitimizes van Meteren's notion that he was in fact serving the Law, of which temporal law is only a distant shadow, in executing Piet Verboom. As an Agent of the Law he seems to rise above the more constrained agents of Amsterdam's diminished law who must, even though they respect him, condemn his "outside" actions. Thus, at least in this first novel in the series, van de Wetering manages to have things both ways: he can endorse the extra-legal actions of van Meteren without ultimately questioning the State's statutes which are only a shadow of the "true" Code.

If there is a danger in the position mapped out by van de Wetering in *Outsider in Amsterdam*, it is that he can be accused of rather simplistic romanticization, a suggestion that the "noble savage" of West Irian can, merely by virtue of his origins, rise above the jaded agents of the State in Amsterdam. Such is clearly not his intent, and as the series progresses the commissaris argues on a number of occasions that vigilante action against those who would challenge the dominant culture is ultimately destructive of both the law and the Law. Indeed, the number of occasions on which precisely this question is raised confirms its centrality to the thematic concerns of all the Grijpstra and de Gier novels.

After *Outsider in Amsterdam*, van de Wetering goes on to juxtapose Dutch society to the cultures of its former possessions on a regular basis. In the second novel of the series, *Tumbleweed*, the key to the murder of Maria Van Buren once again lies in the conflict between the values of Curaçao and those of the Netherlands, though van de Wetering attempts to broaden his analysis by including as suspects not only a Dutch businessman but also a Belgian diplomat and an American colonel. That is, he brings cultural conflict to bear on a figurative NATO alliance, here united only by its members' desires for the sexual favors of Maria van Buren. But this putative NATO, composed of the forces of commerce, the State, and the military, parodically replicates the role of the police and the State in the first novel of the series. They strive to preserve order and an orderly past even while the forces of sexual desire released by Maria challenge Dutch middle-class values.

That this is Maria's role is evident from the furnishings of her houseboat, especially the statuary: "De Gier stopped a second in front of a statue carved out of wood, depicting three female figures standing on top of one another. Their breasts were exaggerated, pointed, with long nipples. The lips were thick and the foreheads low. The three tongues, lolling in three open mouths, had been painted red, and the very white teeth were pointed seashells. An African fertility symbol perhaps, he thought, but there was more than fertility in the three figures. They seemed to radiate some strong power" (T 19). On the one hand, of course, the statues simply reproduce Western stereotypes of other, darker races by emphasizing "primitive" sexuality and fertility, but, on the other, they also overturn the assumed Western domination of those same colonized regions since power radiates from them just as Maria's sexual power has dominated her three clients. Her murder, then, replicates the crushing of the colonial slave revolts of an earlier imperial age. Here it is the Dutch businessman, the direct descendant of the colonizers, who manipulates Maria's sexually repressed brother, himself a dislocated and disoriented colonial in the service of the State (ironically as a nature reserve ranger on Schiermonnikoog where he attempts to maintain the area's pristine beauty from the pollution of outside forces), into eliminating the dangerous power of the Other which has come to control him.

Perhaps the most sophisticated example of the way in which van de Wetering uses figures from the Netherlands' colonial past to challenge contemporary values is in *The Streetbird*. The elaboration of the Surinamer Luku Obrian in the ninth novel of the series is foreshadowed as early as *The Corpse on the Dike* where de Gier, waiting on the Dam Square beneath "the immense white concrete phallus pointing at heaven to remind everyone that the War had been terrible and had taken many Dutch lives," observes "some elegant black beauties" who

> were talking to each other in the dialect of Surinam, the last Dutch colony on the South American continent. Now threatened by independence, it was losing its population in a steady trickle via Schiphol airport at the rate of at least one full four-engined jet plane a day. Dutch welfare provided these young people with their bell-bottomed trousers, striped shirts and high-heeled boots. And here they were in the shadow of the phallus enjoying their sudden freedom from the claws of hunger and disease, trying to get used to a new environment that, so far, showed few signs of accepting them. De Gier had been looking at them for some time, the great-great-great-grandchildren of slaves taken some hundreds of years ago by Arab and Dutch vessels from the west coast of Africa to the new promising colony of sugar and cotton fields – slaves who died like rats on ships and plantations but who were always replaced by fresh deliveries. (CD 146)

The sympathy which de Gier evidences here is almost immediately called into question by his encounter with two hashish dealers; by terming them "Evil yogis, perverted fakirs with black souls full of hatred and greed and spite" (CD 147), van de Wetering comes close to lapsing into the "black equals other and thus evil" stereotype, though the fact that the two are indeed drug-dealers, a group to which van de Wetering is quite hostile in virtually every case, suggests that the characterization is not so simplistic. The real point to be made, of course, is that the attitudes revealed in this brief moment of an early novel of the series predict the complexities of van de Wetering's treatment of Luku Obrian later on.[21]

Although Surinam attained Dominion status in 1954, it continued to be a part of the Kingdom of the Netherlands until 1975, when it gained full independence. Prior to that time, there had been a long history of two-way travel between Surinam and the Netherlands for both economic and educational reasons. Dutch colonists, intermarrying in the Dutch West Indies as they had in the East, sent their children by both Dutch and Negro wives (and mistresses) to the Netherlands to be educated, thus helping to create an educated middle class that was in many cases unwilling to return to Surinam and accept a lower status in the colony (Bagley 114–16). There was, however, relatively little hostility to the settlement of Surinamers in the Netherlands.

The situation has changed considerably since the early 1970s when the Surinamers lost their free right of entry to the Netherlands as they gained full independence. As a result, in the years just prior to the change in status, there was a frantic rush to move to the Netherlands with, for example, 40,000 immigrants settling there in 1975 alone (Cross and Entzinger 8). While it is true that migration to the Netherlands from the Caribbean has never been primarily to fill gaps in the labor market since the Dutch have traditionally recruited their guest workers from Southern Europe, " . . . there have been growing numbers of migrants [from the Caribbean] who preferred the material certainties of the welfare state to the uncertainties of vulnerable and one-sided economies. Their Netherlands passports or, as in the case of Surinam since 1975, the existence of so many close family ties with Netherlands citizens of Surinamese origin, have enabled them to do so without any guaranteed job prospects in the metropolis" (Cross and Entzinger 10). While immigration to the Netherlands prior to the 1970s was apparently relatively smooth, it is clear that this was largely due to the fact that those arriving were doing so in order to obtain education and were already generally familiar with Dutch society; in short, they were relatively well off and they essentially "fit in": "What happened in the 1970s was that there was a marked increase in the numbers of immigrants, particularly from Surinam, who were totally unprepared. A growing percentage of those arriving at Schiphol airport knew little about the Netherlands and had insufficient background or education to adjust to a society that was totally alien to them. The contrast between the culture of the Surinamese lower classes and the 'Dutch' was obviously enormous. . . . In any case, the Dutch viewed all this primarily as a problem rather than as an addition to their own culture" (Oostindie 67). In short, whether one agrees that the Netherlands was fundamentally free of racial prejudice in regard to immigrants from its former colonies or not, it is clear that, at least with the advent of large-scale immigration by Surinamers in the early 1970s, there has been a clear increase in hostility to non-whites and, apparently, a tendency to focus on the possibility of a criminal minority in the population (Bagley 146).

In *The Streetbird*, then, Obrian's biography, at least as it is narrated by Sergeant Jurriaans, itself reveals the myriad ways in which "the rebellious chaos of the colony" (S 63), the "primitive" legacy of the Dutch imperial past, can disrupt and unsettle the bourgeois welfare state:

"What do we have here?" Jurriaans asked. "A dead pimp. Who? Luku Obrian, black, born in Paramaribo, Surinam, formerly Dutch Guiana on the South American east coast thirty-eight years ago. Who his father was is unknown, but we may assume that his grandfather, in any case his great-grandfather, was a slave, originating in Africa. Our contemporary corpse arrived five years ago at Amsterdam airport, before independence, but not out of fear for the potentially shaky future of his country or because of small-minded greed, knowing that he could apply for social security and never work again, but because of spite. He wished to avenge the fate of his forefathers. He told me so the night of his arrival, when he was dragged into this station, accused of unruly behavior. Drunks do not always speak the truth, but Obrian wasn't lying when he predicted that he would *disconcert* us. The expression is his, for he spoke perfect Dutch, better than we do, and phrased his thoughts accurately, using excellent grammar. He *did* disconcert us, during five long and terrible years, us and the civilians, and last night he was finally taken away from our midst by means of six nine-millimeter bullets fired from an automatic weapon." (S 27–28)

What is perhaps the most telling element of Obrian's plan to "avenge his forefathers" is his method; he intends to "disconcert" the Dutch, to cause them discomfort rather than to attack them physically, to challenge the conventionality which is the reputed bedrock of the "Dutch mind."[22] That is, apparently knowing full well that he will be dealt with in terms of racial stereotypes upon his arrival, Obrian himself carefully reduces his opponents to stereotypes, thus replicating the process of enslavement practiced upon his ancestors. Like Opete, the vulture which Obrian incubates in his armpit during the flight to Amsterdam (S 81) and the "streetbird" of the title, Obrian himself is incubated in Surinam but is (re)born in Amsterdam.

Exploited in the jungles of Surinam, Luku transforms himself into the exploiter in "The Quarter," the jungle of Amsterdam where "anything goes" (S 41). Becoming a powerful pimp in the inner city, itself originally funded by the proceeds of the slave trade, Obrian enslaves the capital. Choosing to live on the Keizersgracht, the Emperor's Canal, in a patrician house, Luku becomes the "Prince of the Quarter," the only figure prepared to challenge Sergeant Jurriaans, embodiment of the State and "King of the Quarter." As de Gier looks through Obrian's apartment, his "long arms swung, indicating all parts of the room. 'Theft,' the sergeant said. 'Everything here is stolen. We are disconcerted, because we have been robbed. He even took our women, enslaved the poor creatures we cherish'" (S 63). What is, of course, so striking about de Gier's sympathy for "the poor creatures" in Obrian's power is that he, like the pimp, uses them as counters in the game played by Obrian and the police.

The evidence of Obrian's power is not solely the number of women in his stable, however. It is, more importantly, the power he exercises over women who are meant to be beyond his reach. He initially demonstrates his control by compelling "'a whore here by the name of Madeleine, a most extraordinarily beautiful woman who acted like a lady and worked for her own account'" to perform an act of fellatio on him on the "cast-iron bridge on the Oldside Canal, pedestrians only, with lions' heads on the railing, many centuries old, a cherished antiquity the tourists gape at" (S 30–31). Because Madeleine was a favorite of the police at the local station, a prostitute whose sexual allure they admired but whose independence impressed them the most, her public humiliation becomes one of Obrian's most spectacular ways to "disconcert" the authorities; her subsequent heroin addiction and eventual suicide merely finalize her public "death" on the bridge under the helpless gaze of the police and the "lions' heads" of the Dutch State. Thus it is perfectly logical that what prompts Obrian's murder by Sergeant Jurriaans is his attempt to compel Adjutant Adele, the beautiful and popular policewoman attached to the station in the Quarter, to perform precisely the same act on precisely the same spot, "'in uniform . . . in full view of everybody'" (S 236). The rebellious colonial Prince of the Quarter finally provokes the wrath of the King of the Quarter, now the extra-legal representative of the State.[23] Although the State itself provides welfare services to immigrants like Obrian in the hope of integrating them fully into Dutch society, van de Wetering sees a constant guerilla war being fought at the point at which the immigrant meets the agents of control.[24]

This struggle, with its reliance on the extra-legal, highlights one of the central dilemmas at the cultural core of van de Wetering's novels. If a figure like Obrian is the "wild man" from Surinam, Jurriaans' actions evoke fears of the return of "the wild men from the early ages who once populated the swamp that, now, today, was called Holland" (OA 260). Like Conan Doyle, who accurately invokes Victorian England's fear of atavism in a figure like Selden in *The Hound of the Baskervilles*, van de Wetering reminds his readers of the primitive just below the surface of even those sworn to uphold Dutch laws. De Gier, the most sophisticated and urbane member of the squad, is also the most susceptible to the return of the repressed. At the end of *The Streetbird*, for example, he dreams that he is paddling "a hollowed-out tree trunk across a wide river" (S 253), with Luku Obrian steering from the bow. Although Obrian is apparently in charge as they head toward a waterfall and destruction, he tells de Gier, "'We're going the right way . . . because that's the direction you chose'" (S 253). Thus it comes as no surprise that at the end of *Hard Rain* de Gier flees Amsterdam and its confines for the putative freedom of New Guinea, presumably to join van Meteren.

These dream images therefore serve as emblems of the breakdown of the "civility," "decorum," "self-possession" and "sense of duty and responsibility" that had heretofore defined the Dutch ideal (Goudsblom 126). Van de Wetering clearly sees *civitas* as endangered by a contemporary tide – of heroin, immigrants and mayhem – that the citizens of the Netherlands are either ill-prepared or unwilling to stem. In this respect, he reproduces a similar debate within Dutch society. As Punch points out, "From the middle 1970s there was a moral panic surrounding the consequences of the drugs-aliens-crime connection which has continued unabated to the present and which initially accentuated the futility of the battle, the hopeless weakness of the police, and the laxity of legal provision" (*Conduct* 56).[25] The moral "laxity" that pervades the Grijpstra and de Gier series is thus related to van de Wetering's perception of a Holland once again fallen victim to nemesis. Like his seventeenth-century counterparts, who imagined themselves subject to God's wrath if they wallowed in "complacency and affluence" (Schama 48), van de Wetering yearns for a return to virtue and moderation.[26]

Thus, van de Wetering follows in a long tradition of Dutch Jeremiahs who exalt Dutch values by pointing out the failings of their contemporaries and warning of the wages of sin. During the Golden Age, Jacob Cats's moralizing emblem books, addressed to all social classes, likewise attempted to instill virtue in a populace threatened by the vices that came with luxury and leisure (Schama 326; 567). Even the graphic representations of children's games which were so popular in the seventeenth century combined "a Rabelaisian pleasure in compilation" with the desire to generate "normative hierarchies" and make "distinctions between categories of virtue and vice, wisdom and folly, good and ill" (Schama 497–98). The inextricable relationship between the ludic and the moral which Schama finds in paintings, emblem books, and commentaries of the seventeenth century remains undiminished three hundred years later in the police procedurals of Janwillem van de Wetering. In fact, the habit of mind which automatically joins the moral and the ludic enables van de Wetering to claim, apparently in all seriousness, that he is "not interested in the moral impact of crime at all" (Filstrup 100) even as the parodic elements of his fiction enact a worldview in which Calvinist principles play a leading role. Thus the comedy is that of the nervous laugh, the shock of recognition that, while the author is far enough removed from Calvinism to be able to stand aside and laugh at it, he remains Dutch enough to call upon police scrutiny to keep his fellow Amsterdammers in check.

Notes

CHAPTER 1 ASPECTS OF THE POLICE PROCEDURAL

1. Jameson is following Norman Holland's "revision" of Freud's notion of repression in *The Dynamics of Literary Response* (141).
2. All translations of Eisenzweig are the authors'.
3. For additional views of Golden Age detective fiction in this same regard, see, for example, Charney; Grella, "Murder and Manners: The Formal Detective Novel"; Panek; and Porter.
4. Mandel traces the rise of the hard-boiled detective novel to the gangsterization of American society; that is, to "the real coming of age of organized crime in bourgeois society" (33).
5. For similar judgments about hard-boiled detective fiction, see, for example, Durham; Porter; Rabinowitz; Grella, "The Hard-Boiled Detective Novel"; Reilly, "Classic and Hard-Boiled Detective Fiction"; Isaac, "The Changing Face of Evil in the Hard-Boiled Novel"; and Hulley.
6. In Mandel's view, the primary difference between the Golden Age detective and the hard-boiled dick is the latter's degree of cynicism combined with his penchant for sentimentality (35).
7. A similar shift from individual to corporate hero can also be seen in the thriller formula. Jerry Palmer argues, under the rubric of "competitive individualism," that the espionage novel focuses on the conflict between the professional spy and the bureaucrat. The thriller, while resolving the contradiction between individuality and sociality in favor of the former, nonetheless foregrounds the notion of the elite (204).
8. Mandel argues that the "ascendancy" of the police in the crime story of the 1940s reflects transformed bourgeois values towards the power of the state; the police, as defenders of private property and a shield against organized crime, "came to be seen as the embodiment of social good in the eyes of the bourgeoisie" (53–54). This view fails to recognize the complex and problematic relationship of the police to their fellow citizens. George Dove comes closer to our perspective on the police when he notes that, because the policeman (and his family) are themselves members of the larger community, they, too, are affected by the "common condition." The policeman must therefore be seen as a "servant of the community" who is judged by the community and whose success may well be determined by that community (*Procedural* 68).
9. This is precisely the trap into which Mandel falls; while arguing that statistics for crimes of violence are in fact down since World War II, he claims that those for petty crimes against property are up, thus suggesting that the "crime scare" is primarily a response to

bourgeois fears of the "'criminal classes.'" Mandel goes on to note, however, that a climate of violence was established, at least in the United States, by the prevalence of "anonymous, gratuitous, and mass crimes" during the 1960s and 1970s (93). These statistics find their "corresponding expression in the evolution of the crime story," which after the war is characterized by a "greater preoccupation with violence than with the unravelling of any mystery" (93–94).

10. Eisenzweig makes a similar point when he notes that the policing apparatus requires its own representation. That is, the beginnings of the detective novel are coterminus with the establishment of the police because, in order to function, the police need a parallel cultural narrative of their work to legitimize their enterprise (188; 259–60).

11. For a similar discussion from a sociological point of view, see Erikson, whose "study in the sociology of deviance" scrutinizes the ways in which communities maintain their "boundaries" by labelling marginal behavior as "deviant."

12. In a later study of Ed McBain's 87th Precinct novels, Dove notes that there are mystery writers, like Sjöwall and Wahlöö, who incorporate social criticism into their series, and that McBain is particularly "light" in this regard (*The Boys from Grover Avenue* 143). Dove seems, however, to posit "social criticism" as background to the formula rather than as an inherent feature of the ideology of the text.

13. The authors of "Popular Culture and Hegemony in Post-War Britain" argue, in a similar vein, that to see the rise of the spy thriller simply as a reflection of Cold War tensions ignores the fact that spy novels are more than just fiction about espionage; they may well be keyed to areas that are not overtly concerned with foreign policy, such as sexuality and class relationships (27). Eric Homberger suggests that in the case of John le Carré's fiction, the "small world of spies" stands for Britain "in all of its moral seediness" (27). In his view, then, le Carré uses "the formulae of the spy thriller . . . for profound and fully serious investigations of the central issues of our time. Le Carré *uses* the spy thriller to write 'real' novels" (104).

CHAPTER 2   BRAVE NEW SWEDEN

1. The novels in the series are: *Roseanna*, 1965 (R); *The Man Who Went Up in Smoke*, 1966 (MS); *The Man on the Balcony*, 1967 (MB); *The Laughing Policeman*, 1968 (LP); *The Fire Engine That Disappeared*, 1969 (FE); *Murder at the Savoy*, 1970 (SAV); *The Abominable Man*, 1971 (AM); *The Locked Room*, 1973 (LR); *Cop Killer*, 1974 (CK); *The Terrorists*, 1975 (T).
2. See also Williams; Duffy; Blom (334); and Dove, *Procedural* (217–18).
3. See Zetterberg (19) and Hancock, *Sweden* (ix, 32).
4. Such a view undercuts attempts by critics to divide their work into three distinct stages. See, for example, Blom, who argues that the first three novels of the series are reminiscent of Simenon, the middle four

of McBain, and the final three "have found an audience outside of 'mere' mystery readers" (334).
5. All translations of Eisenzweig are the authors'.
6. It is interesting to note that, in their recreation of the locked room mystery of Svärd's death, Sjöwall and Wahlöö deliberately recall the archetype of the genre, Poe's "Murders in the Rue Morgue." They do so by having Martin Beck discover, as Dupin did, that the solution to the crime hinges on a closed window which was in fact open at the exact moment of the murder.
7. See, for example, Hancock, "Post-Welfare" (235); Gyllensten (286); and Samuelsson.
8. See Gyllensten (282) on Tingsten's *From Ideas to Utopia* published in 1966 and Lewin (300).
9. According to Fleisher and others, this term is current coinage for the welfare state (17).
10. Liahna K. Babener, in her useful discussion of California as "a fallen paradise, violated by the social sins of modern man" (77), notes that for Raymond Chandler, Dashiell Hammett and Ross MacDonald, "California is the modern Babylon, the site of the apocalypse of the American dream" (78). Other critics have linked Sjöwall and Wahlöö to this hard-boiled tradition (see Becker 158–59, for example), but none have carefully explored their use of landscape for ideological purposes.
11. For a contrasting view of setting in the hard-boiled detective novel as mythic, see Mahan (90–91).
12. This scene is immediately preceded by a description of Mariatorget, once a beautiful square distinguished by its gardens and old buildings, now (according to Lennart Kollberg), a place "where schoolchildren and other young people met the small-scale dope pushers" (MB 122).
13. It is interesting that Sjöwall and Wahlöö's portrayal of the mugger runs counter to the portraits drawn by many popular novelists and scriptwriters in America and Great Britain. Alan Clarke notes that in the 1970s the mugger was the catalyst for "a moral panic" in which he came to "represent the decay of society" and was used "as a vehicle to call for the restoration of standards, the maintaining of discipline, a return to the ideals of consensus [in order to] shore up a crumbling hegemonic position," that of the New Right (52–53).
14. In *The Fire Engine That Disappeared* and in *The Locked Room*, parks play a relatively minor but significant role. The former is bracketed by references to parks, initially serving as posts from which to observe criminals (FE 7–12) and finally as probable loci for the discovery of missing female adolescents (FE 210–11). In *The Locked Room* the enigmatic murder of Svärd is in fact solved by Martin Beck who realizes that the victim has been shot from a post in Kronoberg Park. He finds the empty cartridge "lying between two stones, partially covered by leaves and dirt. . . . Dogs and other animals had been trampling about up here; certainly humans too – for example, those who took it into their heads to break the law by drinking beer in a

public place" (253). Once again, then, parks are places where both police and criminals stalk their victims.

15. In fact, the policeman has died of an allergic reaction to a wasp sting. Occhiogrosso notes that *Cop Killer* is an "ironic title, for the criminal sought here has not only *not* killed any cops but in the end has to be rescued from the police who are out to murder *him*" (176). Occhiogrosso fails to notice that the cop killer of the title is actually Lennart Kollberg.

16. For example, Roseanna's killer, Folke Bengtsson, is under suspicion here.

17. The notion that the murder victims are frequently the true criminals is also discussed by Occhiogrosso (176), Maxfield (71), and Lundin (1554). Dove discusses Sweden's "malaise" and urban redevelopment, but he locates the authors' focus in the "novels of the middle and last periods" (*Procedural* 218–19). Porter discusses similar issues with regard to Dashiell Hammett, arguing that novels like *Red Harvest* and *The Glass Key* are "direct reflections of contemporary American anxieties and manifestations of a national dream turned nightmare" with the city seen "as a realm of the rich and the poor, of work, money, organized exploitation, corruption, death, and dying" (197).

18. For a discussion of the notion of cooperative individualism, see, for example, Hancock, *Sweden* (32), whose analysis is typical. In the more strictly literary realm, it might be argued that this theme of alienation is merely an outgrowth of existentialist ideas that dominated Swedish literature in the 1940s and 1950s (see Gyllensten 298), but Sjöwall and Wahlöö clearly locate the sources of anomie in urban life rather than some nameless, universal *angst*.

19. The role of the American detective also initiates another recurring leitmotif. Whenever the Swedish police confront extremes of pathological behavior, they rely on psychological profiles produced in America. They are forced to do so, they say, because Sweden is such a well-adjusted society that it has no real history of, for example, mass murders (LP 94). The fact that the profile based on American sources is completely wrong in *The Laughing Policeman* does not obviate the fact that, according to Sjöwall and Wahlöö, Sweden is inevitably becoming precisely the sort of society that will generate its own psychopaths in increasing numbers.

20. See Fleisher (189–203) for a description of the nature of these institutions, which range from the new and pleasant to the old and horrible.

21. See, for example, FE (2–3) and LR (60–64).

22. See Fleisher, quoting Lo-Johansson (197–99).

23. For a fuller discussion of recidivism and carceral theory in general, see Foucault, especially 229–308.

24. See, for example, LP (98–99), where two Turks, an Arab, two Spaniards, a Finn and a Greek share a room that measures "about 23 feet by 16." These six guest workers each pay 350 kronor per month for "palatial" lodgings in which they are not even allowed

to make coffee. The publication of *The Laughing Policeman* in 1968, the year the Commission was established, confirms our claim that Sjöwall and Wahlöö are participating directly in the radical critique conducted by the New Left in Sweden. One should take note of the fact that Sweden's immigration policies have become more restrictive since the late 1970s (Childs 163).

25. Occhiogrosso is correct to suggest that Sjöwall and Wahlöö emphasize "a growing malaise in the country" in the latter novels of the series (175); as we have demonstrated, however, earlier novels do in fact contain the ideological seeds of the authors' class analysis, and his claim that they "underscore the basically sound nature" (175) of Sweden in the first several novels is certainly arguable at best.

26. As Hancock points out, "If established elites fail to sanction significant changes in authority relations, the result might be an intensification of critical consciousness and mass alienation. Under such circumstances it is not inconceivable that many young academicians and workers would refuse to be coopted by the existing pluralist system, thereby deepening sociopolitical malaise and increasing the potential for revolutionary acts" (*Sweden* 276).

27. The bitterness of Sjöwall and Wahlöö's critique is evident in the object of Rebecka's assault. It is clear from their description of the Prime Minister (T 232) that he is in fact Olof Palme, who was one of the leading Social Democrats in Sweden and who had received worldwide acclaim for his championing of the rights of the powerless. Palme's subsequent assassination in 1986 has, of course, yet to be solved. It is indeed curious that the Swedish police have yet to isolate a single political group from the multitude that apparently had reason to wish Palme dead. Perhaps the most ironic feature of the investigation is the possibility that Palme's own Social Democrats appear to wish the crime to remain unsolved, since it may reveal a connection between the government and illegal arms sales by "neutral" Sweden to the Middle East. See Reeves (22).

28. See, for example, *The Abominable Man*, *The Locked Room*, and *Cop Killer*.

29. Clarke addresses specifically British television crime series, and he is concerned with showing that the shift from the cop in uniform to the plainclothes policeman between the 1950s and 1970s throws into relief the conflict between collective and bureaucratic responsibility for law enforcement and an individualist and "anti-statist" response to re-establishing social order (50–52). Again, one of the essential differences between Clarke's series and the Beck novels is that the former covertly enter the discussion while Sjöwall and Wahlöö foreground the question of what ideology will control the state apparatuses.

30. See, for example, Melander's remark that, "'most people react with either fear or contempt when the police, in one way or the other, interfere in their existence or disturb their peace of mind'" (LP 103–4).

31. Williams (126) denies that there is a serious connection between the plot of *The Laughing Policeman* and the Vietnam material.
32. See, for example, Nordin's experience when he interviews a potential witness who watches him produce his police identification card "with alarm, as if expecting him to take out a bomb or a machine gun or a condom" (LP 117).
33. See Clarke's discussion of the "anomic hero" charged with "enforcing values which are in conflict with the people he confronts . . . for the benefit of the majority of law abiding citizens. These are depicted as thankless individuals, which increases the detective's feeling of anomie and emphasizes the need for decisive individual action" (50).
34. Dove discusses this phenomenon, arguing that "Kollberg's sense of alienation is more intense than the one experienced by other policemen, but most of them share his qualms, if only to a lesser degree" (*Procedural* 88–89). Dove does not, however, comment on the narrative function of Kollberg's ruminations.

CHAPTER 3   ANATOMIZING THE OTHER

1. The novels of McClure's series are: *The Steam Pig*, 1971 (SP); *The Caterpillar Cop*, 1972 (CC); *The Gooseberry Fool*, 1974 (GF); *Snake*, 1975 (S); *The Sunday Hangman*, 1977 (SH); *The Blood of an Englishman*, 1980 (BE); *The Artful Egg*, 1984 (AE).
2. Schleh, too, mentions that "it is impossible to write a novel of daily life in South Africa without some allusions to 'the system'" (100); his essay, however, concentrates primarily on documenting McClure's relatively accurate quotidian details without addressing the ways in which the author mediates the ideological implications of writing about the "system." Wall notes that South Africa under apartheid provides McClure "with a richly complicated cultural matrix within which to write" his series, and he goes on to discuss the ways in which the laws governing apartheid are fully integrated into the process of detection itself ("Apartheid," 348–49). Wall repeats this assertion in "Achievement" (8).
3. McClure claims that South Africa "is a very alien country to most people" and that attempting to produce a portrait of South African life is akin to writing science fiction (Wall, "Interview" 12). Andreski makes the interesting argument that "The true explanation of the worldwide unanimity against Apartheid has little to do with internal injustice . . . but stems from the incompatibility of the South African system of stratification with the requirements of polite intercourse between the governments and elites of the world." That is, since South Africans equate even non-white leaders of foreign nations with inferior groups, apartheid is a threat to "the dark-skinned elites throughout the world" (29).
4. The difficulty inherent in McClure's attempt to recapture South

African experience is hardly unique; it is a problem inherent in the experience of the exile. For example, when Arthur Ravenscroft, a South African who left to teach at the University of Leeds, returned to his native land in 1974 to discuss "South African English Literature," he noted that "returning here has severe handicaps. One is deeply conscious that one's own conclusions about English-speaking South Africanness are based on what *was*, more than a decade ago. On the one hand, listening to what some have called the breast-beatings at this conference has struck a chill in my heart – it's as if time has stood still for more than ten years. On the other hand, there is the chill of sheer bewilderment, for some important things *seem* different . . . but one hasn't had a chance to assess their significance yet, or judge whether they in fact *are* any different" (317).

5. Probably the 1960s. See McBain (95). McClure himself notes that he is influenced by the procedurals of Ed McBain as well as by the writings of John D. MacDonald, Lawrence Sanders, Chester Himes, and Joseph Wambaugh (Wall, "Interview" 8–9; 13–14).

6. See also White (29).

7. Interestingly, McClure mentions Sjöwall and Wahlöö's *Cop Killer* as a book that "fascinated" him "because of its Kramer & Zondi-like relationship between the Swedish public and the police" (Wall, "Interview" 16). He thus seems to suggest that he has deliberately deflected the political to the personal, a method which, as we will show, is ideologically problematic.

8. Only *The Sunday Hangman* has been banned, and only because it deals with proscribed materials, i.e., state executions (Wall, "Interview" 9; 19–22). McClure's series has in fact been well-received in South Africa, appearing regularly, for example, in the list of most borrowed books from public libraries. This suggests that many South African readers agree with McClure's pronouncement that "the main function [of his series] is entertainment" and that he is reaching "conservative" readers, "ordinary folk," and "not only the sort of 'concerned' who usually read books about South Africa." Indeed, "The Kramer and Zondi series has even become something of a cult among the South African Police because they appreciate the accurate portrayal of police work" (Wall, "Achievement" 23).

9. It is perhaps not coincidental that the medical examiner, whose other roles include certifying that prisoners are fit for corporal punishment, is named Strydom; J. G. Strydom Hospital is a whites-only facility in Johannesburg. See Lelyveld (209).

10. Andreski notes that the "efficiency of the machinery of coercion . . . enables it to avoid the bloodier methods of repression" (25). This is his explanation for the fact that official South African violence is still relatively restricted by comparison with other African and Latin American states. Mathews contends that what we are calling the panoptic model of Bentham does apply to South Africa, since laws like those which can be used to endorse troublesome blacks to their homelands automatically mean the loss of employment and income: "A power like this need not be exercised frequently;

the threat will generally be enough" (236). Adam and Moodley stress "techniques of sophisticated control" rather than the "use of primitive coercion" (2) since they believe that forms of ideological manipulation exercised through the media of mass culture like television and radio programming are even more important than state surveillance and repression (45). Later in their study, though, they argue that the South African state wants its populace to know that it is brutal, as a form of deterrence (137). Therefore, the fact that South African police are not as brutal as they might be and that surveillance is at least partially internalized does not obviate the claim that South Africa still publicizes its practice of bodily discipline.

11. Although he confines his remarks to listing examples of "petty-Apartheid," Schleh, too, notes that "even the dead bodies of Whites take precedence over those of non-whites" (101).

12. See BE (48–49 and 199–200, for example) where the corpse of a black suicide victim serves to demonstrate the force necessary to fracture wristbones.

13. The hierarchy of bodies is so complete that the Immorality Act extends into death. Nxumalo is ordered out of the examining room by Strydom when a white woman lies exposed on a mortuary slab (BE 200). For Schleh, this scene is indicative only of "the thought processes of South Africans" (101) rather than the politics of power which permeate the society.

14. The choice of Swart as the villain/victim's name is perhaps an ironic one; C. R. Swart was Minister of Justice and later the first President of the Republic of South Africa. During World War II, he was under suspicion of sympathizing with the Nazis, and was himself under investigation by the Special Branch, which tried to entrap him (Sachs 242).

15. Andreski notes that the Immorality Act is enforced without regard to the status or influence of violators and even upper-class white offenders have gone to jail (28). In fact, as Sachs points out, "The more prominent the white person involved and the more salacious the evidence, the wider the press coverage . . . . Almost every year the newspapers carry reports of whites who have committed suicide rather than face the ignominy of such a charge" (176). In *The Steam Pig* McClure is careful to note the "desperation" which governs the actions of Trenshaw and his cohorts in the face of Jackson's blackmail threats. It is true, however, that the sentences inflicted on black transgressors are much more severe than those meted out to whites (Sachs 154).

16. Jarvis here echoes other English South Africans; for example, a drunken driver says to Strydom, "'But I don't supply – suppose you could understand that in your bloody Dutch patois, hey?'" (CC 107). The denigration of Afrikaans and Afrikaner culture in general by those of English heritage is a leitmotif throughout *Caterpillar Cop* as well as other volumes in the series. As Crapanzano notes, the *taal* (the Afrikaans word for language) has ideological power. It confers

identity on the Afrikaners because "it is a product of a historical struggle. . . . It attests to their particularity, their nationhood, and their distinction. It gives them an intimate sense of social and cultural unity . . . " (30). See also Schlemmer, who claims that "Cultural cleavages among Whites are deeply embedded in the institutions" of South African society (129), and Worrall, who charges that the English have helped create Afrikaner hostility through their "attitude of 'benign superiority'" (202).

17. Garson indicates that Afrikaner Nationalists have often charged that "English-speaking South Africans have habitually given South Africa not the single-minded love of country due from a patriot, but only a divided loyalty or dual allegiance arising from their attachment to the British connection" (32). For another discussion of this issue, see Crapanzano (187–200).

18. Schleh notes that "Durban . . . is alien to Kramer, in some part because of so many Indians roaming around" (102); such a reading de-emphasizes the crucial divisions within white South African society which are in fact the focus of McClure's treatment of the city. The issue is actually a good deal more complicated than even an analysis of Afrikaner-English hostility initially suggests. For example, Worrall argues that the image of "English South Africa as the conscience of White society in race relations matters, and as the preservers, if not also the founders, of the liberal tradition" is false (195–97). Welsh indicates that "the South African English have been deeply implicated in the entrenchment of segregation and racial discrimination. For all that every survey shows that the English are generally more liberal than Afrikaners, this remains a difference of degree and not of principle" (236).

19. Lelyveld remarks that townships "are nearly always set off by buffer zones – highways, railway yards, factories, mining dumps – in a manner that plainly reflects meticulous preparation for a military siege" (36–37).

20. Such evictions are carried out by the South African government when it wishes to create a white area on desirable land. Interestingly, McClure's use of the place name "Robert's Halt" may be intended to recall Lord Roberts, the English general who marched successfully to Pretoria during the Boer War (Lelyveld 235). The Black Spot eviction in *The Gooseberry Fool* thus ironically reproduces the earlier British displacement of Afrikaner settlers.

21. Women in domestic service are not consigned to the same low social status as unskilled male laborers. In fact, "Provided she works in one of the upper income group white suburbs, a female domestic worker can earn mention as a 'socialite' in the social columns of the African Press" (Hellmann 161). Hellmann goes on to claim that "The white middle class is the normative reference group for Africans and the degree of westernization is in itself an attribute of status" (172). Although Zondi apparently finds Jele's adoption of white values "contradictory," he has, as we will show, himself internalized Western values.

22. McClure makes it clear that black identity is frequently compromised in other contexts as well. Lucy Kwalumi, the "town wife" of Thomas Shabalala in *The Gooseberry Fool*, is wearing "a Salvation Army hat with the name ribbon sewn on upside down, and a cast-off frock that may have graced an administrator's reception – it had its own separate smell of salmon paste" (18).
23. Sachs confirms this notion of an "anti-world": "To adherents of racial theory it is self-evident that Africans have an ethnic propensity towards violence and plunder, and criminal statistics are seen merely as confirming what every white man is considered to know from common experience" (185). Andreski, on the other hand, argues that recent changes in Afrikaner Nationalist thinking have produced a new view of blacks: "The underprivileged ought no longer to be regarded as inferior, but solely as different" (79). Leatt *et al.* note that Afrikaner Nationalist ideology has moved from *baasskap* (other races are inferior) to guardianship (blacks can come to maturity) to separate development (concessions must be made to separate but equal opportunities and facilities for blacks) (83). In their view, however, separate development is a vehicle by which black unity can be impaired: "The homelands policy, in fact, represents a systematic attempt to 're-tribalize African consciousness' in such a way that the resultant fragmentation into tribal units would obstruct the emergence of an overriding African nationalism in South Africa" (125). It thus creates a legal "anti-world" within the state.
24. The use of the lecherous goat at this juncture in the novel can be read in at least two ways. On the one hand, McClure himself may well be implicated in the process of stereotyping black sexuality. On the other hand, the hyperbolic nature of both the description and the situation may suggest that he is deconstructing a widely-held view. The fact that it is virtually impossible to validate one of these readings indicates how difficult it is to assign an ideological position to McClure. In addition, the noteworthy resemblances between Mama Benghu's brothel and those that regularly appear in Chester Himes's Harlem procedurals suggest that McClure may well be confronting two stereotypes. Coffin Ed and Gravedigger continually wind up at upper-class brothels whose madams they know well and whose customers are inevitably gangsters. In an interview with Wall, McClure indicates that he has been influenced by Himes ("Interview" 8) – and there is a clear similarity here in the treatment of the white view of black sexuality as somehow animalistic.
25. Crapanzano notes this mythification: "The homelands are filled with witch doctors and sorcerers; the locations are filled with *tsotsis* and *skollies* . . . who take on extrahuman proportion" (261).
26. In fact, Shoe Shoe is so unimportant to the police that his original crippling injury is never investigated because, since Shoe Shoe was himself an up-and-coming mobster, "society had been left better off by a crime" (SP 44).
27. Once again, a Himes paradigm is present in the descriptions of problematic police interrogations. See, for example, the methods

Gravedigger and Coffin Ed use to extract information from Chink Charlie in *The Crazy Kill* (126–27).
28. See also Schleh (104–6) and White (29).
29. See Sachs (239–41, for example) for additional information regarding the role of blacks in the South African Police.
30. Sachs notes that blacks cannot expect, however, to rise above the rank of lieutenant in the South African Police, and that even this promotion is reserved for a very small percentage. In any case, they can never command whites (240–41).
31. For a discussion of class structure within the African community, see Hellmann (171–72).
32. These are indeed "secondhand ideas," stemming as they do from Chester Himes's descriptions of Coffin Ed and Gravedigger in plain clothes on the prowl in Harlem. See, for example, *Blind Man with a Pistol* (189).
33. Indeed, Zondi's qualities as a mimic of those whites to whom he reports (see SH 41) bear witness to his shifting identity. In this respect, he comes perilously close to resembling Crusoe's Friday who learns English by mimicking his master. The resemblance is noted by Sergeant Grobbelaar (SP 103), albeit as an insult.
34. See, for example, SP (25); CC (102); and GF (101).
35. Dove also makes this appraisal of Kramer's attitudes. He goes on to suggest, however, that "In contrast to Kramer's Afrikaner bent . . . is his personal regard for Mickey Zondi, whom he privately regards as the equal of any white policeman of the non-commissioned ranks with whom he jokes and whose playful insolence he gruffly endures, and whom he calls 'old son' when nobody is around to hear" (*Procedural* 233). Wall, too, notes that Kramer's "deep concern" for Zondi "must be hidden or disguised, for others would not understand" ("Achievement" 26). Our reading of the series implies a far more problematic relationship between Kramer and Zondi.
36. The fact that this description of Mbopa recreates Kramer and Zondi's "interrogation" of Gershwin Mkize reinforces the problematic nature of the latter's roles.
37. A similar distorted image of the Kramer-Zondi relationship runs throughout the series in the figures of Van Rensburg and Nxumalo. Here the paramilitary hierarchy of the police is doubly reproduced. Just as Van Rensburg criticizes and insults Nxumalo, another example of white-black exploitation, Strydom denigrates and insults Van Rensburg; here the exploitation is based solely on the power of the superior in the hierarchy rather than on any supposed racial superiority. However, as McClure notes, Nxumalo, by virtue of the fact that he fully recognizes the tenuousness of his position, is able to best Van Rensburg and undercut his power in ways that the "mainstream" white cannot do to his own boss. It is interesting to note that McClure has named his mortuary officer Van Rensburg; his name echoes that of a former commander of the *Ossewabrandwag*, an Afrikaner "'cultural' organization," who was himself an admirer of Adolf Hitler (Crapanzano 124).
38. Marshment argues that, in espionage fiction like that of Fleming,

black characters may serve as "aides" to the hero, reproducing "the stereotypic loyalty of the 'good native' to the white man." In *Dr. No*, for example, the loyalty of Quarrel to Bond is a confirmation of "the rightness of the white man's cause" (336). A recent play by two black South Africans, Percy Mtwa and Aubrey Redebe, more accurately portrays the perception of black cops as submissive collaborators. In *Bopha!* the family conflicts that arise when a father is a policeman and a son an activist are amply documented. By contrast, this situation is absent in McClure's series which covers up the issue of why being a black policeman separates one from one's family and one's neighbors. Wall mentions the indifference of black policemen to "black suffering" ("Achievement" 17).

39. See, for example, *The Sunday Hangman*, where the farmer Jackson assumes that there will be ways to circumvent a fictitious new ordinance proposed by Zondi as a pretext to inteview Dorothy Jele: "'So that's how it's done,' Mr. Jackson chuckled . . . . 'A man never knows what they will think of next!'" (176–77).

40. See Isaac, who notes that "As in the rest of the social order of South Africa, these ["several running investigations"] are kept apart, almost hermetically separated from each other." In addition to writing accurate procedural stories, McClure is also emphasizing "the great distance between the various segments of the nation's people . . . by the force of Apartheid" ("Black and White" 16). Wall makes a similar point about the Danny Govender sub-plot in *The Caterpillar Cop*, noting the irony that the boy's death impedes the primary police investigation ("Apartheid" 350). Much the same might be said of the Ramjut Pillay sub-plot in *The Artful Egg* where once again an important clue is buried, along with Pillay, in a mental institution. Adam and Moodley note that the role of Indians as shopkeepers and relatively privileged residents of South Africa places them in a particularly vulnerable position: they are targets of both white and black anger (84). McClure accurately represents their position through Govender and Pillay, but he introduces this theme as early as *The Steam Pig*, where Moosa and Gogol, residents of Trichaard Street, inhabit a shopping area "within Trekkersburg's sole nonwhite zone, which meant it did the job of ten streets elsewhere in the town" (93). Zondi exploits their tenuous position to obtain information on Gershwin Mkize.

41. See Dove (*Procedural* 128). The use of multiple plots can, of course, bear an ideological function. Recall, for example, Sjöwall and Wahlöö's use of sub-plots to reflect class differences.

42. See, for example, the cases of Theresa le Roux in *The Steam Pig* and of Hugo Swart in *The Gooseberry Fool*.

43. Isaac's judgment that "McClure has blended police procedural mysteries with a unique fury extending past the official policy to a deep anger at the people who tolerate the situation" is troubling. His notion that McClure has "blended" social commentary and an essentially apolitical form denies that the form itself, indeed popular fiction in general, is fundamentally ideological. He reduces Kramer's

reaction to torture, for example, to "background commentary" rather than seeing it as central to the problematic role of the police in South African society ("Black and White" 13). While asserting that "McClure's fiction does not represent an on-going diatribe against the injustices and tensions of the country" ("Achievement" 23), Wall concludes that the relationship between Kramer and Zondi is an "ultimately inspiring example of how men of good will can still rise above the institutionalized narrowness of their culture" ("Achievement" 29).

44. Zondi's relatively stable life in Kwela Village and later in Hamilton actually reverses what is typically the case in South Africa. As Lelyveld notes (44), the perturbation of black family life in the townships is a frequent topic in advice columns in black newspapers. The fact that Zondi need not commute long distances to his job may explain the stability of his marriage.

45. In the context of these Oedipal conflicts, one might well recall the "regression to covert childhood" (SP 213) of Trenshaw and his cohorts in the Albert Club. Because these men are in fact Trekkersburg councillors, their adolescent rebellion against the older generation may well be the first instance of McClure's oedipal-political matrix.

46. Lelyveld notes that, during his stay in South Africa, he found a number of signs which served as reminders "that most individuals, white and black, were basically sane, that they could rise above their inheritance, or, at least, adapt to it when left with no other choice; that, finally, it was the inheritance and the situation it produced that were deranged" (371).

47. Sachs notes that the same inability to address structural change is actually enhanced by the nature of the South African judiciary: "In general terms, by placing a limitation on the powers of the rulers, the courts facilitate the accommodation of the dominated to the dominators, and thereby make rule more secure. What might otherwise be seen as a large question of social relationships gets converted into a series of small questions about individual guilt according to narrowly defined criteria" (262). Because the judiciary is subordinated to the legislature, blacks are "dispossessed by the processes of law," and "the penalisation by the courts of black and white rebels can be justified in terms of the courts' duty to help maintain the public peace" (263).

48. See Adam and Moodley (107–16) for a discussion of collective black identity as it expresses itself in group action.

CHAPTER 4 THE HOUSE OF KEEPING

1. The novels in the Van der Valk series are: *Death in Amsterdam*, 1962 (DA); *Because of the Cats*, 1963 (BC); *Gun Before Butter*, 1963 (GB); *Double Barrel*, 1964 (DB); *King of the Rainy Country*, 1965 (KRC); *Criminal Conversation*, 1966 (CC); *Strike Out Where Not Applicable*,

1967 (SO); *Tsing-Boom!*, 1969 (TB); *The Lovely Ladies*, 1971 (LL); *Auprès de ma Blonde*, 1972 (AB).

2. Shloss's excellent essay is an assessment of the polarization between public and private life in late capitalism in which she concludes that, while "absolute surveillance remains an implicit strategy of state control, . . . Freeling's novels can be read as records of that goal's failures" (171). Although she discusses the evolution of the Van der Valk series towards a greater privatization of the investigation, she does not consider Freeling's use of the fictional intertext to open a dialogue with his predecessors.

3. It should be noted that Freeling, echoing Conan Doyle's actions of a century ago, has recently brought Van der Valk back from the dead in *Sand Castles*. This book does not figure in our analysis.

4. Both Elsa de Charmoy and Martin in *Death in Amsterdam* are "tainted" by their foreignness. Elsa is partly Belgian and has relatives in both hemispheres; Martin is a sort of pan-European figure who has resided throughout the continent and in England. Hjalmar Jansen, the man behind the crimes in *Because of the Cats*, has "lived in Sweden, Belgium and Germany" (26); his commando ideas are borrowed from both fascist and communist movements throughout Europe. Lucienne Englebert flees Holland to take up residence in Belgium; her lover, Stam, is a Belgian masquerading as a Dutchman (GB 128). In *Double Barrel*, both the burgomaster and the husbands victimized by the anonymous letter-writer are "foreigners" from outside Drente (144), while Besançon/Müller is a former S.S. Lieutenant General. Van der Post, the murderous doctor in *Criminal Conversation*, has family roots in colonial Indonesia (173). Anne-Marie Marschal is Belgian (KRC 27), and her husband Jean-Claude, another pan-European character, has been educated in England (KRC 28). Dickie, the putative murderer in *Strike Out Where Not Applicable*, is half-French (77), while his victim Bernhard Fischer is a transplanted German whose father "was on comfortable terms" with the occupying army during World War II (82). The protagonists of *Tsing-Boom!* are French and Belgian, locked in a relationship that dates back to the French-Indochinese War. In *The Lovely Ladies* the murderer, Denis Lynch, is an Irishman; he is egged on by the daughters of an old Dutch family now living in Dublin. It is only the last novel of the series that foregrounds a purely Dutch cast, but here, of course, the victim is the very un-Dutch Inspector Van der Valk, and the chief investigator is his French wife, Arlette.

5. Eisenzweig, playing upon the "eccentric" nature of the Great Detective, focuses on the formal aspects of his discourse. He notes that a structural contradiction arises when the detective "de-centers" the problem, removing it from inside the "textual universe" towards the "paratext" (152) – that is, towards the corpus of previous detective fiction against which it will be measured. Such de-centering directs the reader's attention away from reality and towards its substitute: the world of fiction itself. All translations of Eisenzweig are the authors'.

6. This shift in emphasis may well have its roots in Freeling's biography, since he moved from Holland to France while he was writing the Van der Valk series. As we will show, however, the French experience in Indochina is more adapted to a study of European neurosis than Holland's colonial disengagement.
7. Van der Valk's "archaeological dig" unearths cultural history as well; the text of *Tsing-Boom!* identifies *Wozzeck* as its aesthetic analogue (229).
8. The protagonists of Golden Age detective fiction are outsiders in terms of their personal eccentricities, but are generally committed to the central values of their society. Hard-boiled protagonists are marginalized by their critique of society's hypocrisy; a private investigator like Philip Marlowe actually embodies the values society claims to endorse, when in fact it subverts them for gain.
9. Interestingly, Erikson also uses Salem as an example of a community engaged in boundary maintenance. Freeling's source appears to be some combination of Sartre's *Les Sorcières de Salem* (a screenplay adapted from Miller's *The Crucible*) and Starkey's *The Devil in Massachusetts*. The inclusion of the Besançon/Müller sub-plot, in particular, suggests some knowledge of Starkey's work, which compares the "persecution" of the alleged witches in Salem to the persecution of the Jews by the Nazis.
10. Eisenzweig notes that this form of detective fiction, often referred to as the "Great Policeman" school to distinguish its protagonists from "Great Detectives" like Sherlock Holmes or Lord Peter Wimsey, is exemplified by Maigret, who, though a functionary, is constantly differentiated from his peers. Eisenzweig argues that, because individual identity is required by detective fiction, the investigator must therefore cease to be the symbol of a system: "The police must become a policeman." For this reason, in fiction like that of Simenon there is a conflict between the policeman as a representative of the system and the policeman as a character in a narrative. Maigret, although he fulfills his function within the bureaucracy, is consistently opposed to the methods of that bureaucracy (274–75).
11. Eisenzweig, commenting on the numerical disparity between the more than eighty Maigret novels and the much more limited production of novels featuring hard-boiled detectives, reasons that, because Simenon envisions society as composed of an infinite number of individuals capable of committing crimes, the Maigret series could theoretically be "perpetually renewed." In the case of hard-boiled fiction, however, the guilty party is "always more or less the same" ("a social class, a political system") and the sense of failure at the end of the investigation is so "radical" that the despair which marks such a vision prevents the series from continuing indefinitely (324). As we will suggest in our analysis of the Van der Valk series as a whole, Freeling is trapped between these two visions: he finds systemic causes for the crimes he describes, but the procedural formula insists that he label a specific person as "criminal."

12. We would agree with Jenny that rewriting the *architext* is not merely a case of "the anxiety of influence," identified by Harold Bloom, who, in any event, restricts this idea to poetry (36). We do not believe that Freeling's use of Chandler reflects a simplistic desire for originality *vis-à-vis* either hard-boiled detective fiction or the police procedural.
13. This poem is the only one in Baudelaire's short "spleen cycle" specifically to allude to a figure other than the poet himself – either Charles IX of France or Philip IV of Spain. While critics disagree as to the identity of the king in question, in all likelihood he is Charles IX (1550–74), given the specific reference to the Saint Bartholomew's Day Massacre in the line "subjects dying beneath his balcony" (Baudelaire 976–77). It is interesting that even this reference to "high art" is not unrelated to the history of detective fiction; Baudelaire was Poe's first French translator.
14. Freeling returns to this narrative technique in his Castang series, the subject of Chapter 5.
15. Porter's appraisal of this description of Amsterdam is that it supplies "cultural information . . . about one of the world's great cities . . . in the acerbic voice of a narrator of the world." In this respect, such "digressive elements" are calculated to appeal "to the reader as tourist" (73). This analysis ignores the political subtext which permeates the novel.
16. *The King of the Rainy Country* displays on its surface examples of "'weak' intertextuality" (Jenny 40), mere quotations or resemblances that are not in themselves sufficient to open up the intertextual space to a full-fledged investigation. The rubric of superficial intertextuality would apply to the case of similarities in names between *The King of the Rainy Country* and *The Big Sleep*, such as Canisius/Canino, Marschal/Mars, and Sylvester Marschal/General Sternwood. The latter is a translinguistic pun that plays on the French *sylvestre* (woody) and the military meaning of marshal/*maréchal*. One could even argue that Freeling's choice of the name Sopexique echoes Chandler's Cypress Club. Surface intertextuality also includes resemblances in settings, such as Marschal's baroque bathroom and Sternwood's steamy conservatory. The former, with its fountains, gardens, and orchids (KRC 29), deliberately recalls Sternwood's greenhouse, with its humidity, heat, and orchids (TBS 5). Both settings are important for the insight they give into the characters of their owners; the overdone bath exemplifies the fatally romantic streak in Jean-Claude Marschal while Sternwood's conservatory is emblematic of the corruption that runs through the family blood. Porter discusses Marschal's bathroom briefly, as an example of "traditional realist detailing" (73), without noting its intertextual relationship to Chandler.
17. In *The Big Sleep* Marlowe reveals that he, too, had once been a cop (106, 112). Freeling's re-presentation of Chandler's knight and chess game sequence might well be considered an instance of the the sort of repetition in fiction identified by J. Hillis Miller. There, following

Deleuze, he distinguishes between Platonic repetition which posits an "archetypal model" and Nietzschean repetition which assumes "a world based on difference" (5–6). According to Miller, " . . . each form of repetition inevitably calls up the other as its shadow companion. You cannot have one without the other, though each subverts the other" (16). Such an analysis substantiates our claim that readers of *The King of the Rainy Country* necessarily are aware of the formulaic elements of both the police procedural and Chandler's hard-boiled *The Big Sleep*, mutually deconstructing each simultaneously. The result is precisely Miller's "heterogeneous" form that characterizes much of canonical literature (17–18). Generic irresolution in Freeling is emblematic of this process.

18. One of the earliest analyses of Marlowe as knight appears in Durham (90–98). Other examples include: Grella, "The Hard-Boiled Detective Novel"; Cawelti, *Adventure* (180–181); and Rabinowitz.

19. The knight sequence is an example of *metaphoric isotopy*, in which "a textual fragment is brought into a context because of semantic analogy to it. . . . these analogies are often the result of more or less conscious reflection by the author about his own work. They serve to clarify the meaning of a passage, to enrich it with the play of remembered associations, to indicate through another's voice a direction for reading to follow" (Jenny 53).

20. The paperback edition of *The King of the Rainy Country* contains a misprint. It begins the third sentence of the quotation with the ambiguous pronoun "He" rather than the more logical "One" which appears in the original. See *The King of the Rainy Country* (New York: Harper & Row, 1965) 139.

21. Freeling's echoes of Chandler's prose are so exact that, just as Carmen "hisses" at Marlowe (TBS 147), Anne-Marie "spits" at Van der Valk (KRC 124).

22. Throughout the second half of *The King of the Rainy Country* Freeling uses the term "amateur" simply to denote the non-policeman; he does not distinguish explicitly among "the brilliant amateur detective X" (132) of classic detective fiction, the paid private investigator of the hard-boiled, or the international operative like James Bond (see 132–34). This same imprecision also appears in *Auprès de ma Blonde*.

23. Porter notes that "Marlowe need have looked no further for his criminal than the first character he meets after the butler on entering the Sternwood mansion, namely . . . Carmen." For this reason, the text of *The Big Sleep* "takes the ironic form of an unnecessary journey" (39). A similar structuring principle governs *The King of the Rainy Country* where Van der Valk meets first Marschal's butler, and then Anne-Marie, as he begins his investigation.

24. In order to deflect attention away from the alienation of earlier stages of capital and thus reaffirm the dominant ideology, Golden Age detective fiction created a facade of non-conformism though nothing ideological actually separated this type of detective from the police (Eisenzweig 276). Sherlock Holmes, for example, upholds the same Victorian values as the hapless Inspector Lestrade.

25. For other versions of this fatally romantic streak, see, for example, Hugo van der Post in *Criminal Conversation* who seeks to live the life of the artist in an appropriately tawdry garret, a role that is at odds with his position and function in Holland's "rigid social order" (205). *Strike Out Where Not Applicable* provides a portrait of the bourgeoisie in Lisse which imagines itself a new aristocracy dedicated to art. Denis Lynch in *The Lovely Ladies* is "a young romantic boy" who burns "to change an evil world" (269–70).
26. In the case of Esther Marx, in fact, several bureaucracies and institutions of surveillance are implicated in her death. The investigation becomes an elaborate cover-up for the behavior of French forces in Indochina. Only by circumventing a long series of bureaucratic stumbling blocks and insisting on the value of Esther Marx as a person rather than a bureaucratic cipher can Van der Valk finally discover the truth.
27. In fairness to Dove, he does point out that Van der Valk has "an unorthodox approach to police work" which "is rooted in his attitude toward people and justice." Dove reasons that "Van der Valk does not subscribe to the myth of police work as part of the struggle of Good versus Evil: he has found, in his job, that there are very few good men and perhaps even fewer bad ones, and crime has little to do with absolutes like Right and Wrong" (214). In leaving Van der Valk's position at this point, however, Dove fails to take into account the ways in which Freeling calls into question the larger social determinants operating within a culture, such as the legacy of History.
28. Shloss (171) and Bakerman (352) argue that the Arlette series builds on this quality of the heroine.
29. Another element in Arlette's French background may also contribute to her discomfort at engaging in surveillance. The French bureaucracy is one of the most Argus-like in Europe; Freeling will go on to explore the centralized French state in the Castang series.
30. In *Strike Out Where Not Applicable* Arlette is again asked to provide information; here it takes the form of thumbnail biographies of the members of the *manège*, a riding establishment near Lisse. The distance Arlette has come from her earlier horror at prying into the lives of others is obvious: "Arlette lit a cigarette slowly, remembering an occasion in the north of Holland when she had been told to study the habits of a suburban street. She had been horrified – younger then. She was no longer alarmed that people she habitually met and talked to were criminals" (33). By this point in her life, she has clearly internalized the policeman's view of society, one of generalized suspicion. In *Tsing-Boom!*, she has so far internalized the mindset of a detective that it shapes her relationship with Ruth, the young girl she and Van der Valk adopt (136). It is no wonder, then, that she is prepared, as well as eager, to conduct the investigation into Van der Valk's death in *Auprès de ma Blonde*.
31. Shloss argues that the "feminization" of Van der Valk's methods is finally a hopeful sign. She bases her argument largely on Arlette's

successful solution of Van der Valk's murder in *Auprès de ma Blonde*, as well as on the roles of other feminine "helpers" over the course of the series. At the same time that she sees the evolution of female characters in the novels as the basis for this hope, Shloss overlooks the fact that social change in Europe is inevitably determined by the cultural past.

32. Echoes of *The Big Sleep* return again in, for example, Larry Saint's exotic pornography shop, The Golden Apples of the Hesperides, a distant cousin of Geiger's pornographic lending library.

33. The voice of Freeling's persona here is precisely the same as that which he uses to write Van der Valk's "biography" in Otto Penzler's *The Great Detectives*, and so the voice is clearly "outside" the space of the series. (See Freeling, "Inspector Van der Valk.") In his use of the "I"-narrator, Freeling comes much closer to the sort of "auto-representation" that Eisenzweig characterizes as a major transtextual activity in detective fiction (154–55). That is, Freeling intrudes a voice which insists that the narrative is an "authentic" document. This "real" voice, expressing its grief at the shocking death of Piet Van der Valk, helps to defuse the readers' "grief" even as it reengages them in the fictional world by recounting Arlette's investigation. She conquers her grief as she, too, becomes a reader, here of Van der Valk's notes. Freeling is thus returning to one of detective fiction's archetypal problems – convincing the reader of the reality of the created world. Interestingly, the "I"-narrator here inverts the structure of Simenon's *Les Mémoires de Maigret*, in which Maigret recounts his early life as a Paris policeman and in which he evokes his former colleagues, including Simenon himself.

34. Dove's discussion of *Auprès de ma Blonde* implies a false distinction between "Fiction" and "Reality" in this text. He suggests that Van der Valk's private investigation constitutes "fiction," into which the "reality" of his death at the hands of "real" criminals intrudes (215). This seems to us to bear out Eisenzweig's notion that detective fiction must constantly insist on its own "reality." Dove therefore falls into the trap set by the generic code: mistaking a fictional version of reality for the real itself.

35. Freeling's experiments with detective fiction are by no means limited to their appearance in the Van der Valk series. Since *Auprès de ma Blonde*, Freeling has continued to write three different variants of the mystery novel simultaneously: the police procedural Castang series, the amateur Arlette series, and a group of unrelated international conspiracy novels. It is interesting to note that Freeling begins the Arlette series with an extended reference to *The Big Sleep*. See Freeling, *The Widow* (1–3).

36. Porter makes a similar point when he discusses the ways in which Chandler, Hammett, and the hard-boiled tradition as a whole reveal a "nostalgia for a mythical past," that of the American frontier (181).

37. In fact, he was awarded a Golden Dagger by the Crime Writers in 1963, the Grand Prix du Roman Policier in 1965, and an Edgar (by the Mystery Writers Association) in 1966.

38. Freeling's debt to Simenon goes beyond the Maigret series. *Criminal Conversation*, as the text overtly proclaims, reproduces the structure of Simenon's *Lettre à mon juge*; the female protagonist, Martine Englebert, also furnishes a surname for Lucienne in *Gun Before Butter*.
39. See, for example, the following references: Sir Arthur Conan Doyle (LL 208; AB 29–31); S. S. Van Dine (SO 29); Dorothy Sayers (AB 162); Edgar Wallace (AB 158–59, 168); Raymond Chandler (DA 140–41; GB 152; CC 23, 26; TB 126, 141; AB 29–31); Dashiell Hammett (CC 55); G. K. Chesterton (DB 76); Ian Fleming (DB 76; KRC 134; AB 64); Rex Stout (TB 11); and Len Deighton (TB 105). This list is hardly exhaustive, but it does serve to indicate Freeling's ability to range throughout the works of his predecessors and contemporaries. In addition to detective fiction, Freeling also includes references to appropriate films, particularly those of Alfred Hitchcock (see, for example, DB 118), and an occasional television series like *Dixon of Dock Green* (AB 21).

CHAPTER 5   A FAMILY AFFAIR

1. The key term for the Castang series is *"perceived* devolution." As Stuart Hall *et al.* have shown, a "moral panic" is not necessarily created in a society by, say, an actual rise in crime but rather by a public consensus that such an increase is taking place. Thus, the crucial element is not the *"deviant act"* itself but *"the relations between the deviant act and the reaction of the public and the control agencies to the act"* (13–17). Control agencies, the press, and the public thus respond not to "a simple set of facts but a new *definition of the situation* – a new construction of the social reality of crime." While this "new construction" necessarily implies important ideological shifts, ideological change takes the form of a "moral panic" which obscures the structural and economic realities that underlie crime (29; 115). While Hall *et al.* concentrate on the role of the media in shaping – indeed, in producing – "moral panics," it is clear that detective fiction also responds to these "panics," though at some chronological remove.
2. All translations of Peyrefitte are the authors'.
3. In fact, many of Freeling's Castang novels demonstrate that he is aware of the ongoing debate crystallized by contemporary social critics. See, for example, Peyrefitte (8; 412).
4. The novels in the ongoing Castang series are: *Dressing of Diamond*, 1974 (DD); *The Bugles Blowing*, 1975 (BB); *Sabine*, 1976 (S); *The Night Lords*, 1978 (NL); *Castang's City*, 1980 (CC); *Wolfnight*, 1982 (W); *The Back of the North Wind*, 1983 (BNW); *No Part in Your Death*, 1984 (NPD).
5. For a discussion of the peasant hearth as a "symbolic domicile of the family," see Joseph *et al.* (23). In the nineteenth century, for

example, theoreticians of the family believed that it was necessary to "recreate" for the working-class family "the warmth [and] . . . the gratifications of family life to which the bourgeoisie had exclusive rights and privilege" and "which the rural family knew how to preserve" (173). All translations of Joseph et al. are the authors'.
6. Under the *ancien régime*, the family constituted a "plexus of dependent relations that were indissociably private and public," but after the fall of the Bastille the state intruded directly into the life of the family, ending the patriarchal alliance between father and king, in order to "take charge of its citizens, to become the agency responsible for the satisfaction of their needs" (Donzelot 48–51).
7. Hall et al. discuss the creation of scapegoats as a means to avoid facing up to the ideological implications of changes in traditional values (156–57).
8. The link between Soulay and Stendhal's Verrières in *The Red and the Black* is oblique but nonetheless clear; local politics invade the private sphere in both towns. Freeling's familiarity with Stendhal is evident from both the Van der Valk and Castang series.
9. As we shall see, the whole question of justifying illegal actions in the name of some transcendent belief is raised to the overtly political level in later novels.
10. Shloss argues that, in the Van der Valk series, women act as helping figures who possess "privileged knowledge of the victim" (166). Their understanding of character and motive makes them superior "detectives" to those who act only within official bureaucratic channels, and the earlier series thus ends with the private triumphing over the public (170–71). It is clear from Vera's involvement in Castang's cases that Freeling has not yet resolved this private-public tension.
11. For the convent as a site of discipline, see Foucault (143).
12. Peyrefitte discusses compartmentalization (*cloisonnement*) as a feature of French bureaucracy which alienates the public and allows hierarchies to avoid assuming responsibility (318). Freeling's point is that the attempt to avoid personal responsibility in one's public role results in a similar alienation on the private level.
13. The family structure dominates commercial, agricultural, and industrial areas of French life, forming "hierarchized micro-societies" much like those in the civil service. When these begin to disintegrate from within, the society as a whole is threatened (Peyrefitte 369–70). We argue that the *perception* of disintegration is sufficient to provoke a crisis.
14. Peyrefitte, though not specifically discussing the bourgeoisie, underlines a French tendency to create clandestine groups which both compensate for and reveal a hatred of official society. He points out that these adult groups can become "delinquent communities" but that this form of "marginal heroism" has appealed to "centurions" and "mercenaries" throughout French history (396–97).
15. The La Touche daughters reject the rigid moral standards of their father in *The Bugles Blowing*, and in *Sabine* Gerard does not respond

to his parents' dedication to the patrimony at either the personal or the national level. In *Castang's City* Thierry Marcel never succeeds in establishing his position within the Marcel family and seeks to compensate for his "loss" by joining Maresq's sect. *Dressing of Diamond* shows that Marie-Thérèse's anomalous position, caught between the worlds of the rural peasantry and the Parisian lower classes, causes her to strike out at what is for her a logical target – a close-knit, successful family. Laetitia Toth's fascination with sex and violence in *The Night Lords* seems to be ascribed to her "gypsy" origins, the union of a French mother and a Malaysian father; as an orphan, she, too, strikes out at a successful family, the Armitages.

16. While Hall and his co-authors limit their discussion to Britain in the 1970s, their claims regarding the role of the family can clearly be generalized to contemporary Western societies.

17. The Armitage-Castang exchange sounds very like the platform articulated by the British Conservative Party in 1977, one year before the publication of *The Night Lords*. In *The Right Approach*, the Tories indicate that "what we have to set out, and it is in the mainstream of Conservatism for us to do so, is a political philosophy that goes beyond the State and the individual, and begins to express in human terms the complex network of reciprocal rights and duties in an orderly society" (quoted in Clarke, "Television Police Series" 54). Clarke argues that the "moral entrepreneurs of the New Right" reveal here "a long term strategy aimed at securing a new hegemony on the revived morality of individualism" (53–54). He goes on to claim that the struggle between the responsibility of the individual and that of the state is worked out in television police series which foreground the tension between official methods of solving crime and unofficial, extra-legal enterprise (56–57). This is precisely the direction Freeling takes in the later novels in the Castang series, and his familiarity with British political debates can reasonably be assumed.

18. Jameson uses *The Godfather* as an example of the way in which mass culture can at times protect the dominant ideology from attack: "the Mafia can be understood . . . as the substitution of crime for big business, as the strategic displacement of all the rage generated by the American system onto this mirror-image of big business provided by the movie screen and the various tv series . . . ." This narrative insists that "the deterioration of daily life in the United States today is an ethical rather than an economic matter, connected, not with profit, but rather 'merely' with dishonesty, and with some omnipresent moral corruption whose ultimate mythic source lies in the pure Evil of the Mafiosi themselves." Such a narrative also proposes a "Utopian" or "fantasy message" as well – "the family itself, seen as a figure of collectivity and as the object of a Utopian longing, if not a Utopian envy" ("Reification" 146). Homberger makes a similar point about the compensatory family with regard to le Carré's *The Little Drummer Girl* and *A Perfect Spy* (90).

19. George Dove contends that the discussion of "family" is a recurring

theme in the police procedural generally. For Dove, however, the family functions as a "frame of reference" which concretizes the threat to society represented by crime (*Procedural* 84). Rather than using the families of policemen as background material, Freeling emphasizes both police and non-police families as parts of the larger social system of control.

20. Freeling perhaps also has in mind another traitorous organization, the Charlemagne division, composed of Frenchmen who served under the SS in World War II on the Eastern front.

21. Freeling's location of the Martindale-Sevenhampton conspiracy in England confirms that the crisis in discipline he describes is endemic in advanced Western capitalism.

22. In his portrait of the Gaboriau-Moustier family, Freeling might be accused of reducing "the definition of the environment from one embracing the hidden mechanisms of housing, poverty and race to one involving simply the surface appearance of dirt and dereliction," thus suppressing "the possible mediations between environment and crime." By displacing larger social ties onto "biographical pieces," Freeling avoids having to develop the complex relationships between "the deteriorated physical environment, patterns of cultural organisation and individual acts of crime . . . . " Instead, he appears to rely on his reader's making "the inference . . . that a derelict and neglected house or street infects the inhabitants with a kind of moral pollution" (Hall *et al.* 115). Thus, although he makes clear that the conflict between the Gaboriau-Moustier clan and the Delavigne family is rooted in class antagonism, he does not go as far as Sjöwall and Wahlöö in exploring the structural sources of the crime.

23. The fact that, due to his position within his class and the English judicial system, he will be treated with great leniency for the crime to which he confessed in the Jesuit garden suggests a "jesuitical" logic within the "simplicity" of the Code itself.

24. In *The Bugles Blowing* Freeling describes the interrogation room at police headquarters as a "convent parlor" where the nuns have been replaced by detainees and religious artifacts have been superseded by "a forbidding portrait of the General" (63).

25. Freeling traces the institution of counter-balancing police forces back to Napoleon who "had had a healthy distrust of conspiracies while he was away, and distrusted his Minister of Police more than anyone else" (NL 61). This same heritage of Napoleonic "distrust" that marks the larger judicial system is reproduced in the hierarchy of French police forces whose purviews are, theoretically, strictly defined in order to assuage popular fears of police abuse. The police are thus organized in a compartmentalized fashion within the highly centralized State.

26. Erikson, of course, would see these examples of surveillance as part of the larger social system of "boundary maintenance" which necessarily begins at the private level, well before official intervention can occur.

27. Donzelot argues that, beginning in the late nineteenth century,

"What was at issue ... was the transition from a government of families to a government through the family." In order "to achieve the maximum harmony between the principle of family authority ... and the procedures of socialization of its members," the "tutelary complex" comes into being: " ... within this double network of social guardians and technicians, the family appears as though colonized" and the "concentric circles" of "tutelary authority" finally destroy patriarchal authority (92–103). Although Donzelot emphasizes the decline of familial power, it is obvious that in Freeling's novels the family and the state can still work together, although the state is gaining the upper hand.

28. It is interesting to note that by the time of *Castang's City* Freeling has included a woman in the ranks of those who have become official agents of surveillance; while Vera continues the tradition established by Arlette in the Van der Valk series, as the embodiment of a feminine intuition which penetrates private defenses outside the bureaucracy (Shloss 170), Liliane's intuition has been co-opted into the service of the State. Shloss's conclusion that the Van der Valk series revalidates the feminine through Arlette's actions in *Auprès de ma Blonde* is thus undercut here by a potentially troubling development, Liliane's full integration into the ranks of the *police judiciaire*.

29. Freeling repeats here a sequence from the Van der Valk series, the Peeping Tom incident at the end of *Double Barrel*, which also raises questions of integrity for the protagonist.

30. Shloss notes that in the Van der Valk series the detective occasionally disguises himself to forestall the "fear and resistance" of the citizenry: "These methods are condoned or even initiated by the police bureau; it is common knowledge that the police operate in the face of suspicion and hostility" (164). Shloss uses her discussion of disguise to talk about Van der Valk's conformity to the methods that are required of him; we are interested, rather, in the very different tone that disguise scenes take in the Castang series.

31. For a discussion of the thriller formula, see Palmer (especially 82–89).

32. Such a description is applicable to Freeling's own thriller, *Gadget*, for example.

33. Homberger finds a similar tension in the works of le Carré who explores "the political dilemmas of post-imperial Britain": "The state and the claims it makes upon the consciences of its servants and victims are traditionally the terrain of the liberal novelist, and are le Carré's ultimate subject" (14).

34. Similar metaphors appear, for example, in *Castang's City*. There Castang refers to his work as stirring up "the compost heap" with "his pointed stick" (20) and, later, makes an analogy between policemen and sewer cleaners (305). These descriptions do a good deal more than define police work as a "dirty job," of course; they suggest that its sphere of influence is that criminal stratum of society labelled as "human waste." Such a classification is central to the

typical police procedural since it ensures reader identification with the protagonists intent upon defending society from the spreading stain of crime. It establishes the "us versus them" paradigm, with "us" always victorious. However, as Sjöwall and Wahlöö have shown, such a traditional formulation can in fact be transformed to deny that the "real" criminals within a society are the "lower" strata and to redefine them as, for example, those who profit from the misery produced by governing social structures.

35. The identification of the reader with the police in procedurals is the culmination of a shifting narrative center in detective fiction. In Golden Age novels, for example, the reader is provided with a surrogate in the form of a Watson-like narrator who demystifies the textual world while simultaneously contributing to the mythic stature of the brilliant Great Detective. The hard-boiled insistence on the protagonist as an "ordinary guy," coupled with the presence of first-person narration, is much closer to the procedural's method, but the return to third-person narration implies a more "objective" narrative that ought to provide the reader with the "safe" distance from the criminal world. Freeling seems to be aware of the naturalizing tendencies in contemporary detective fiction and exploits indirect quotation (*style indirect libre*) in order to draw the reader into the investigation. He thus suppresses narrative distance stylistically.

36. It is interesting to note that in his Castang series Freeling comes to ask questions about the efficacy of restoring order to a corrupt state which are strikingly similar to those raised by Dashiell Hammett in hard-boiled novels like *The Glass Key* and *Red Harvest*. Freeling's foregrounding of the police makes Hammett's "unofficial" approach overtly political.

37. Castang's reference to "botanising" recalls, for example, Rousseau's endeavors in Switzerland. He assumed that Nature was ordered according to divine laws which were ultimately comprehensible by human intelligence.

CHAPTER 6   IMPERFECT INVIGILATION

1. The novels in van de Wetering's Grijpstra and de Gier series are: *Outsider in Amsterdam*, 1975 (OA); *Tumbleweed*, 1976 (T); *The Corpse on the Dike*, 1976 (CD); *Death of a Hawker*, 1977 (DH); *The Japanese Corpse*, 1977 (JC); *The Blond Baboon*, 1978 (BB); *The Maine Massacre*, 1979 (MA); *The Mind-Murders*, 1981 (MI); *The Streetbird*, 1983 (S); *The Rattle-Rat*, 1985 (RR); *Hard Rain*, 1986 (HR).

2. Although Michielsen carefully catalogs the descriptive aspects of Amsterdam employed by van de Wetering, he sees the relationship between physical architecture and social reality as unproblematic: "The author is skillful at evoking both the beauty and the richness of the life in the city that is admired by those who visit it and live in it, and miserable lives of some of the inhabitants with whom the

3. police come into contact. The acceptance of both of these aspects and the juxtaposition of the ugliness and the crimes committed within these surroundings is one important factor in his novels" (47).
3. This sequence is followed by references to apocalyptic scenes from the "Mad Max" movie series, further underlining the desperate straits in which, according to Griipstra and de Gier, Holland currently finds itself.
4. Bagley points out that deference to social and governmental authority is a crucial guarantor of social stability in the Netherlands. The characteristics of parent-child relationships (respect for authority, kindness and love) are reproduced in the society at large, where obedience is rewarded with integration (20–29). The commissaris' position within the squad is thus that of loving but stern patriarch.
5. The Cat is so nicknamed because he resembles a lion, since the seventeenth century the symbol of the Netherlands state (CD 72).
6. In both *The Japanese Corpse* and *The Maine Massacre*, books which take the commissaris and de Gier out of the Netherlands, the connections between villainy and commerce remain important. In the former, in particular, the daimyos simultaneously rule both "the big companies" and the yakusa, the Japanese mafia (JC 21).
7. Throughout the series van de Wetering insists upon the commissaris' service in the Resistance during World War II. This biographical note automatically elevates the commissaris to a "higher" moral plane since, as Punch points out, the reputation of the Amsterdam police generally has suffered as a result of their collaboration with the Nazis: "The Dutch police were inextricably involved in enforcement with the Nazi occupiers and, in a city like Amsterdam which was a major Jewish city before the war, this has left a legacy of distrust . . . " (*Conduct* 6). In *Death of a Hawker* Louis Zilver makes explicit the widely held distrust of the police, and it is only the commissaris' anti-Nazi past which leads Zilver to cooperate, ultimately saving the commissaris' life (DH 36–37; 213–14). See also CD 11; S 82; and RR 39.
8. Fernandus is, of course, the ultimate "false father," since he engineers the murder of his own son.
9. Simon Schama, quoting Paul Claudel's essay on *The Night Watch*, notes that the anachronistic quality of this painting and other militia pieces represents the disintegration of the group, a "setting-off and a coming-apart" that is itself symbolic of the Dutch "state of organic flux, forever composing, decomposing and recomposing itself" (11).
10. The fact that his drum set comes from the lost property department may well be an ironic confirmation of the devolution van de Wetering anatomizes.
11. Bagley's work, of course, builds on Goudsblom's earlier study of Dutch culture.
12. In *The Japanese Corpse* the commissaris notes explicitly that "'The laws we defend were religious once, in origin anyway'" (90).
13. The fact that throughout the scene Karate is dressed in drag so

Notes to pp. 173–180   223

that he will "fit in" with the *outré* appearance and behavior of the
Quarter's regular denizens links van de Wetering's purpose here to
the social critique of Sjöwall and Wahlöö. The latter use the antics
of Kristiansson and Kvant to undercut the whole policing enterprise
in Sweden which they see as a tool of oppressive State power.

14. This conversation takes place in the commissaris' back garden as
Turtle, the commissaris' pet, wanders through the weeds. In Dutch
emblem books, the turtle is traditionally associated with morality
(Schama 389). During the conversation about Jurriaans, however,
the policemen are free to talk precisely because "'Turtle isn't really
interested'" (S 244).

15. Clearly, the "stable Dutch deviant community" that was the red-light
district in Amsterdam has evolved into a "plural cultural and ethnic
melting-pot with a predatory criminal element": "Initially informal
policies led to the creation of a normative ghetto where deviance
could flourish and where accommodation was reached between
police and underworld in the interests of regulating social life in the
area. This segregation, which was somewhat hypocritically sold to
the outside world as an indication of 'tolerance' . . . began to break
down when a combination of factors . . . fundamentally altered
the character of the area" (Punch, *Policing* 186). Just as Jurriaans,
therefore, found it necessary to challenge Luku Obrian for "control"
of the Quarter, so, too, do contemporary Amsterdam policemen rely
upon Surinamers as "ideal scapegoats for the 'decline' of the area"
(Punch, *Policing* 188).

16. Goudsblom notes that, while one's place of residence in the Netherlands is declining in importance, there are still "at least three major
dividing lines splitting the Dutch population into distinct social
categories: the 'West-rest,' the North-South, and the urban-rural
divisions" (58). Since the mid-1960s Amsterdam in particular has
come to be known as a "'troublesome city' and the Amsterdam
police as a problem-ridden force" (Punch, *Policing* 33). Interestingly
enough, among the inner-city policemen themselves an "anti-public"
attitude has developed, particularly in regard to the "archetypal
Amsterdammer, who [is] held to be volubly and spontaneously
against authority." Of course, this apparently anomalous attitude
has its real roots in "the fact that many policemen [are] not
themselves from Amsterdam" (Punch, *Policing* 124). See also Punch,
Conduct 59.

17. The Ary-Fritz story line is, of course, reminiscent of police overkill
of the sort dramatized by Sjöwall and Wahlöö in *The Abominable
Man*. Punch notes that "the Dutch Police is moving towards a
substantial reorganisation along familiar lines – more technology,
larger units, more specialised and centralised groups, and so on –
with the primary purpose of increasing 'efficiency' . . . and . . . this
reflects developments elsewhere where preoccupation with means
has obscured the classification of ends" (*Policing* 181). Van de
Wetering's Arrest Teams are thus a comic version of Sjöwall and
Wahlöö's far more vicious, space-age robocops.

18. Both the parodic elements of *The Rattle-Rat* and the Oppenhuyzen-heroin-Chinese plot confirm that van de Wetering is "keeping up" with events in the Amsterdam police department. Maurice Punch's study, *Conduct Unbecoming* (1985), details a major police scandal which the press chronicled in the late 1970s. The corruption which was uncovered had its roots in the heroin trade, presided over by powerful Chinese triads. Punch shows that relatively minor graft (the occasional pay-off to allow a Chinese gambling establishment to continue operating) grew to major proportions with the arrival of lucrative Asian heroin in 1972. He suggests that the press was so interested in detailing this scandal precisely because it was connected to the wave of concern over hard drugs and Amsterdam's place as a major international transshipment point. Ultimately, though, little was done to excise the corruption at a systemic level. Scapegoats were prosecuted, but police and government overseers joined forces to limit the damage. Van de Wetering's handling of this affair, in ways which quite accurately reproduce the events (though several years after the fact), reconfirms that popular forms like the police procedural must necessarily be seen as interventions in ongoing debates within the cultures which produce them. Although van de Wetering insists that he is not writing with a moral purpose (Filstrup 100; Cooper-Clark 153), he inevitably produces texts which confront and mediate moral concerns. Thus it seems logical to assume that distress at governmental complacency must have been one of van de Wetering's motives in writing a novel like *The Rattle-Rat* which quite literally explodes the myths of the new, hi-tech police of the Netherlands.
19. As we have seen, Nicolas Freeling evokes specific episodes from the pan-European colonial past to provide a broader perspective on post-war European history. Van de Wetering, on the other hand, seeks "depth" rather than "breadth": he uses the Other to probe a specifically Dutch national character.
20. That van de Wetering should be sensitive to interactions between cultures is only logical given his peripatetic life. For biographical information on van de Wetering, see Filstrup, Cooper-Clark, and Schultze.
21. The race of the hash dealers is actually a bit uncertain though the context suggests they are black. If in fact they are white, then van de Wetering seems to be claiming that the "outside," the source of the hashish, has corrupted the "inside" of Dutch society, making it "evil" and hence "black." His presentation of race remains problematic in either case.
22. In 1973 Bagley argued that "Immigrants to the Netherlands from Indonesia, and from Surinam and the Antilles are strongly oriented to the 'motherland'. They are loyal to her institutions, they speak her language, they share her national sentiments" (225). Van de Wetering's picture of Luku Obrian accords with more recent scholarship on immigrants to the Netherlands. While, as we have seen, the Papuan van Meteren conforms to the image of the "loyal

subject" because he is a "brown Dutchman" who shares the cultural values of the Netherlands, the Surinamer Obrian demonstrates the more complicated, post-1975 immigration patterns (see Oostindie 67; Reubsaet 109–17; Koot and Venema 194–202; and Rath 267).

23 As with the plot of *The Rattle-Rat* discussed earlier, it seems clear that elements of *The Streetbird* are drawn from the same corruption scandal detailed by Punch in *Conduct Unbecoming*. The identification of Jurriaans' station with the precinct in the Warmoesstraat (the site of much of the 1970s scandal) is surely no accident, and the fact that it is the most powerful policeman of the Quarter who is the murderer must be read as van de Wetering's commentary on the whole sordid affair. For a fuller discussion of the Quarter in Amsterdam, see Punch, *Policing the Inner City*.

24. Opete, on the other hand, is finally banded by Grijpstra with a miniature Dutch flag, evidence that he has been "integrated" into Dutch culture (S 152). In fact, he helps lead the squad to the murderer.

25. Recent information on drug-related crime in the Netherlands indicates, however, that the problem is no longer as serious as van de Wetering suggests. The decriminalization of marijuana and hashish has not led to a crime wave, for example. In 1985 the Ministry of Justice likewise ordered the police not to use their strong powers to enforce laws against hard drugs; the result has been an increase in the number of junkies seeking institutional help and a decrease in dealer-related crime (see "War" 50).

26. Schama notes that "the arms of Holland bore the device of a lion rampant, guarding a fertile, fenced garden. His sword remained raised, but how to wield it with dexterity and virtue remained the problem of the lay guardians of the new Israel. Solomon had to remain wise, Josiah pure and Hezekiah repentant – or else the citadel and the temple within it would be razed" (48). It is tempting to see van de Wetering's squad as a latter-day incarnation of the "lay guardians," not only because each member suggests Schama's description, but because the series articulates the same dilemma.

Select Bibliography

Adam, Heribert and Kogila Moodley. *South Africa Without Apartheid: Dismantling Racial Domination.* Berkeley: University of California Press, 1986.
Andreski, Stanislav. "Reflections on the South African Social Order from a Comparative Viewpoint." *South Africa: Sociological Perspectives.* Ed. Heribert Adam. London: Oxford University Press, 1971. 24–36.
Babener, Liahna K. "California Babylon: The World of American Detective Fiction." *Clues* 1:2 (1980): 77–89.
Back, Pär-Erik. "How Sweden is Governed." *Sweden in the Sixties.* Ed. Ingemar Wizelius. Trans. Rudy Feichtner. Stockholm: Almqvist & Wiksell, 1967. 49–71.
Bagley, Christopher. *The Dutch Plural Society: A Comparative Study in Race Relations.* Published for the Institute of Race Relations, London, by London: Oxford University Press, 1973.
Bailey, O. L. "On the Docket." *The Saturday Review* 28 October 1972: 84; 89.
Bakerman, Jane S. "Arlette: Nicholas [sic] Freeling's Candle Against the Dark." *The Armchair Detective* 16:4 (1983): 348–53.
Baudelaire, Charles. *Oeuvres complètes.* Ed. Claude Pichois. Vol. 1. Paris: Gallimard, 1975. 2 vols.
Becker, Jens Peter. "The Mean Streets of Europe: The Influence of the American 'Hard-Boiled School' on European Detective Fiction." Trans. Ian E. Oliver. *Superculture: American Popular Culture and Europe.* Ed. C. W. Bigsby. Bowling Green, OH: Bowling Green University Popular Press, 1975. 152–9.
Blom, K. Arne. "Polis! Polis!." *Murder Ink: The Mystery Reader's Companion.* Ed. Dilys Winn. New York: Workman Publishing, 1977. 334–5.
Boucher, Anthony. "Criminals at Large." *New York Times* 27 November 1966, VII: 64.
Broyard, Anatole. "A Crime Against the Reader." *New York Times* 19 July 1972: 35.
Callendar, Newgate. "Criminals at Large." *The New York Times Book Review* 1 September 1974: 14.
———, "Criminals at Large." *The New York Times Book Review* 1 February 1981: 31.
Cawelti, John G. *Adventure, Mystery, and Romance: Formula Stories as Art and Popular Culture.* Chicago: University of Chicago Press, 1976.
———, "Chinatown and Generic Transformation in Recent American Films." *Film Theory and Criticism.* Eds. Gerald Mast and Marshall Cohen. 2nd edn. New York: Oxford University Press, 1979. 559–79.
Chandler, Raymond. *The Big Sleep.* 1939. New York: Vintage Books, 1976.
———, "The Simple Art of Murder." 1944. Rpt. in *The Simple Art of Murder.* 1950. New York: Ballantine, 1972. 1–21.

Charney, Hanna. *The Detective Novel of Manners: Hedonism, Morality, and the Life of Reason*. Rutherford, NJ: Fairleigh Dickinson University Press, 1981.
Childs, Marquis W. *Sweden: The Middle Way on Trial*. New Haven: Yale University Press, 1980.
Clarke, Alan. "Television Police Series and Law and Order." *Politics, Ideology and Popular Culture (2)*. Milton Keynes: Open University Press, 1982. 37–57.
Cooper-Clark, Diana. "Interview with Janwillem van de Wetering." *Designs of Darkness*. Bowling Green, OH: Bowling Green University Popular Press, 1983. 145–57.
Crapanzano, Vincent. *Waiting: The Whites of South Africa*. New York: Random House, 1985.
Cross, Malcolm and Hans Entzinger. "Caribbean Minorities in Britain and in the Netherlands." *Lost Illusions: Caribbean Minorities in Britain and the Netherlands*. Eds. Malcolm Cross and Hans Entzinger. London: Routledge, 1988. 1–33.
Donzelot, Jacques. *The Policing of Families*. 1977. Trans. Robert Hurley. New York: Pantheon, 1979.
Dove, George. *The Boys from Grover Avenue*. Bowling Green, OH: Bowling Green University Popular Press, 1985.
———, *The Police Procedural*. Bowling Green, OH: Bowling Green University Popular Press, 1982.
Duffy, Martha. "Martin Beck Passes." *Time* 11 August 1975: 58–9.
Durham, Philip. *Down These Mean Streets a Man Must Go: Raymond Chandler's Knight*. Chapel Hill: University of North Carolina Press, 1963.
Eisenzweig, Uri. *Le Récit impossible: forme et sens du roman policier*. Paris: Christian Bourgois Editeur, 1986.
Elvander, Nils. "Democracy and Large Organizations." *Politics in the Post-Welfare State: Responses to the New Individualism*. Eds. M. Donald Hancock and Gideon Sjoberg. New York: Columbia University Press, 1972. 302–24.
Erikson, Kai T. *Wayward Puritans: A Study of the Sociology of Deviance*. New York: John Wiley, 1966.
Filstrup, Chris and Janie. "An Interview with a Black Sheep of Amsterdam." *The Armchair Detective* 13:2 (1980): 98–107.
Fleisher, Wilfrid. *Sweden: The Welfare State*. Westport: Greenwood Press, 1956.
Foote, Timothy. "Once More with Freeling." *Time* 31 July 1972: 59.
Foucault, Michel. *Discipline and Punish: The Birth of the Prison*. 1975. Trans. Alan Sheridan. New York: Vintage, 1979.
Freeling, Nicolas. *Arlette*. 1981. New York: Vintage, 1982.
———, *Auprès de ma Blonde*. 1972. New York: Vintage, 1979.
———, *The Back of the North Wind*. 1983. Harmondsworth: Penguin, 1984.
———, *Because of the Cats*. 1963. Harmondsworth: Penguin, 1965.
———, *The Bugles Blowing*. 1975. New York: Vintage, 1980.
———, *Castang's City*. 1980. New York: Vintage, 1981.
———, *Criminal Conversation*. 1966. New York: Ballantine, 1967.
———, *Death in Amsterdam*. (originally *Love in Amsterdam*.) 1962. New York:

Ballantine, 1964.
———, *Double Barrel*. 1964. New York: Vintage, 1981.
———, *Dressing of Diamond*. 1974. Harmondsworth: Penguin, 1976.
———, *Gadget*. 1977. Harmondsworth: Penguin, 1979.
———, *Gun Before Butter*. 1963. New York: Vintage, 1982.
———, "Inspector Van der Valk." *The Great Detectives*. Ed. Otto Penzler. Boston: Little, Brown, 1978. 249–57.
———, *The King of the Rainy Country*. 1965. Harmondsworth: Penguin, 1968.
———, *The Lovely Ladies*. 1971. New York: Vintage, 1981.
———, *The Night Lords*. 1978. New York: Vintage, 1980.
———, *No Part in Your Death*. New York: Viking, 1984.
———, *Sabine*. (originally *Lake Isle*.) 1976. New York: Harper & Row, 1976.
———, *Sand Castles*. New York: The Mysterious Press, 1990.
———, *Strike Out Where Not Applicable*. 1967. Harmondsworth: Penguin, 1969.
———, *Tsing-Boom!*. 1969. New York: Ballantine, 1971.
———, *The Widow*. 1979. New York: Vintage, 1980.
———, *Wolfnight*. 1982. New York: Vintage, 1983.
Garson, N. G. "English-Speaking South Africans and the British Connection: 1829–1961." *English-Speaking South Africa Today: Proceedings of the National Conference, July 1974*. Ed. André de Villiers. Cape Town: Oxford University Press, 1976. 17–39.
Gordimer, Nadine. *July's People*. 1981. Harmondsworth: Penguin, 1982.
———, "Living in the Interregnum." *The New York Review of Books* 20 January 1983: 21–8.
Goudsblom, Johan. *Dutch Society*. New York: Random House, 1967.
Grella, George. "Murder and Manners: The Formal Detective Novel." *Novel* 4 (1970): 30–48. Rpt. in *Dimensions of Detective Fiction*. Eds. Larry Landrum, Pat Browne, and Ray Browne. Bowling Green, OH: Bowling Green University Popular Press, 1976. 37–57.
———, "Murder and the Mean Streets: The Hard-Boiled Detective Novel." *Contempora* 1 (1970): 6–15. Rpt. as "The Hard-Boiled Detective Novel." *Detective Fiction: A Collection of Critical Essays*. Ed. Robin W. Winks. Englewood Cliffs: Prentice-Hall, 1980. 103–20.
Gyllensten, Lars. "Swedish Radicalism in the 1960s: An Experiment in Political and Cultural Debate." *Politics in the Post-Welfare State: Responses to the New Individualism*. Eds. M. Donald Hancock and Gideon Sjoberg. New York: Columbia University Press, 1972. 279–301.
Hall, Stuart, Chas Critcher, Tony Jefferson, John Clarke, and Brian Roberts. *Policing the Crisis: Mugging, The State, and Law and Order*. London: Macmillan, 1978.
Hancock, M. Donald. "Post-Welfare Modernization in Sweden: The Quest for Cumulative Rationality and Equality." *Politics in the Post-Welfare State: Response to the New Individualism*. Ed. M. Donald Hancock and Gideon Sjoberg. New York: Columbia University Press, 1972. 223–45.
———, *Sweden: The Politics of Postindustrial Change*. Hinsdale, IL: Dryden, 1972.
Haverkamp-Begemann, E. *Rembrandt: The Nightwatch*. Princeton: Princeton University Press, 1982.

Hellman, Ellen. "Social Change among Urban Africans." *South Africa: Sociological Perspectives*. Ed. Heribert Adam. London: Oxford University Press, 1971. 158–76.
Himes, Chester. *Blind Man With a Pistol*. New York: William Morrow, 1969.
———, *The Crazy Kill*. 1959. Chatham, NJ: Chatham Booksellers, 1973.
Homberger, Eric. *John Le Carré*. New York: Methuen, 1986.
Hulley, Kathleen. "From the Crystal Sphere to *Edge City*: Ideology in the Novels of Dashiell Hammett." *Myth and Ideology in American Culture*. Lille: Pub. de l'Univ. de Lille III, 1976. 111–27.
Isaac, Fred. "Black and White and Dead: James McClure's South Africa." *The Mystery FANcier* 6:4 (1982): 12–18.
Isaac, Frederick. "The Changing Face of Evil in the Hard-Boiled Novel." *The Armchair Detective* 16:3 (1983): 241–7.
Jameson, Fredric. *The Political Unconscious: Narrative as a Socially Symbolic Act*. Ithaca: Cornell University Press, 1981.
———, "Postmodernism, or The Cultural Logic of Late Capitalism." *New Left Review* July–August 1984: 53–92.
———, "Reification and Utopia in Mass Culture." *Social Text* 1:1 (1979): 130–48.
Jenny, Laurent. "La Stratégie de la forme." *Poétique* 27 (1976): 257–81. Rpt. in *French Literary Theory Today*. Ed. Tzvetan Todorov. Paris: Maison des sciences de l'homme; London: Cambridge University Press, 1982. 34–63.
Joseph, Isaac et al., *Disciplines à Domicile*. Fontenay-sous-Bois: Recherches, 1977.
Koot, Willem and Petrien Uniken Venema. "Education: The Way Up for Surinamese in the Netherlands?" *Lost Illusions: Caribbean Minorities in Britain and the Netherlands*. Eds. Malcolm Cross and Hans Entzinger. London: Routledge, 1988. 185–203.
Leatt, James, Theo Kneifel, and Klaus Nurnberger. *Contending Ideologies in South Africa*. Cape Town and Johannesburg: David Philip, 1986.
Lelyveld, Joseph. *Move Your Shadow*. New York: Times Books, Random House, 1985.
Lesser, Wendy. "Kungsholmsgatan Blues." *The Threepenny Review*. Summer, 1983: 18–19.
Lewin, Leif. "The Debate on Economic Planning in Sweden." *Sweden's Development from Poverty to Affluence, 1750–1970*. Ed. Steven Koblik. Trans. Joanne Johnson. Minneapolis: University of Minnesota Press, 1975. 282–302.
Lijphart, Arend. *The Politics of Accommodation: Pluralism and Democracy in The Netherlands*. Berkeley: University of California Press, 1968.
———, *The Trauma of Decolonialization: The Dutch and West New Guinea*. New Haven: Yale University Press, 1966.
Lundin, Bo. "Wahlöö, Per (1926–75), and Maj Sjöwall (1935)." *Twentieth-Century Crime and Mystery Writers*. Ed. John M. Reilly. New York: St. Martin's, 1980. 1553–4.
Mahan, Jeffrey H. "The Hard-Boiled Detective in the Fallen World." *Clues* 1:2 (1980): 90–9.

Mandel, Ernest. *Delightful Murder: A Social History of the Crime Story*. Minneapolis: University of Minnesota Press, 1984.
Marshment, Margaret. "Racist Ideology and Popular Fiction." *Race & Class* 19:4 (1978): 331-44.
Mathews, A.S. "Security Laws and Social Change in the Republic of South Africa." *South Africa: Sociological Perspectives*. Ed. Heribert Adam. London: Oxford University Press, 1971. 228-48.
Maxfield, James F. "The Collective Detective Hero: The Police Novels of Maj Sjöwall and Per Wahlöö." *Clues* 3:1 (1982): 70-9.
McBain, Ed. "The 87th Precinct." *The Great Detectives*. Ed. Otto Penzler. New York: Little, Brown, 1978. 89-97.
McClure, James. *The Artful Egg*. 1984. New York: Pantheon, 1986.
——, *The Blood of an Englishman*. 1980. New York: Pantheon, 1982.
——, *The Caterpillar Cop*. 1972. New York: Pantheon, 1982.
——, *The Gooseberry Fool*. 1974. New York: Pantheon, 1983.
——, *Snake*. 1975. New York: Pantheon, 1984.
——, *The Steam Pig*. 1971. New York: Pantheon, 1982.
——, *The Sunday Hangman*. 1977. New York: Pantheon, 1984.
Michielsen, John. "Van de Wetering's Amsterdam." *Clues* 7:1 (1986): 39-48.
Miller, J. Hillis. *Fiction and Repetition: Seven English Novels*. Cambridge: Harvard University Press, 1982.
Occhiogrosso, Frank. "The Police in Society: The Novels of Maj Sjöwall and Per Wahlöö." *The Armchair Detective* 12:2 (1979): 174-7.
"One Man's Mote." *Times Literary Supplement* 20 January 1966: 37.
Oostindie, Gert J. "Caribbean Migration to the Netherlands: A Journey to Disappointment?" *Lost Illusions: Caribbean Minorities in Britain and the Netherlands*. Eds. Malcolm Cross and Hans Entzinger. London: Routledge, 1988. 54-72.
Palmer, Jerry. *Thrillers: Genesis and Structure of a Popular Genre*. New York: St. Martin's, 1979.
Panek, Leroy Lad. *Watteau's Shepherds: The Detective Novel in Britain, 1914-1940*. Bowling Green, OH: Bowling Green University Popular Press, 1979.
Peyrefitte, Alain. *Le Mal Français*. Paris: Plon, 1976.
"Popular Culture and Hegemony in Post-War Britain." *Politics, Ideology and Popular Culture (1)*. Milton Keynes: Open University Press, 1982. 7-29.
Porter, Dennis. *The Pursuit of Crime: Art and Ideology in Detective Fiction*. New Haven: Yale University Press, 1981.
Punch, Maurice. *Conduct Unbecoming: The Social Construction of Police Deviance and Control*. London: Tavistock, 1985.
——, *Policing the Inner City: A Study of Amsterdam's Warmoesstraat*. London: Macmillan, 1979.
Rabinowitz, Peter J. "Rats Behind the Wainscoting: Politics, Convention, and Chandler's *The Big Sleep*." *Texas Studies in Literature and Language* 22:2 (1980): 224-45.
Rath, Jan. "Mobilization of Ethnicity in Dutch Politics." *Lost Illusions: Caribbean Minorities in Britain and the Netherlands*. Eds. Malcolm Cross and Hans Entzinger. London: Routledge, 1988. 267-84.

Select Bibliography

Ravenscroft, Arthur. "South African English Literature." *English-Speaking South Africa Today: Proceedings of the National Conference, July 1974.* Ed. André de Villiers. Cape Town: Oxford University Press, 1976. 317–29.

Reilly, John M. "Classic and Hard-Boiled Detective Fiction." *The Armchair Detective* 9:4 (1976): 289–91; 334.

Reeves, Richard. "The Palme Obsession." *New York Times Sunday Magazine* 1 March 1987: 20–28, 56, 82.

Reubsaet, Theo. "On the Way Up? Surinamese and Antilleans in the Dutch Labour Market." *Lost Illusions: Caribbean Minorities in Britain and the Netherlands.* Eds. Malcolm Cross and Hans Entzinger. London: Routledge, 1988. 106–125.

Sachs, Albie. *Justice in South Africa.* Berkeley: University of California Press, 1973.

Samuelsson, Kurt. "The Philosophy of Swedish Welfare Policies." *Sweden's Development From Poverty To Affluence, 1750–1970.* Ed. Steven Koblik. Trans. Joanne Johnson. Minneapolis: University of Minnesota Press, 1975. 335–53.

Schama, Simon. *The Embarrassment of Riches.* New York: Knopf, 1987.

Schleh, Eugene. "Spotlight on South Africa: The Police Novels of James McClure." *Clues* 7:2 (1986): 99–107.

Schlemmer, Lawrence. "English-Speaking South Africans Today: Identity and Integration into the Broader National Community." *English-Speaking South Africa Today: Proceedings of the National Conference, July 1974.* Ed. André de Villiers. Cape Town: Oxford University Press, 1976. 91–135.

Schultze, Sydney. "Zen and the Art of Mystery Writing: The Novels of Janwillem van de Wetering." *The Armchair Detective* 18:1 (1984): 20–31.

Shannon, Dell [Elizabeth Linnington]. "Lieutenant Luis Mendoza." *The Great Detectives.* Ed. Otto Penzler. New York: Little, Brown, 1978. 149–53.

Shloss, Carol. "The Van der Valk Novels of Nicolas Freeling: Going by the Book." *Art in Crime Writing: Essays on Detective Fiction.* Ed. Bernard Benstock. New York: St. Martin's, 1983. 159–73.

Sjöwall, Maj, and Per Wahlöö. *The Abominable Man.* Trans. Thomas Teal. 1971. New York: Vintage, 1980.

——, *Cop Killer.* Trans. Thomas Teal. 1974. New York: Vintage, 1978.

——, *The Fire Engine That Disappeared.* Trans. Joan Tate. 1969. New York: Vintage, 1977.

——, *The Laughing Policeman.* Trans. Alan Bair. 1968. New York: Vintage, 1977.

——, *The Locked Room.* Trans. Paul Britten Austin. 1973. New York: Vintage, 1980.

—— *The Man on the Balcony.* Trans. Alan Bair. 1967. New York: Vintage, 1977.

—— *The Man Who Went Up in Smoke.* Trans. Joan Tate. 1966. New York: Vintage, 1976.

——, *Murder at the Savoy.* Trans. Amy and Ken Konespel. 1970. New York: Vintage, 1977.

——, *Roseanna.* Trans. Lois Roth. 1965. New York: Vintage, 1976.

—— *The Terrorists.* Trans. Joan Tate. 1975. New York: Vintage, 1978.

Stromholm, Stig. "The Law and its Administration." *Sweden in the Sixties.*

Ed. Ingemar Wizelius. Trans. Rudy Feichtner. Stockholm: Almqvist & Wiksell, 1967. 95–111.
Wall, Donald C. "The Achievement of James McClure." *Clues* 10:1 (1989): 1–29.
——, "Apartheid in the Novels of James McClure." *The Armchair Detective* 10:4 (1977): 348–351.
——, "An Interview with James McClure." *Clues* 6:2 (1985): 7–25.
"War by Other Means." *The Economist* February 10, 1990.
Welsh, David. "English-Speaking Whites and the Racial Problem." *English-Speaking South Africa Today: Proceedings of the National Conference, July 1974*. Ed. André de Villiers. Cape Town: Oxford University Press, 1976. 217–39.
Wetering, Janwillem van de. *The Blond Baboon*. Boston: Houghton Mifflin, 1978.
——, *The Corpse on the Dike*. 1976. New York: Pocket Books, 1978.
——, *Death of a Hawker*. 1977. New York: Pocket Books, 1978.
——, *Hard Rain*. 1986. New York: Ballantine, 1987.
——, *The Japanese Corpse*. 1977. New York: Pocket Books, 1978.
——, *The Maine Massacre*. Boston: Houghton Mifflin, 1979.
——, *The Mind-Murders*. 1981. New York: Pocket Books, 1983.
——, *Outsider in Amsterdam*. 1975. New York: Ballantine, 1986.
——, *The Rattle-Rat*. 1985. New York: Ballantine, 1986.
——, *The Streetbird*. 1983. New York: Pocket Books, 1985.
——, *Tumbleweed*. 1976. New York: Pocket Books, 1978.
White, Jean M. "Wahlöö/Sjöwall and James McClure." *The New Republic* 31 July 1976: 27–9.
Williams, Thomas E. "Martin Beck: The Swedish Version of Barney Miller Without the Canned Laughter." *Clues* 1:1(1980): 123–8.
Wizelius, Ingemar. "Literature" in "The Arts in Sweden." *Sweden in the Sixties*. Ed. Ingemar Wizelius. Trans. Rudy Feichtner. Stockholm: Almqvist & Wiksell, 1967. 242–5.
Worrall, Dennis. "English South Africa and the Political System." *English-Speaking South Africa Today: Proceedings of the National Conference, July 1974*. Ed. André de Villiers. Cape Town: Oxford University Press, 1976. 193–215.
Wright, Will. *Six Guns and Society: A Structural Study of the Western*. Berkeley: University of California Press, 1975.
Zetterberg, Hans L. "Sweden – A Land of Tomorrow?" *Sweden in the Sixties*. Ed. Ingemar Wizelius. Trans. Rudy Feichtner. Stockholm: Almqvist & Wiksell, 1967. 13–21.

Index

Adam, Heribert and Kogila Moodley 77–9, 84, 88, 203–4 (n. 10), 208 (n. 40), 209 (n. 48)
Andreski, Stanislav 88, 202 (n. 3), 203–4 (n. 10), 204 (n. 15), 206 (n. 23)

Babener, Liahna K. 20, 199 (n. 10)
Back, Pär-Erik 50
Bagley, Christopher 164, 172, 185–7, 192–3, 222 (n. 4), 222 (n. 11), 224–5 (n. 22)
Bailey, O. L. 53
Bakerman, Jane S. 214 (n. 28)
Baudelaire, Charles 103–4, 212 (n. 13)
Becker, Jens Peter 199 (n. 10)
Bentham, Jeremy, see Panopticon
Blom, K. Arne 16–17, 198 (n. 2), 198–9 (n. 4)
Bloom, Harold 212 (n. 12)
Boucher, Anthony 124
Broyard, Anatole 124
Bureaucracy 2, 6–7, 12–13, 16, 28–9, 33–4, 42–6, 94–6, 100–1, 105, 108–10, 112–14, 116–25, 128, 137, 140–1, 145–6, 150–1, 160–1, 179–80

Callendar, Newgate 53–4
Cawelti, John G. 3–5, 101–2, 130–1, 213 (n. 18)
Chandler, Raymond 12, 27, 30–1, 122–3, 125, 199 (n. 10), 211 (n. 8), 212 (n. 12), 215 (n. 32), 215 (n. 35), 215 (n. 36), 216 (n. 39)
  The Big Sleep 102–4, 106–11, 212 (n. 16), 212–3 (n. 17), 213 (n. 18), 213 (n. 21), 213 (n. 23), 215 (n. 32), 215 (n. 35)
  "The Simple Art of Murder" 109–10

Charney, Hanna 197 (n. 3)
Chesterton, G. K. 216 (n. 39)
Childs, Marquis W. 20, 34, 36, 41, 200–1 (n. 24)
Clarke, Alan 7, 15, 40, 150, 160–1, 199 (n. 13), 201 (n. 29), 202 (n. 33), 218 (n. 17)
Cooper-Clark, Diana 224 (n. 18), 224 (n. 20)
Crapanzano, Vincent 52–3, 59–63, 67, 69, 73, 204–5 (n. 16), 205 (n. 17), 206 (n. 25), 207 (n. 37)
Cross, Malcolm and Hans Entzinger 192

Deighton, Len 216 (n. 39)
De Quincey, Thomas 8
Detective fiction, *see* Golden Age detective fiction; hard-boiled detective fiction; police procedural
Deviance 8, 11–12, 33, 40, 46, 94, 99–100, 113, 176–7, 198 (n. 11), 223 (n. 15)
Donzelot, Jacques 127, 130–3, 140, 147, 217 (n. 6), 219–20 (n. 27)
Dove, George
  The Boys from Grover Avenue 198 (n. 12)
  The Police Procedural 9–10, 47, 116, 125, 154–5, 197 (n. 8), 198 (n. 2), 200 (n. 17), 202 (n. 34), 207 (n. 35), 208 (n. 41), 214 (n. 27), 215 (n. 34), 218–19 (n. 19)
Doyle, Sir Arthur Conan 4, 30, 125, 195, 210 (n. 3), 211 (n. 10), 213 (n. 24), 216 (n. 39)
Duffy, Martha 198 (n. 2)
Durham, Philip 197 (n. 5), 213 (n. 18)

Eisenzweig, Uri 3–4, 18, 92–3,

98, 101, 125, 181–2, 198 (n. 10), 210 (n. 5), 211 (n. 10), 211 (n. 11), 213 (n. 24), 215 (n. 33), 215 (n. 34)
Elvander, Nils   29
Entzinger, Hans, *see* Cross, Malcolm and Hans Entzinger
Erikson, Kai T.   99, 198 (n. 11), 211 (n. 9), 219 (n. 26)

Filstrup, Chris and Janie   196, 224 (n. 18), 224 (n. 20)
Fleisher, Wilfrid   34–6, 199 (n. 9), 200 (n. 20), 200 (n. 22)
Fleming, Ian   124–5, 207–8 (n. 38), 213 (n. 22), 216 (n. 39)
Foote, Timothy   124
Foucault, Michel   7–8, 33, 43–6, 51, 54–6, 90, 94, 130, 145–8, 152–3, 162, 200 (n. 23), 217 (n. 11)
Freeling, Nicolas (*see below for* WORKS)
  and Algeria   96–7
  and Amsterdam   105, 112, 117, 120, 212 (n. 15)
  and the *ancien régime*   134, 136–7, 217 (n. 6)
  and bureaucracy   12–13, 94–6, 100–1, 105, 108–9, 112–14, 116–25, 128, 137, 140–1, 145–6, 150–2, 160–1, 214 (n. 26), 214 (n. 29), 217 (n. 12)
  and Calvinism   94, 100, 118
  and the *Code Napoléon*   127–30, 137, 144–7, 162, 219 (n. 23), 219 (n. 25)
  and Dutch bourgeois values   12, 95, 112–14, 119
  and the Dutch judicial system   93–4, 114–16
  and foreigners   93, 97–9, 117
  and the French bourgeois family   13, 130–5, 138–9, 143–5, 157, 216–17 (n. 5), 219 (n. 22), 219–20 (n. 27)
  and the French judiciary   128–9, 131–2
  and the French police   127,
131–2, 135–6, 144–6, 148–9, 152–3, 155–6, 219 (n. 25), 220 (n. 28)
  and Golden Age detective fiction   12, 90–3, 96, 98, 101–2, 109, 126, 130–1, 140, 144, 153–4, 161, 211 (n. 8), 213 (n. 22), 213 (n. 24), 221 (n. 35)
  and hard-boiled detective fiction   12, 90, 101–4, 106–11, 122, 126, 211 (n. 8), 211 (n. 11), 212 (n. 12), 212–13 (n. 17), 213 (n. 22), 215 (n. 36)
  and Indochina   96–8, 113, 211 (n. 6), 214 (n. 26)
  and intertextuality   12, 102–4, 106–9, 122, 124, 150–1, 212 (n. 16), 212–13 (n. 17), 213 (n. 19), 213 (n. 21), 215 (n. 32), 216 (n. 38), 216 (n. 39)
  and the New Right   138–9, 141–3, 152, 156–9, 161, 218 (n. 17), 219 (n. 21)
  and the police procedural   12–13, 90–2, 99–111, 115–16, 119–26, 211 (n. 11), 212 (n. 12), 212–13 (n. 17), 214 (n. 27), 218–19 (n. 19), 220 (n. 30), 220–1 (n. 34), 221 (n. 35)
  and the private investigator   106–11, 120–3
  and private life (opposed to the public sphere)   12–13, 94–8, 100–1, 128, 130–5, 137–44, 147–8, 151, 157–60, 210 (n. 2), 217 (n. 10)
  and the thriller   124–5, 150–1, 213 (n. 22), 220 (n. 31), 220 (n. 32)
Freeling, Nicolas (WORKS)
  Auprès de ma Blonde   95–6, 102, 112, 120–4, 128, 213 (n. 22), 214 (n. 30), 214–15 (n. 31), 215 (n. 34), 215 (n. 35), 216 (n. 39), 220 (n. 28)
  The Back of the North Wind   131,

Index

141–2, 148–9, 152, 157, 159–60
Because of the Cats 95–6, 115, 120, 125, 210 (n. 4)
The Bugles Blowing 129, 133–4, 138, 143–4, 146, 151, 153, 217–18 (n. 15), 219 (n. 24)
Castang's City 130, 137–8, 142–3, 147–9, 153–7, 217–18 (n.15), 220 (n. 28), 220–1 (n. 34)
Criminal Conversation 210 (n. 4), 214 (n. 25), 216 (n. 38), 216 (n. 39)
Death in Amsterdam 93–4, 114–15, 119, 125, 210 (n. 4), 216 (n. 39)
Double Barrel 93–4, 98–100, 115–19, 210 (n. 4), 216 (n. 39), 220 (n. 29)
Dressing of Diamond 129–33, 143, 146–7, 149, 152–3, 162, 217–18 (n. 15)
Gadget 220 (n. 32)
Gun Before Butter 98–9, 112, 115, 125, 210 (n. 4), 216 (n. 38), 216 (n. 39)
"Inspector Van der Valk" 91–2, 215 (n. 33)
The King of the Rainy Country 93, 102–11, 120–2, 124, 210 (n. 4), 212 (n. 16), 212–13 (n. 17), 213 (n. 20), 213 (n. 21), 213 (n. 22), 213 (n. 23), 216 (n. 39)
The Lovely Ladies 113, 210 (n. 4), 214 (n. 25), 216 (n. 39)
The Night Lords 128, 135–7, 141, 144–5, 153, 155, 217–18 (n. 15), 218 (n. 17), 219 (n. 25)
No Part in Your Death 142–3, 146–7, 149–52, 157–60
Sabine 134–5, 146–7, 153–4, 217–18 (n. 15)
Sand Castles 210 (n. 3)
Strike Out Where Not Applicable 95, 114, 122, 210 (n. 4), 214 (n. 25), 214 (n. 30), 216 (n. 39)
Tsing-Boom! 93, 96–8, 117, 119, 125, 210 (n. 4), 211 (n. 7), 214 (n. 30), 216 (n. 39)
The Widow 215 (n. 35)
Wolfnight 138–42, 147, 149–51, 154, 156–7, 160–2

Garson, N. G. 205 (n. 17)
Golden Age detective fiction 3–5, 8–9, 12–13, 90–3, 96, 98, 101–2, 109, 126, 130–1, 140, 144, 153–4, 161, 163–4, 181–2, 197 (n.3), 197 (n.6), 211 (n. 8), 213 (n. 22), 213 (n. 24), 221 (n. 35)
Gordimer, Nadine
July's People 52, 54
"Living in the Interregnum" 64
Goudsblom, Johan 164, 195, 223 (n. 16)
Great Detective 3, 9, 101, 125, 131, 210 (n. 5), 211 (n. 10), 221 (n. 35)
Grella, George
"The Hard-Boiled Detective Novel" 197 (n. 5), 213 (n. 18)
"Murder and Manners" 197 (n. 3)
Gyllensten, Lars 20, 38, 199 (n. 7), 199 (n. 8), 200 (n. 18)

Hall, Stuart *et al.* 13, 139–40, 145, 159, 216 (n. 1), 217 (n. 7), 218 (n. 16), 219 (n. 22)
Hammett, Dashiell 16, 26–7, 199 (n. 10), 200 (n. 17), 215 (n. 36), 216 (n. 39), 221 (n. 36)
Hancock, M. Donald
"Post-Welfare Modernization in Sweden" 19–20, 199 (n. 7)
Sweden 19–20, 38, 41, 50–1, 198 (n. 3), 200 (n. 18), 201 (n. 26)
Hard-Boiled detective fiction 4–6, 12, 14, 16, 20–1, 90, 101–3, 106–7, 111, 122, 126, 197 (n. 5), 197 (n. 6), 199 (n. 10), 199 (n. 11), 200 (n. 17), 211 (n. 8), 211 (n. 11), 212 (n. 12), 212–13 (n. 17), 213 (n. 22), 215 (n. 36), 221 (n. 35), 221 (n. 36)

Haverkamp-Begemann, E.   171–2
Hellman, Ellen   70–1, 205 (n. 21),
   207 (n. 31)
Himes, Chester   203 (n. 5),
   206 (n. 24)
   Blind Man with a Pistol   207
      (n. 32)
   The Crazy Kill   206–7 (n. 27)
Hitchcock, Alfred   216 (n. 39)
Homberger, Eric   198 (n. 13), 218
   (n. 18), 220 (n. 33)
Hulley, Kathleen   197 (n. 5)

Isaac, Fred   75, 82, 208 (n. 40),
   208–9 (n. 43)
Isaac, Frederick   197 (n. 5)

Jameson, Fredric
   The Political Unconscious   90
   "Postmodernism, or The
      Cultural Logic of Late
      Capitalism"   151
   "Reification and Utopia in Mass
      Culture"   1–3, 86, 141, 152,
      218 (n. 18)
Jenny, Laurent   102–3, 212 (n. 12),
   212 (n. 16), 213 (n. 19)
Joseph, Isaac *et al.*   216–17 (n. 5)

Koot, Willem and Petrien Uniken
   Venema   224–5 (n. 22)

Leatt, James *et al.*   88, 206 (n. 23)
le Carré, John   198 (n. 13), 218
   (n. 18), 220 (n. 33)
Lelyveld, Joseph   66, 71, 77–8, 80,
   85, 203 (n. 9), 205 (n. 19), 205
   (n. 20), 209 (n. 44), 209 (n. 46)
Lesser, Wendy   25, 30
Lewin, Leif   199 (n. 8)
Lijphart, Arend
   *The Politics of Accommoda-
      tion*   164
   *The Trauma of Decoloniza-
      tion*   186–8
Lundin, Bo   16–17, 50, 52,
   200 (n. 17)

Mahan, Jeffrey H.   199 (n. 11)

MacDonald, John D.   203 (n. 5)
MacDonald, Ross   20, 199 (n. 10)
Mandel, Ernest   1–2, 6, 10, 197
   (n. 4), 197 (n. 6), 197 (n. 8),
   197–8 (n. 9)
Marshment, Margaret   207–8
   (n. 38)
Mathews, A. S.   203–4 (n. 10)
Maxfield, James F.   17, 200 (n. 17)
McBain, Ed   14–15, 53, 101, 198
   (n. 12), 198–9 (n. 4), 203 (n. 5)
McClure, James (*see below for
   WORKS*)   90–2, 103
   and Afrikaner culture   53,
      57, 59–63, 75, 82–8, 204–5
      (n. 16), 205 (n. 17), 205
      (n. 18), 206 (n. 23)
   and Anglo-Boer hostility   11,
      60–3
   and apartheid   11–12, 52–4,
      58–9, 62, 64, 67, 71, 73, 75–8,
      83–8, 202 (n. 2), 202 (n. 3),
      204 (n. 11), 206 (n. 23),
      208 (n. 40)
   and the Boers, *see* Afrikaner
      culture
   and evictions   65–6, 79,
      205 (n. 20)
   and homelands   80, 203 (n. 10),
      206 (n. 25)
   and the Immorality Act   58–9,
      204 (n. 13), 204 (n. 15)
   and the police procedural
      11–12, 53–6, 85, 88–9,
      203 (n. 7), 208 (n. 40),
      208–9 (n. 43)
   and the South African judici-
      ary   209 (n. 47)
   and the South African
      police   60–1, 76, 82–3, 88,
      203 (n. 8), 203–4 (n. 10),
      207 (n. 29), 207 (n. 30),
      207 (n. 37), 207–8 (n. 38),
      208–9 (n. 43)
   and townships, 56, 66, 70, 88, 205
      (n. 19), 209 (n. 44)
McClure, James (WORKS)
   The Artful Egg   57, 61–2, 68,
      78–9, 81–3, 86–8, 208 (n. 40)

Index

The Blood of an Englishman 55,
  57, 61, 65, 69–70, 81–2, 204
  (n. 12), 204 (n. 13)
The Caterpillar Cop 57, 59–61,
  66–7, 72, 76, 82, 204–5
  (n. 16), 207 (n. 34), 208 (n. 40)
The Gooseberry Fool 57, 65–6,
  77, 79–82, 86, 205 (n. 20), 206
  (n. 22), 207 (n. 34), 208 (n. 42)
Snake 57, 64–5, 67–9, 71–2, 75–6,
  84, 86–7
The Steam Pig 57–9, 62–4, 67,
  69, 74, 80–1, 204 (n. 15),
  206 (n. 26), 207 (n. 33),
  207 (n. 34), 208 (n. 40), 208
  (n. 42), 209 (n. 45)
The Sunday Hangman 57, 63–4,
  68–9, 71, 77, 81–2, 84, 203
  (n. 8), 207 (n. 33), 208 (n. 39)
Michielsen, John 221–2 (n. 2)
Miller, Arthur 211 (n. 9)
Miller, J. Hillis 212–13 (n. 17)
Moodley, Kogila, *see* Adam,
  Heribert and Kogila Moodley

Night Watch, The, *see* Rembrandt

Occhiogrosso, Frank 24–5, 200
  (n. 15), 200 (n. 17), 201 (n. 25)
"One Man's Mote" 124
Oostindie, Gert J. 192–3,
  224–5 (n. 22)

Palme, Olof 201 (n. 27)
Palmer, Jerry 197 (n. 7),
  220 (n. 31)
Panek, Leroy Lad 197 (n. 3)
Panopticon 7–8, 45–6, 51, 55, 146,
  148–9, 203–4 (n. 10)
Peyrefitte, Alain 128, 140, 143,
  161, 216 (n. 3), 217 (n. 12), 217
  (n. 13), 217 (n. 14)
Poe, Edgar Allan 199 (n. 6)
Police Procedural 10–13, 16–18,
  21, 39–40, 47, 53–6, 85, 88–92,
  99–111, 115–16, 119–26, 163–4,
  196, 197 (n. 8), 198 (n. 10), 198
  (n. 12), 203 (n. 7), 208–9 (n. 43),
  212 (n. 12), 212–13 (n. 17), 214

(n. 27), 218–19 (n. 19), 220 (n.
  30), 220–1 (n. 34), 221 (n. 35)
"Popular Culture and Hegemony
  in Post-War Britain" 10, 15,
  51
Porter, Dennis 21, 26–7, 30–1,
  39–40, 92, 197 (n. 3), 197 (n. 5),
  200 (n. 17), 212 (n. 15), 212
  (n. 16), 213 (n. 23), 215 (n. 36)
Punch, Maurice
  Conduct Unbecoming 195–6, 222
    (n. 7), 223 (n. 16), 224 (n. 18),
    225 (n. 23)
  Policing the Inner City 176, 223
    (n. 15), 223 (n. 16), 223 (n.
    17), 223 (n. 23)

Rabinowitz, Peter J. 197 (n. 5),
  213 (n. 18)
Rath, Jan 224–5 (n. 22)
Ravenscroft, Arthur 202–3 (n. 4)
Reilly, John M. 197 (n. 5)
Reeves, Richard 201 (n. 27)
Rembrandt 171–2, 178
Reubsaet, Theo 224–5 (n. 22)
Rousseau, Jean-Jacques 221 (n. 37)

Sachs, Albie 52, 204 (n. 14), 204
  (n. 15), 206 (n. 23), 207 (n. 29),
  207 (n. 30), 209 (n. 47)
Samuelsson, Kurt 199 (n. 7)
Sanders, Lawrence 203 (n. 5)
Sartre, Jean-Paul 211 (n. 9)
Sayers, Dorothy 211 (n. 10),
  216 (n. 39)
Schama, Simon 164, 167, 175–6,
  196, 222 (n. 9), 223 (n. 14),
  225 (n. 26)
Schleh, Eugene 76, 202 (n. 2), 204
  (n. 11), 204 (n. 13), 205 (n. 18),
  207 (n. 28)
Schlemmer, Eugene 204–5 (n. 16)
Schultze, Sydney 224 (n. 20)
Shannon, Dell [Elizabeth
  Linnington] 14–15
Shloss, Carol 91–2, 97–8, 100–1,
  114, 119, 159, 210 (n. 2), 214
  (n. 28), 214–15 (n. 31), 217
  (n. 10), 220 (n. 28), 220 (n. 30)

Simenon, Georges   30–1, 92, 124–5,
  198–9 (n. 4), 211 (n. 10), 211
  (n. 11), 215 (n. 33), 216 (n. 38)
Sjöwall, Maj and Per Wahlöö (see
  below for WORKS)   52–4, 90–2,
  155, 208 (n. 41), 219 (n. 22),
  220–1 (n. 34), 222–3 (n. 13),
  223 (n. 17)
  and bureaucracy   16, 28–9,
    33, 42–6
  and capitalism   10–11, 17–19,
    38–9, 43
  and the environment   10, 20–31,
    199–200 (n. 14)
  and hard-boiled detective
    fiction   16, 20–1, 199 (n. 10),
    199 (n. 11), 200 (n. 17)
  and immigration   36–7,
    200–1 (n. 24)
  and the Left   10, 16–17, 19, 29,
    37–8, 50–1
  and the ombudsman   50–1
  and police alienation   46–9, 202
    (n. 33), 202 (n. 34)
  and the police procedural
    10–11, 16–18, 21, 39–40, 47
  and the Social Democrats
    19–20, 32–5, 38, 201 (n. 27)
  and urban alienation   10, 30–2,
    200 (n. 18), 201 (n. 26)
  and the Vietnam War   40–4, 49
  and the welfare state   10–11,
    16–17, 18–20, 32–6, 46, 50–2
Sjöwall, Maj and Per Wahlöö
  (WORKS)
  The Abominable Man   18, 29–30,
    42–5, 201 (n. 28), 223 (n. 17)
  Cop Killer   18, 20, 26–8, 31–2,
    34, 44, 46, 49, 200 (n. 15), 201
    (n. 28), 203 (n. 7)
  The Fire Engine That Disap-
    peared   28, 33–5, 43, 199–200
    (n. 14), 200 (n. 21)
  The Laughing Policeman   28,
    37–8, 40–2, 200 (n. 19), 200–1
    (n. 24), 201 (n. 30), 202 (n. 32)
  The Locked Room   18–19, 33, 36,
    39, 42–5, 199–200 (n. 14), 200
    (n. 21), 201 (n. 28)

The Man on the Balcony   21–5,
  27–30, 34–5, 40, 47–8,
  199 (n. 12)
The Man Who Went Up in
  Smoke   25–6, 45
Murder at the Savoy   28–9, 32, 36,
  38, 46, 48–9
Roseanna   18, 20, 27–8,
  30–1, 46–7
The Terrorists   29, 38–9, 45,
  49–50, 201 (n. 21)
Starkey, Marion   211 (n. 9)
Stendhal   217 (n. 8)
Stout, Rex   216 (n. 39)
Stromholm, Stig   16, 34, 50
Surveillance   6–8, 12, 30, 36, 43–4,
  51, 54–5, 67–8, 94, 99, 117–19,
  132, 136–8, 145–9, 151–2, 158,
  219 (n. 26), 220 (n. 28)

Thrillers   124–5, 150–1, 197 (n. 7),
  198 (n. 13), 207–8 (n. 38), 213
  (n. 22), 220 (n. 31), 220 (n. 32)

Van Dine, S. S.   216 (n. 39)
Venema, Petrien Uniken, see Koot,
  Willem and Petrien Uniken
  Venema

Wahlöö, Per, see Sjöwall, Maj and
  Per Wahlöö
Wall, Donald C.
  "The Achievement of James
    McClure"   202 (n. 2), 203
    (n. 8), 207 (n. 35), 207–8
    (n. 38), 208–9 (n. 43)
  "An Interview with James
    McClure"   60, 86, 202 (n. 3),
    203 (n. 5), 203 (n. 7), 203
    (n. 8), 206 (n. 24)
  "Apartheid in the Novels of
    James McClure"   58, 75–6,
    202 (n. 2), 208 (n. 40)
Wallace, Edgar   216 (n. 39)
Wambaugh, Joseph   203
  (n. 5)
"War by Other Means"   225
  (n. 25)
Welsh, David   205 (n. 18)

Index

Wetering, Janwillem van de (see below for WORKS)
  and Amsterdam 13, 164–72, 174, 176–9, 183, 188–90, 193–4, 221–2 (n. 2), 223 (n. 16), 224 (n. 18), 225 (n. 23)
  and bureaucracy 179–80
  and Calvinism 164–5, 174, 196
  and Civic Guards, see schutterijen
  and civility, see Dutch bourgeois values
  and decolonization 13–14, 181–95, 224–5 (n. 22)
  and drugs 167, 169–70, 176, 183–5, 191, 195, 224 (n. 18), 225 (n. 25)
  and Dutch bourgeois values 163–4, 167–8, 170–6, 180–1, 195–6
  and Dutch genre painting 175
  and Dutch Golden Age 13–14, 163–4, 167–78, 183–4, 196
  and emblem books 196, 223 (n. 14)
  and Golden Age detective fiction 163–4, 181–2
  and *The Night Watch* 171–2, 178, 222 (n. 9)
  and police corruption 223 (n. 16), 224 (n. 18), 225 (n. 23)
  and the police procedural 13, 163–4, 196
  and Rembrandt, see *The Night Watch*

  and schutterijen 171–2, 176–8, 180
Wetering, Janwillem van de (WORKS)
  The Blond Baboon 165, 167–9
  The Corpse on the Dike 168–9, 173–4, 191, 222 (n. 5), 222 (n. 7)
  Death of a Hawker 166, 168, 222 (n. 7)
  Hard Rain 165, 167–71, 195
  The Japanese Corpse 222 (n. 6), 222 (n. 12)
  The Maine Massacre 222 (n. 6)
  The Mind-Murders 174–5
  Outsider in Amsterdam 183–5, 188–90, 195
  The Rattle-Rat 177–83, 222 (n. 7), 224 (n. 18), 225 (n. 23)
  The Streetbird 167, 170–2, 175–7, 191–5, 222 (n. 7), 223 (n. 14), 225 (n. 23), 225 (n. 24)
  Tumbleweed 164–6, 172–3, 190–1
White, Jean M. 203 (n. 6), 207 (n. 28)
Williams, Thomas E. 198 (n. 2), 202 (n. 31)
Wizelius, Ingemar 20
Worrall, Dennis 204–5 (n. 16), 205 (n. 18)
Wright, Will 5–6

Zetterberg, Hans L. 198 (n. 3)

OHIO